Te

E-mail:

This book is due

mes Joyce's
Ulysses

EBOOK

CASEBOOKS IN CRITICISM

JAMES JOYCE'S

Ulysses

◆　◆　◆

A CASEBOOK

Edited by
Derek Attridge

OXFORD
UNIVERSITY PRESS

2004

OXFORD
UNIVERSITY PRESS

Oxford   New York
Auckland   Bangkok   Buenos Aires   Cape Town   Chennai
Dar es Salaam   Delhi   Hong Kong   Istanbul   Karachi   Kolkata
Kuala Lumpur   Madrid   Melbourne   Mexico City   Mumbai
Nairobi   São Paulo   Shanghai   Taipei   Tokyo   Toronto

Copyright © 2004 by Oxford University Press, Inc.

Published by Oxford University Press, Inc.
198 Madison Avenue, New York, New York 10016

www.oup.com

Oxford is a registered trademark of Oxford University Press

Library of Congress Cataloging-in-Publication Data
James Joyce's Ulysses : a casebook / edited by Derek Attridge.
p. cm.—(Casebooks in criticism)
Includes bibliographical references.

ISBN: 978-0-19-515831-1

1. Joyce, James, 1882–1941. Ulysses. 2. Dublin (Ireland)—In
literature. I. Attridge, Derek. II. Series.
PR6019.09 U6583 2004
823'.912—dc21   2003007745

Credits

The editor and publisher are grateful to the authors and publishers listed below for permission to reprint the essays in this volume.

Leo Bersani, "Against *Ulysses*." Reprinted by permission from *Raritan: a Quarterly Review* 8, no. 2 (Fall 1988). Copyright © 1988 by Raritan.

Frank Budgen, *James Joyce and the Making of "Ulysses."* Extracts reprinted by permission of Indiana University Press. Copyright © 1960 by Indiana University Press.

Maud Ellmann, "The Ghosts of *Ulysses*," in *The Languages of Joyce*, edited by R. M. Bolletieri Bosinelli, C. Marengo Vaglio, and Christine van Boheemen. Reprinted by permission of John Benjamins Publishing Co. Copyright © 1992 John Benjamins B.V.

Cheryl Herr, "Art and Life, Nature and Culture, *Ulysses*," in *Joyce's "Ulysses": The Larger Perspective*, edited by Robert D. Newman and Weldon Thornton. Reprinted by permission of Associated

University Presses. Copyright © 1987 by Associated University Presses, Inc.

Hugh Kenner, *James Joyce's "Ulysses."* Extract reprinted by permission of Taylor & Francis Books Ltd. Copyright © 1980 George Allen & Unwin (Publishers) Ltd.

Vicki Mahaffey, "Intentional Error: The Paradox of Editing Joyce's *Ulysses*," in *Representing Modernist Texts: Editing as Interpretation*, edited by George Bornstein. Reprinted by permission of the University of Michigan Press. Copyright © 1991 by the University of Michigan.

Emer Nolan, *James Joyce and Nationalism.* Extracts reprinted by permission of Taylor & Francis Books Ltd. Copyright © 1995 by Emer Nolan.

Fritz Senn, "Book of Many Turns," in *"Ulysses": Fifty Years*, edited by Thomas F. Staley. Reprinted by permission of Indiana University Press. Copyright © 1974 by Indiana University Press.

Henry Staten, "The Decomposing Form of Joyce's *Ulysses*." Reprinted by permission of the Modern Language Association of America from *PMLA* 112 (1997): 380–92. Copyright © 1997 by the Modern Language Association of America.

Mark A. Wollaeger, "Reading *Ulysses*: Agency, Ideology, and the Novel," in *Joyce and the Subject of History*, edited by Mark A. Wollaeger, Victor Luftig, and Robert Spoo. Reprinted by permission of the University of Michigan Press. Copyright © 1996 by the University of Michigan.

Ewa Ziarek, "The Female Body, Technology, and Memory in 'Penelope,' " in *Molly Blooms: A Polylogue on "Penelope" and Cultural Studies*, edited by Richard Pearce. Reprinted by permission of the University of Wisconsin Press. Copyright ©1994 by the University of Wisconsin Press.

Abbreviations

<table>
<tr><td>CW</td><td>The Critical Writings. Ed. Ellsworth Mason and Richard Ellmann. New York: Viking, 1959; reprint, Ithaca, N.Y.: Cornell University Press, 1989.</td></tr>
<tr><td>D</td><td>James Joyce, Dubliners. Ed. Jeri Johnson. Oxford: Oxford University Press, 2000.</td></tr>
<tr><td>FW</td><td>James Joyce, Finnegans Wake. London: Faber & Faber, 1939. References in the form: page number.line number (e.g., FW 318.24). All editions have the same pagination.</td></tr>
<tr><td>JJ1</td><td>Richard Ellmann, James Joyce. New York: Oxford University Press, 1959.</td></tr>
<tr><td>JJ2</td><td>Richard Ellmann, James Joyce. Rev. ed. New York: Oxford University Press, 1982.</td></tr>
<tr><td>Letters I, II, III</td><td>James Joyce, Letters. Ed. Stuart Gilbert and Richard Ellmann. 3 vols. New York: Viking, 1957–1966.</td></tr>
<tr><td>P</td><td>James Joyce, A Portrait of the Artist as a Young Man.</td></tr>
</table>

Ed. Jeri Johnson. Oxford: Oxford University Press, 2000.

SL   James Joyce, *Selected Letters*. Ed. Richard Ellmann. London: Faber, 1975.

U   James Joyce, *Ulysses: The Corrected Text*. Ed. Hans Walter Gabler, with Wolfhard Steppe and Claus Melchior. New York: Random House; London: Bodley Head and Penguin, 1986. References in the form: episode number.line number (e.g., *U* 13.950).

Contents

James Joyce's
Ulysses

A CASEBOOK

Introduction

DEREK ATTRIDGE

✦   ✦   ✦

*U*LYSSES IS THE MOST FAMOUS literary work, in any language, of the twentieth century: this claim would be hard to dispute, subjective though it is. The book's fame—or, more accurately perhaps, its notoriety—does not necessarily mean that it is the most widely read of twentieth-century literary works, though it would probably appear high on a list of works most frequently begun and never finished. Its difficulty is one of the main ingredients of its reputation, the others being its length, its psychological realism, and (connected to this) its explicitness about sexual and other bodily matters. The first two seem calculated to deter the reader; the second two are more likely to attract him or her, out of curiosity if for no other reason.

To those who are familiar with the novel—we might as well call it a novel, although it could equally be called an antinovel— this caricature is misleading in many ways. For one thing, it leaves out the fact that *Ulysses* is, to those who tap into its humor, one of the funniest novels ever written. Allied to this is the sheer pleasure with which the writing is imbued and in which the reader is invited to participate. Joyce is said to have boasted, "I have discovered that I can do anything with language I want,"[1] and many readers would testify that this sense of an almost boundless capacity to exploit the potential of language—the English language in particular—is an important part of their enjoyment.

There is no denying, however, that *Ulysses* is a difficult novel, and it must have seemed an impossibly difficult novel to many who picked it up soon after its publication in 1922 (not an easy thing for most English-speaking readers to do, for reasons we shall explore). Its great length did not help. Readers who grew up enjoying the novels of George Eliot and Thomas Hardy, or even Henry James and Joseph Conrad, would not have known what to do with this bloated monster of a book in which the rules of the English language seem to count for nothing; there is no consistency of style after the first few chapters; it is often difficult to know what is actually happening; and what *can* be fathomed of the narrative content bears little relation to anything that would normally be considered a conventional plot line. Even today, when the long, difficult novel that flouts the conventions of writing and reading is not an uncommon phenomenon (thanks in part to Joyce's example), *Ulysses* presents the newcomer with a challenge.

Yet countless readers, young and old, have been entertained, delighted, and even changed by the experience of getting to grips with Joyce's novel. They have given it the time and the commitment it asks for and have not been inhibited by the book's fearsome reputation. A good way of overcoming initial obstacles is tackling it in a group or comparing notes with other readers; and for those who are reading on their own there is a wide array of guides and companions to assist the beginner. Most important, however, is an open-mindedness toward the text, a willingness to press on even through apparently impenetrable passages, and an alertness to the play of language, the contours of speech and thought, and the mundane details of daily existence.

These qualities are also valuable in responding to the other two aspects of the book that I have mentioned as being central to its reputation: its psychological realism and its bodily and sexual frankness. While literary critics since the late 1970s have tended to emphasize the way the novel undermines the certainties upon which we depend in our use of language, in our relations with one another, and in our sense of self, there can be no doubt that *Ulysses* would have long ago been consigned to the pile of interesting but fruitless experiments were it not for the vividness with which it conveys the twists and turns of people's minds as they go about their daily business. Or, more accurately, minds and bodies: the explicit details of sexual thoughts and activities, of the physical needs and experiences that traverse our everyday lives, are there as part of a rich texture of interpenetrating mental and physical worlds—desires, aversions, fears, hopes, moments of insight or self-deception, memories, observations, and speculations, presented either with remarkable directness in what is known as "interior monologue" or playfully mediated by one of a number of styles that Joyce developed for the later chapters.

There are many ways of reading *Ulysses*, and there is no reason that an individual reader should not try several of them. For a first reading, however, it is best not to worry too much about the many historical and cultural allusions, the intricate web of cross-references, the detailed Homeric correspondences, the ethical and political nuances, the undermining of novelistic and linguistic conventions. There are characters to get to know, relationships to follow up, minutely realized details of lives and thoughts to register. If the first episode, or chapter, seems hard going, little is lost by skipping to episode 4 and following the experiences of the book's central character, Leopold Bloom, for three episodes (which take place at 8, 10, and 11 A.M.) before returning to the opening three episodes, which focus on Stephen Dedalus and take place at exactly the same times in different parts of Dublin. (Leopold's and Stephen's paths cross once in the sixth episode.) It is easy to establish a rapport with Leopold Bloom's mental world, which is full of pragmatic responses to the exigencies of his surroundings; Stephen Dedalus's rarefied musings, however, though deliciously funny and entirely absorbing when you become familiar with them, can take some getting used to. (If you are reading an edition that—as Joyce wanted—lacks episode numbers, it might be helpful to write these in.)

The style of these first six episodes—known to critics as the "initial style"—is not hard to tune in to; the interior monologue, in which the thoughts of the character (Stephen or Bloom) are represented by grammatically imperfect, present-tense bits of language, quickly becomes second nature as we read. After something of a departure in episode 7, the eighth episode reverts to the initial style, but all the episodes that follow utilize other stylistic devices, either in conjunction with interior monologue or moving away from it altogether. Part of the fun of reading *Ulysses* is reaching the end of one of the later episodes and taking a deep breath before plunging into the next one, knowing that it will offer not only a different scene and new events but a quite different way of representing this outward reality in language.

Even on a first reading, some guidance can be a godsend, providing much-needed signposts—but it is important to remember that the puzzles in *Ulysses* are there to be enjoyed, and the premature use of notes to solve them takes away most of the pleasure. It helps in understanding the opening three episodes, for instance, to have read Joyce's earlier novel *A Portrait of the Artist as a Young Man* or, at least, to know that at the end of that work Stephen Dedalus, who imagines a future for himself as a writer, is about to leave Ireland for Paris. Finding him back in Dublin at the opening of *Ulysses*, then, the knowledgeable reader will wonder what has happened to those aspirations and look for clues about his time in Paris and the reason for his return. Some understanding of Irish history prior to June 16, 1904 (when the novel is set) and of Dublin geography will help, and most introductions to the novel will provide information about the events that really did occur on that day, such as the running of the Gold Cup horse race at Ascot in England, which impinge on the characters' lives. But most important of all is to find one's own way of engaging with Joyce's consistently inventive language in the process of creating and recreating a city as it was eighteen years earlier (for Joyce when he published the book) and a hundred years ago (for us) and the words, thoughts, emotions, and sensations of some of its citizens; and then to begin to explore the powers of discourse itself as they are staged in the novel, the many varieties of language that dominate but also make possible our lives as social beings. The essays in this collection are all attempts, from a range of perspectives, to do just that.

THAT JOYCE EVER COMPLETED *ULYSSES* is one of the most extraordinary facts about it. He began the book in 1914 at the age of thirty-two while living in Trieste, the city where he and Nora Barnacle had made a home for themselves when, ten years earlier, they had left Ireland to begin a new life free from the oppressive conditions of their native country. When Joyce started work on *Ulysses*, the career as a writer to which he had dedicated himself (like Stephen Dedalus) was only just beginning to bear fruit. *Dubliners*, his collection of short stories, was published in that year after nearly a decade of frustrating negotiations with anxious publishers, and 1914 also saw the beginning of the serialization of *A Portrait of the Artist as a Young Man* in a journal edited by Ezra Pound. Although he could not at that point foresee what *Ulysses* would become, it is testimony to Joyce's faith in himself as an artist that he could embark on a project of such scope and originality when the world had given only the most meager signs of appreciating his art.

The outbreak of the First World War did not make the early stages of composition any easier. James and Nora, with their two small children, were forced to leave Trieste (then a part of the Austro-Hungarian empire) and make a temporary home in Zurich, in neutral Switzerland. Here Joyce, with very little money (as in Trieste, private English lessons were his main source of income), living at several addresses, learning a new language, following reports of the war and of the Irish struggle for independence, persevered with *Ulysses*. To make matters worse, his eye troubles, which had begun in Trieste, worsened and were to plague him for the rest of his life. Yet by the time he left Zurich in 1919 he had completed the initial versions of twelve of the book's eighteen episodes, and he had also arranged—again with

Pound's help—for it to appear in serial form in an American magazine, *The Little Review*. Money problems had abated somewhat, thanks largely to the generosity of a new benefactor in England, Harriet Shaw Weaver.

After a short stay back in Trieste (where Joyce wrote two more chapters), the family moved to Paris, the city in which they were to live for twenty years—until forced into exile by another world war. Paris was their home throughout the completion and publication of *Ulysses* (and after that, the writing of Joyce's last and even more challenging book, *Finnegans Wake*). These last eighteen months of work on *Ulysses* are perhaps the most difficult of all to comprehend. Although the success of *Dubliners* and *A Portrait of the Artist* had by now secured Joyce's reputation, he was still beset by medical and financial problems and had to devote a large amount of energy to the business of finding affordable rooms in which he could write without endangering his eyes and to the frequent moves that this necessitated. It is a telling comment on Joyce's ability to work in a small apartment amid the bustle of family life that when the French author Valery Larbaud let him spend a summer in his Paris apartment, which included a sound-proofed room especially designed for writing, the Irishman found it "like writing in a tomb."[2]

As the pace of Joyce's writing increased, he often worked for sixteen hours a day, going to bed at three or four in the morning, until one evening he collapsed while attending a music-hall performance. After this, he tried to restrict the number of hours he put in each day. In spite of his precautions, an eye attack laid him up for five weeks as he was finishing the last chapter. For most of the time that he was writing *Ulysses*, he had no guarantee that he would ever find a publisher: he could persuade no one in Britain or the United States to touch the scandalous work, and even the serialization he had arranged with Pound was halted after the thirteenth episode when the editors of the magazine—three issues of which had already been confiscated and burned by the U.S. Post Office—were found guilty of publishing obscenity. Only when, in 1921, he received an offer of publication from an American bookseller in Paris, Sylvia Beach (another of the many women without whose support Joyce would have achieved little), was he able to work with the image of a published book in his mind.

Under these unpropitious conditions, Joyce wrote the final four chapters and revised the whole book, using the successive proofs to keep adding material. Four chapters and proof correction may not sound like a great deal of work, unless you know that these final chapters constitute about two-fifths of the entire book and that Joyce enlarged *Ulysses* by approximately one-third through additions to the proofs. With changes being made up to the very last minute, the printer, whose efforts were nothing short of heroic, was able to produce a copy in time for Joyce's fortieth birthday celebration on February 2, 1922.

FOR TWELVE YEARS after its publication, *Ulysses* lived a clandestine existence: banned in the English-speaking world, the book had to be smuggled in under plain covers from abroad. In consequence, its reputation as pornography grew among the general public, while those with a serious interest in literature had to rely more than is usually the case upon what the critics had to say about it. And the critics were divided. There were those who regarded it as immoral, or tasteless, or boring, or arcane, or imbecilic, or a hoax, or a combination of two or more of these. But there were also those who hailed it as a work of genius, confirming the achievement of *Dubliners* and *A Portrait of the Artist* and securing Joyce's place as one of the leading writers of the day. Among the influential figures who championed the work were Pound, Valery Larbaud, T. S. Eliot, and Edmund Wilson—although reading their highly diverse responses makes it hard to believe they had the same book in front of them. The novel continued to sell steadily, and one sign of its success was that an American editor started to publish a pirated version in a monthly magazine; publication had reached the end of the fourteenth episode in 1927 before the legal proceedings initiated by Joyce took effect.

Those who could not get access to the book or who found it too great a challenge to read were thrown a lifeline in 1930 by

Joyce's friend Stuart Gilbert in the shape of his study *James Joyce's "Ulysses,"*³ which summarized the chapters and quoted liberally. Gilbert's book made public for the first time a plan of *Ulysses* that Joyce had shown a few acquaintances but not hitherto allowed to appear in print. This "schema"—Clive Hart's version of which is reproduced, with some modifications, as an appendix to this volume—provides detailed correspondences between the chapters of *Ulysses* and Homer's *Odyssey*, including the Homeric chapter titles, which Joyce at first planned to use but then dropped. These titles have become the standard way of referring to the episodes of *Ulysses*, and students of Joyce's novel sometimes find it hard to keep in mind that they are not part of the published book.

The schema also gives a time for each episode except the last, showing how the novel covers a single day from eight in the morning to the small hours of the next (it is from the novel itself that we learn that these days are June 16 and 17, 1904). And it proposes an elaborate system of correspondences with the organs of the body, the arts, and various colors, symbols, and stylistic techniques (what Joyce calls "technics"). Just as many parts of the novel are parodies of ways of writing novels while remaining highly effective exploitations of the novel tradition, so this schema seems to poke fun at overly elaborate systematizations of literature while at the same time offering some useful keys to the novel's interpretation. Gilbert, who was advised by Joyce in preparing his study, made a great deal of the systematic organization of the book and provided a solid account of its narrative content, so that even readers who could not, or did not want to, get hold of the book were able to feel they had acquired some sense of its singular qualities.

The other early book that Joyce helped into existence and that provided readers—and nonreaders—with useful insights into the novel and a good selection of quotations was Frank Budgen's *James Joyce and the Making of "Ulysses,"* published in 1934. Budgen and Joyce had become friends in Zurich and kept in touch after Joyce had left, and Budgen's book interlaces its full account of the novel with reminiscences about the author. Joyce felt no inhibitions about making suggestions to Budgen about what he should include, so part of the value of the book is its closeness to the author's own views (though as the overelaboration of the schema suggests, we should always take Joyce's self-commentaries with a grain of salt). A selection of Budgen's recounted conversations with Joyce about *Ulysses* is included in this volume.

By the time Budgen's book was published, however, one part of its raison d'être had disappeared, since a U.S. court ruling the previous year had exempted *Ulysses* from the charge of obscenity. In 1934, Random House brought out its first edition, which was followed two years later by the first British edition from Bodley Head. Twelve years after he finished it, Joyce's great book could at last be freely bought in the English-speaking world.

JOYCE DIED IN 1941, back in Zurich because of the war, two years after the publication of his last work, *Finnegans Wake*—an even more ambitious and unconventional book, which he had begun soon after the publication of *Ulysses*. In the same year, an American academic, Harry Levin, published a study of Joyce's entire oeuvre (*James Joyce: A Critical Introduction*), which became one of the foundation stones of his reputation as a major writer worthy of inclusion in college syllabi along with Chaucer, Shakespeare, and Milton. It was largely in North America that this reputation was built: important contributions included Richard M. Kain's study of the realism of *Ulysses, Fabulous Voyager* (1947), Hugh Kenner's insightful close reading, *Dublin's Joyce* (1956), and Richard Ellmann's magisterial biography (1959). The achievement of critics like these is that, in addition to propelling *Ulysses* into the canon of great English literature, they helped to make it a text to read with delight, rather than a monument to be in awe of, a hoax to make fun of, or an unnecessarily long book with occasional bits to giggle over. The chapter from Kenner's later study of *Ulysses* (first published in 1980) with which this collection begins is a good example of his brilliance as a critic of Joyce. In it, he explores what he sees as "perhaps the most radical, the most disconcerting innovation in all of *Ulysses*," the use of a consciousness—he takes over David Hayman's phrase "the Arranger"—that does not coincide with any of the characters or with a traditional narrator.

The remainder of the English-speaking world was slower to recognize Joyce's achievement, partly because of the influence in schools and universities of F. R. Leavis, a critic who had little time for Joyce's experimental playfulness. But in continental Europe—Joyce's home for most of his life—his work found many admirers. In Switzerland, for instance, his writing caught the attention of a young man who was to become one of his most penetrating commentators: Fritz Senn. Senn's essay reprinted here exemplifies both his careful attention to Joycean detail (and in particular the way Joycean detail responds to Homeric detail) and his general argument that to do justice to Joyce the reader must be suspicious of any claims to fixed and final answers.

In the late 1970s, Anglo-American literary criticism began to undergo a sea change under the impact of French theoretical writings, and *Ulysses* (along with Joyce's other works, notably *Finnegans Wake*) achieved a new significance and a new status. (This is hardly surprising, since Joyce's work had been an important influence on many of the French theorists themselves, including Jacques Derrida, Jacques Lacan, Julia Kristeva, and Hélène Cixous.) Readers found new ways of enjoying its play with the conventions of representation and the operations of language and stopped worrying about its moral assumptions and apparent lapses of taste. Essays in this collection especially responsive to these developments are those by Maud Ellmann, Ewa Ziarek, Mark Wollaeger, and Henry Staten, although each of them works with a different set of theoretical models and produces a distinctive reading of *Ulysses*. Ellmann draws on philosophy and psychoanalysis to bring out the surprising importance of ghosts in *Ulysses* (especially in relation to Joyce's, and Stephen's, preoccupation with Shakespeare); Ziarek finds Walter Benjamin particularly helpful in understanding the role of the female body in the final episode and makes use of the insights of Freud and Derrida; Wollaeger shows how Althusser's account of interpellation can illuminate the encounters with British imperialism that Joyce stages; and

Staten ranges from Aristotle to Derrida in the course of an exploration of the novel's engagement with textual realism and fidelity. Psychoanalytic accounts of fecality and anality also prove unexpectedly relevant to *Ulysses'* dealings with the material realm in Staten's highly original reading.

Approaches to literature and culture that stress the social and the political also proved highly productive in rereading Joyce. These included some varieties of Marxism, like that of Theodor Adorno (and unlike that of the Stalinist culture managers, who had condemned *Ulysses*, or the Hungarian Marxist Georg Lukács, who saw in Joyce an exemplar of irresponsible subjectivism), and the renewed interest in the historical contexts of literature inspired largely by the writing of Michel Foucault. This concern with the material world reflected by, and absorbed into, Joyce's work is evident in Cheryl Herr's essay in this volume, which examines the relation between nature and culture in *Ulysses*, while Wollaeger locates *Ulysses* in the context of Ireland's subject status within the British Empire in 1904. The question of Ireland's colonial situation has stimulated a good deal of interesting criticism, spurred by the growth of postcolonial studies in the final decade of the twentieth century, and for the first time Irish critics contributed in a substantial way to the body of work about Joyce. Emer Nolan's *James Joyce and Nationalism* (1995), a section of which is reprinted in this volume, approaches *Ulysses* as a novel in part about the Irish struggle for national independence, although she does so with some misgivings about the theoretical bases of much postcolonial criticism and is prepared to challenge traditional readings of Bloom as a positive embodiment of political values.

Feminist approaches to literature have also opened up new ways of responding to *Ulysses*, and Ziarek's essay in this casebook is one example of a wide variety of critical engagements with the role of women in Joyce's writing. To register the impact of feminist thought on the criticism of *Ulysses*, one has only to compare two edited volumes, published twenty-five years apart, which devote a chapter to each episode: *James Joyce's "Ulysses": Critical Essays*, edited by Clive Hart and David Hayman in 1974, and *"Ulysses": En-Gendered Perspectives*, edited by Kimberly J. Devlin and Marilyn

Reizbaum in 1999. The first volume is an extremely valuable compendium of commentaries by many of the leading critics of the time, and yet it shows very little interest in the concerns that animate the readings in the second volume, another gathering of contributions by leading critics, who this time were asked to discuss the importance of gender in each episode. Herr's and Ellmann's essays in this collection are also animated in part by feminist concerns—the conventional association of woman and nature, for example, and the place of the maternal in the schemes of Western thought, both of which were of telling interest to Joyce.

Almost all of the huge amount of commentary on *Ulysses* that has accumulated since the 1980s has been approving, if not celebratory. After the initial period of debate about Joyce's revolutionary book, during which some potent negatives were registered (by, for instance, C. G. Jung, D. H. Lawrence, and Virginia Woolf), a virtually unbroken consensus about its brilliance and its importance emerged. One of the few skeptical voices to be heard in recent years has been that of Leo Bersani, whose essay "Against *Ulysses*" is reprinted here—although even Bersani's doubts are colored by enormous admiration and perhaps have more to do with the way we now read Joyce, thanks to the academic institution that has grown up around him, than about the work itself. Yet even this qualification needs qualifying, since we cannot speak of "the work itself" in any straightforward way: *Ulysses* exists for us as a book that has been read and reread, analyzed and psychoanalyzed, summarized and excerpted. The book has filtered into our consciousnesses from multiple sources (often without our being aware of it), so that when we encounter it, we encounter a whole cultural history. Though we might regret this fact and attempt the impossible feat of a "naïve reading" (something Bersani undertakes, knowing that it is impossible), we stand to gain more from accepting it and capitalizing on it.

In addition to critical commentary, reference material, and introductory guides, Joyce scholars have put a great deal of effort into editing *Ulysses*. The conditions under which it was written and printed meant that its first publication was characterized by a large number of errors, and Joyce immediately set about compiling a list of errata. However, every edition that has tried to fix earlier mistakes has ended up introducing new ones. We are now in a better position to appreciate the impossibility of a "definitive" edition; any text we read is the product of a host of editorial decisions (both conscious and unconscious, both principled and idiosyncratic), as well as being subject to all the contingencies of the material processes involved. For anyone who wants to study the text, the standard version is the one edited by Hans Walter Gabler and published by Random House; although some of its editorial decisions remain disputed, it corrects a large number of the errors that have marred earlier editions, and the line numbers it provides are used by commentators to make precise references. If such matters are unimportant to the reader, there are many alternatives; two that many readers find pleasant to handle as material artifacts are, in Britain, the 1960 Bodley Head edition (currently available in Penguin) and, in the United States, the 1961 Random House edition. The best notes are provided by Jeri Johnson in her Oxford edition, though the text—a reprint of the 1922 original—is largely of historical interest. In her essay included in this volume, Vicki Mahaffey, writing from the point of view of the reader and critic, discusses the problems and paradoxes of editing *Ulysses*, highlighting the important contribution made by the Gabler edition to our understanding of Joyce's work and tracing some of the fruitful consequences of Joyce's own creative view of error.

This volume cannot, of course, exhaust the immense variety of approaches to *Ulysses* that have borne fruit in recent years. Important work has appeared on the significance of homosexuality in the novel; the role of commodity culture and advertising has been rewardingly discussed; the insights offered by chaos theory and the mathematical study of complexity have been applied; the ethical implications of Joyce's writing have been explored; the rapid developments in electronic media have had a considerable impact; and the examination of Joyce's manuscripts has thrown light on his working methods. These are only some of the avenues that have proved productive; no doubt others will emerge in future years. The suggestions for further reading at the end of this book can give only the scantiest impression of the riches that are available to those who wish to go further in pursuit of critical studies; they can be complemented by the guidance given in many introductory books on Joyce and by some excellent websites.

But what is most important is direct engagement with Joyce's writing, when the guides and notes are put away. The essays I have chosen for this volume, although they differ widely in their methods of reading and their conclusions about *Ulysses*, are all examples of this direct engagement with, and pleasure in, Joyce's endlessly evocative words.

Notes

1. Eugene Jolas, "My Friend James Joyce," excerpted in Robert H. Deming, *James Joyce: The Critical Heritage* (London: Routledge & Kegan Paul, 1970), 1:384.

2. Arthur Power, *Conversations with James Joyce*, ed. Clive Hart (Chicago, Ill.: University of Chicago Press, 1974), 91.

3. The full citations for books mentioned in this introduction are given in the suggested reading section.

The Arranger

HUGH KENNER

◆　◆　◆

A LINE ACROSS THE PAGE divides, nine and nine, the first extant list of *Ulysses* episodes, the one Joyce sent John Quinn in September 1920 (*Letters* I, 145). Correspondingly, the words "End of First Part of *Ulysses*" appear on the last page of the Rosenbach fair copy of episode 9, "Scylla and Charybdis." If we append to this half its coda, "Wandering Rocks," we have a ten-episode block, homogeneous in its style[1] and reasonably self-contained in its themes and actions. It is instructive to linger on this fragment. What should we make of *Ulysses* if it had ended with "Wandering Rocks"?

We should have, by contrast with the book we know, a moderately orthodox novel of under 100,000 words, its ten chapters each of fairly normal length. The interior monologue, tactfully introduced, would be its striking technical feature: that and a certain penchant for abrupt scene shifting (and both have precedents in Meredith). It would follow, contrapuntally, Stephen Dedalus and Leopold Bloom from 8 A.M. till midafternoon, when the ostensible business of each is done for the day. Bloom, fussing with Keyes's ad, is tacitly acquiescing in cuckoldry. Stephen, placing Deasy's letter with editors, is unresistant to the role of bullockbefriending bard.

We might say, two *Dubliners* stories intercut. Bloom's story—the cuckold-to-be drifting round the city, triumphant only in procuring the porn book his wife wanted—may even be based on the "Ulysses" story Joyce thought of writing late in 1906; the ironic point of the title is simply the faithlessness of Penelope.[2] Stephen's story—the "artist" ruminating, drinking, and placing someone else's letter to the press—resolves, with ironies of its own, "A Little Cloud," the last *Dubliners* story Joyce wrote before he conceived "The Dead." Its artist, though formidably talented by contrast with the story's Little Chandler, has seemingly made his restless peace with the world's Ignatius Gallaghers. Intertwining these two stories, our ten-episode *Ulysses* affirms the usual *Dubliners* message, the futility of Dublin aspirations. A marriage that has come to be defined by masochistic noninterference, a vocation that has lapsed into acquiescence in being, like it or not, a drunken father's bibulous son—these are a Dublin marriage, a Dublin vocation. Ulysses' consort will welcome a brawny suitor; Telemachus is driven by his consubstantial father who is not in heaven nor yet secure in his kingdom. And the tenth episode draws back as though to locate and also lose these two in a fragmented Dublin like that of *Dubliners*, where many other lives are taking their course while Church and State command the passerby's assent.

How Joyce might have talked about *Ulysses* had he planned to end it here is a question not quite beyond speculation; its governing note is irony, relentless irony, like the governing note of *Dubliners*, and we may remark how he refrained from summarizing *Dubliners* stories. In numerous letters he alluded to them in passing and by title, once or twice hinting that a plain blunt reader would miss much that they contained, but thematic summaries he avoided. The theme of a *Dubliners* story and the graph of its happenings are apt to be entirely different things; it is pointless to say that in "Grace" four good-hearted men talk a fifth into amending his ways. For their talk is a monstrous collage of misinformation, and the sermon to which they lead their friend is ingratiatingly unedifying, and as for the title, "Grace," if mysterious grace works like this, summoning Tom Kernan to no more than Father Purdon's preaching, then it is (is it not?) the free gift (*gratia*) of an unworthy God. Groping to summarize, we are back with the word "irony," and to any questions about a much longer work in this vein Joyce's answer might well have been a thin-lipped smile.

But Joyce did discuss *Ulysses*, always with reference to the Homeric parallel. This, we may now note, commences to direct the action only in the second half of the book, where its working-out establishes the requirement that Ulysses and Telemachus shall meet. If its function in a ten-episode *Ulysses* is ironic, in the eighteen-episode *Ulysses* it is coercive. Remove it, and nothing is left to obligate what only chance procures, some kind of confrontation between the two figures who when we last discern them in "Wandering Rocks" are each as shut away in private concerns as two characters in the same book might possibly be. Save in a non-Aristotelean universe, one might suppose, their conjunction could not be plausibly arranged.

And Joyce planned from the start that his principal characters should meet. In 1920 (*Letters* III, 31) he told John Quinn that "Ithaca" and "Penelope"—Bloom with Stephen, Molly's thoughts—had been sketched since 1916, his first year of undivided work on *Ulysses*. Later his first biographer, Herbert Gorman, was to hear that "preliminary sketches for the final sections" dated from early 1914.[3] Whatever their date, they preceded the toil that began at the beginning. Joyce then elaborated the first half of the book in what he was to call "the initial style" (*Letters* I, 129), a manner backed by fluent practice with *Dubliners* and *Portrait*. This took until early 1919—say, three years—and with no disrespect to a prodigious feat of writing we may call it relatively rapid work for a man who had struggled during five and a half years on the five-chapter *Portrait*. Fourteen *Dubliners* stories and twenty-five chapters of *Stephen Hero* had taken but a year and a half; the *Dubliners* irony is useful if one must produce, and it helped him produce unelaborated versions of the early sections of *Ulysses* with some facility. If once in a while two sentences took all day,[4] we may be sure that on other days long passages were blocked out with little hesitation. (At two lines a day, *Ulysses* would have taken forty years.)

And now, at midpoint, new invention was incumbent. Bloom and Stephen were to converge, and one thing needed was a set of narrative conventions that would keep an eye on two main characters simultaneously without acquiescing in Victorian fictionists' puppetry. "Aeolus," the first episode in which Stephen and Bloom are both present though not at the same time, was one precedent. Joyce had already stressed the artifice of its surfaces, making the first sentence of his first version read.

> Grossbooted draymen rolled barrels dullthudding out of Prince's stores and bumped them up on the brewery float. (7.21)

This already seems to foresee the sentence he was later to insert after it:

> On the brewery float bumped dullthudding barrels rolled by grossbooted draymen out of Prince's stores.

Though Bloom is within earshot of the din, the syntactic artifice is not meant to reflect the working of his busy mind: rather, a self-sufficient geometry as indifferent to his presence as are whatever Newtonian equations can describe the momentum of dullthudding barrels. Subsequent to its *Little Review* publication (October 1918) Joyce was greatly to extend the artifice of "Aeolus," multiplying its rhetorical figures, emphasizing their conspicuousness, breaking the text sixty-three times with captions, even introducing the episode with yet more paragraphs of Bloomless material, the tramcars, the bootblacks.[5] "Rhetoric," which is something less personal than pervasive talk and gives a collective identity to disembodied facility with words, corresponds, as it blows through the episode's interstices, to a certain Dublin indifference on the part of the talkers, anonymous as the wind "that changing its direction changes its name." Petty errands, uncon-summated, blow Bloom in and out, unattended to, and no one but Professor MacHugh hears out Stephen's parable.

In "Wandering Rocks"—apparently an addition to plans that had seemed firm as late as May 1918[6]—Joyce extended the principle of pervasive indifference, again inserting Stephen and Bloom into separated parts of the one episode but entrusting the whole to a narrator whose grim delight is to monitor with clock and map the space-time whereabouts of more than thirty characters simultaneously. All these people, plus the many who jostle them and the viceregal cavalcade that sweeps east and then southeast across the city, make a composite synecdoche for Dublin; here as in "Aeolus" a rhetoric that can manage more than one center of awareness is still grounded in Dublin itself.

Once accustomed in "Wandering Rocks" to a narrator with a good deal more in mind than getting on with two men's fortunes, we shall not be allowed to overlook his autonomy again. It is as though a giant were slowly coming awake. In "Sirens" he manifests two more degrees of freedom. For the first time "style," some game the narrator is playing, is more expressive and more apparent than narration, forcing us to pay close attention if we would be sure what the characters are doing. And, in a manner reminiscent of "Wandering Rocks," details commence to find their way on to the page without regard for the consciousness of anyone present, thoroughly subverting the premise of the initial style. In "Wandering Rocks" such details had been cross-links of synchronicity. In "Sirens" their origin is in former time, coming as they do from earlier parts of the book. Bloom munches, and the page comments:

> Leopold cut liverslices. As said before he ate with relish the inner organs, nutty gizzards, fried cods' roes. (11.519)

"As said before" looks back to the first of all the Bloom sentences:

> Mr Leopold Bloom ate with relish the inner organs of beasts and fowls. He liked thick giblet soup, nutty gizzards, a stuffed

roast heart, liver slices fried with crustcrumbs, fried hencod's roes. (4.1)

And, lest the retrospect be missed, the "Sirens" narrator soon repeats, "Bloom ate liv as said before." Some pages later we find Bloom furtively answering Martha's letter. He pens a postscript, "I feel so sad today. So lonely," and reflects:

> Too poetical that about the sad. Music did that. Music hath charms. Shakespeare said. Quotations every day in the year. To be or not to be. Wisdom while you wait.

Whereupon the narrator interpolates:

> In Gerard's rosery of Fetter Lane he walks, greyedauburn. One life is all. One body. Do. But do. (11.904)

And Bloom, as if he had either heard this remark or not heard it, continues, "Done anyhow": meaning he has written what he has written. The narrator has paraphrased and interpolated thoughts about Shakespeare which Stephen framed but did not speak two hours before (9.651). Some mind, it is clear, keeps track of the details of this printed cosmos, and lets escape from its scrutiny the fall of no sparrow.

The intrusion of this consciousness is perhaps the most radical, the most disconcerting innovation in all of *Ulysses*. It is something new in fiction. It is not the voice of the storyteller: not a voice at all, since it does not address us, does not even speak. We do not hear its accents, we observe its actions, which are performed with a certain indifference to our presence: actions such as pasting captions across the pages of "Aeolus" in such wise as to render impossible a straightforward vocal performance of that talk-ridden episode.

For the tale of Bloomsday is not in the old sense, nor in any sense, "told"; it is mimed in words arranged on pages in space. We are urged to read aloud and tripped up if we try. The arranging presence (David Hayman, the first critic to dwell on its intrusions, has even suggested that we say "the Arranger"[7]) enjoys a seemingly total recall for exact forms of words used hundreds of pages earlier, a recall which implies not an operation of memory but access such as ours to a printed book, in which pages can be turned to and fro. Like an author's ideal reader, this Arranger keeps remembering, savoring the choice verbal bits.

We have mentioned a certain indifference to our presence; and yet surely "Bloom ate liv as said before" is marginally aware that we are present to be irritated. "A harsh and awkward narrator," Clive Hart writes of the spirit behind "Wandering Rocks," "whose difficult personality is the most salient thing about the chapter."[8] "Wandering Rocks" was Joyce's earliest exploitation of the Arranger—the captions in "Aeolus" extended his presence retroactively at a late stage of revision—and it is noteworthy that in "Wandering Rocks" the Arranger's difficult personality manifests itself in snares scattered for the reader. "Mr Bloom's dental windows" (10.1115) is a familiar example: a small gratuitous puzzle, apt to annoy if noticed. It will be an exceptional reader indeed who will calmly hold this detail in abeyance until it is resolved some eighty-five pages later in a snatch of dialogue about the Bloom we know:

—Isn't he a cousin of Bloom the dentist? says Jack Power.
—Not at all, says Martin. Only namesakes. (12.1638)

True, we can imagine a reader from whom "Mr Bloom's dental windows" would have instantly invoked the actual Marcus Bloom, dentist, who practiced in 1904 at 2 Clare Street: a reader who would have known that vanished, pre-Rebellion Dublin as intimately as do Joyce's Dubliners. But not even in 1922 can there have been many left alive who both commanded such lore and were capable of reading 250 pages into the difficult *Ulysses*. No, the Arranger can be sure that we readers are probably visiting, and he treats us, when he deigns to notice our presence, with the sour xenophobic indifference Dublin can turn upon visitors who have lingered long enough for hospitality's first gleam to tarnish. Mr. Hart has also detected in the Arranger, the spirit of

Dublin itself, "endowed with a distinctive personality," "capable of a great deal of malice, of deliberate *Schadenfreude*."[9] That spirit does not mind if we misunderstand wholly and never know it, standing unhelpfully by as we read of nonfictional Father Conmee's encounter with a Mrs. Sheehy we may not understand is also nonfictional.

> —Very well indeed, father. And you, father?
> Father Conmee was wonderfully well indeed. He would go to Buxton probably for the waters. And her boys, were they getting on well at Belvedere? Was that so? Father Conmee was very glad indeed to hear that. (10.18)

If we do not know (as we almost certainly do not) that the boys in question, Richard and Eugene Sheehy, were of Joyce's (hence Stephen's) generation and long since out of Belvedere, the Arranger will leave our ignorance undisturbed and will not by the twitch of an eyelid prompt us to remark that we were not allowed to hear what it was that absentminded Father Conmee was very glad to hear.[10] Our innocence will doubtless occasion disgusted comments when we are out of earshot; the Dublin habit of jeering at Joyce enthusiasts has its precedent inside the book itself, where it is an aspect of the Irish citizen's acculturated scorn for anyone whose information or whose sense of things does not coincide precisely with his own.

This is to resay what we began by noticing, that the Arranger's role in the book seems to have been prompted by the needs of two episodes in which neither Stephen nor Bloom but an engulfing Dublin is dominant. Besides civic ubiquity, though, the Arranger has another hallmark, virtuosity. He epitomizes the Dublin knack for performance. Astute readers will have sensed some alien presence well before "Aeolus." Who transcribed the voice of Bloom's cat with such precision? Certainly not Bloom, who utters (4.462) a common "Miaow." Whose phrase registered Bloom's gait in his rush toward the burning kidney, "stepping hastily down the stairs with a flurried stork's legs" (4.383)? The same Arranger, surely, who in contriving the phantasmagoria in "Circe" will make a trolley's gong speak, "Bang Bang Bla Bak

Bludd Bugg Bloo," and have Bloom, as he blunders out of the way, raise "a policeman's whitegloved hand" (15.189). Bloom has no white glove and impersonates no policeman; the whitegloved hand is an expressionistic vividness, in an episode where every passing analogy is rendered visible and audible. By parallel logic the kidney in "Calypso" might have called out as loudly as that trolley and the stork have been as visible as that glove, but the Arranger was not ready to show his hand so early.

In the heyday of the initial style he was content to lie low, imparting at need the little graphic touches whose innovative economy every reader admires:

The felly harshed against the curbstone: stopped. (6.490)

The priest began to read out of his book with a fluent croak. (6.594)

Mr Bloom walked unheeded along his grove by saddened angels, crosses, broken pillars, family vaults, stone hopes praying with upcast eyes, old Ireland's hearts and hands. (6.928)

This does not mean that we are to call him simply "the narrator," since he exists side by side with a colorless primary narrator who sees to the thousand little bits of novelistic housekeeping no one is meant to notice: the cames and wents, saids and askeds, stoods and sats, without which nothing could get done at all. Lounging in this drudge's shadow, the Arranger may now and then show his hand when Bloom is *observed*: when, by a principle we have already dwelt on, the narrative sequence is being responsive to what the character is conscious of:

The mourners knelt here and there in prayingdesks. Mr Bloom stood behind near the font and, when all had knelt, dropped carefully his unfolded newspaper from his pocket and knelt his right knee upon it. He fitted his black hat gently on his left knee and, holding its brim, bent over piously. (6.584)

These are the closely noted actions of a non-Catholic[11] at a Catholic service: aware of kneeling, aware of the danger dust poses to his dark suit, aware of his hat, aware of the need to bend "piously." The Arranger, we may guess, arranged those sentences, snatching the pen from his anonymous colleague to achieve not neologistic vividness but a seriatim accuracy of observation that hovers just this side of being malicious.

Here we need to confront a more general topic, the fluctuating boundary between character and language, since it matters how much "bent over piously" comes from Bloom, how much from the narrative voice. If the former, Bloom is feeling or is trying to feel pious; if the latter, indifference or malice may be remarking that a show of piety is incumbent. The line between such options is often impossible to draw: here even to have asked the question is to have shared a little the Arranger's skepticism, and very often small questions of tone and motive in *Ulysses* turn out to pertain to the ascription of forms of words.*

Yet words, especially in the domain of the initial style, are normally ascribable; thus, whereas in "Calypso" Bloom surely does not spell the catspeech, Stephen in "Proteus" just a few pages previously *may* spell (or imagine spelled) the wavespeech: "seesoo, hrss, rsseeiss, ooos." As a words-on-paper man, he may well be fancying principles of transcription. Or perhaps not: he may only be listening, and whatever hand writes the pages on which he exists may be supplying the transcription from over his shoulder.

That Stephen both exists on printed pages and fancies himself writing at least some of the sentences we read is an old theme for any reader of the *Portrait*, where in letting the style grow as Stephen grew Joyce lets us perceive in style a system of limits

---

* And when mimicry goes on for several pages the effect can be most unsettling, as in the "Wandering Rocks" account (10.1–205) of Father Conmee's walk. "It was idyllic: and Father Conmee reflected on the providence of the Creator who had made turf to be in bogs where men might dig it out and bring it to town and hamlet to make fires in the houses of poor people": so for page after page, and some readers find Father Conmee's naïveté endearing while others think the portrait savage. If we could see the Arranger's face, we might be able to tell.

within which Stephen is somewhere to be found: verbal limits to
locate the expanding limits of an immature but developing character who increasingly likes the thought of being a writer. Thus
chiasmus and "lucid supple periodic prose" reflect Stephen's taste
toward the end of chapter IV, where both are prominent, and
Stephen may be thought of as framing some of the chiasmic
sentences though not all of them. (Once in *Ulysses* Leopold Bloom
exists within an episode he actually fancies himself as writing
[16.1229] and the result is stylistic disaster; the episode is "Eumaeus.")

The essence of limits is that one keeps encountering them, like
the walls of a room; as if to emphasize this principle, Joyce characterized the *Portrait* end to end by a habit of repeating words and
phrases again and again in brief compass:[12]

> And *if* he had judged her harshly? *If her life* were a *simple* rosary
> of hours, *her life simple* and strange as *a bird's life*, gay in the
> morning, restless all day, tired at sundown? *Her heart simple* and
> wilful as *a bird's heart?* (182)

And already two purposes are at work here, Stephen's and Joyce's.
Joyce, shaping the book he was writing, anxious to delimit its
hero, had uses for a rhetoric of repetition which sometimes serves
his purposes a little more nearly than it always describes the
movement of Stephen's thought. But Stephen does have a taste
for such writing. "The spell of arms and voices," he writes in his
diary, "the white arms of roads, their promise of close embraces
and the black arms of tall ships that stand against the moon,
their tale of distant nations" (*P* 252). But other diary entries are
free of this tic, the pervasiveness of which in the book's narrative
texture we may want to ascribe to the author's expressive purposes. Similarly, though Stephen at sixteen has a taste for chiasmus, it was not Stephen's but Joyce's arranging hand that made
the whole book chiasmic, reshuffling manuscript sheets to make
of chapter I's events a reverse mirroring of those of chapter V.[13]

So Stephen exists, for us readers of words, in a zone of interference between "his" habits with words and the practices of

James Joyce. Joyce, let us make no mistake, is always present in *Ulysses*, and no talk of that dyad of technicians, the self-effacing narrator and the mischievous Arranger, should permit us wholly to forget that fact. "O Jamesy let me up out of this," cries Molly Bloom from the chamber pot (18.1128), as if inadvertently calling on her maker.

Early in *Ulysses* Joyce introduced something new, long passages we have learned to call "interior monologue," which profess to transcribe the actual movement of a character's thought. This, we might think, disposes of the perplexity we sometimes feel in the *Portrait,* trying to feel sure whose words we read, Stephen's or the author's. Not wholly, though. The same hand that arranged the events of the *Portrait* into a chiasmus is still writing "Proteus" through Stephen's illusory presence, perhaps spelling out the wavespeech, certainly seeing to it that a young man who thinks he is enacting Hamlet's part (obstinate mourning, soliloquies, disobligingness) shall actually be playing Telemachus, a role that never crosses his mind, and shall accordingly meet an unwitting Ulysses.

And Bloom's unspoken words, are they Bloom's? Not wholly.

> Might meet a robber or two. Well, meet him. Getting on to sundown. The shadows of the mosques among the pillars: priest with a scroll rolled up. A shiver of the trees, signal, the evening wind. I pass on. Fading gold sky. A mother watches me from her doorway. She calls her children home in their dark language. High wall: beyond strings twanged. Night sky, moon, violet, colour of Molly's new garters. Strings. Listen. A girl playing one of those instruments what do you call them: dulcimers. I pass. (4.91)

Bloom's memories of "The Dance of the Hours" have shaded this, and of such books as *In the Track of the Sun* ("sunburst on the titlepage"; later read so much the title page has become detached and vanished; 17.1395). And "what do you call them: dulcimers" is unmistakably Bloom, no doubt fumbling for a classroom memory of "Kubla Khan." The Arranger's merciless eye fastens on "what do you call them," and we are not allowed to forget it when the voice of Si Dedalus in "Sirens" comes to Bloom's ear "like no voice of strings of reeds or whatdoyoucall them dulcimers" (11.675). So much is Bloom. But "their dark language"? "She calls her children home in their dark language": no, those are not Bloom's words, they are surely James Joyce's, supplying a phrase that shall bridge the text's continuity across an instant Bloom did not verbalize, merely felt. So, too, in "Lestrygonians" when Bloom espies Sir Frederick Falkiner, the chief judicial officer of Dublin:

> I suppose he'd turn up his nose at that stuff I drank. Vintage
> wine for them, the year marked on a dusty bottle. (8.1154)

"The year marked on a dusty bottle" seems too many words for Bloom's swift thought; seven words have evidently been supplied for what passed before Bloom as a visual fancy.

So there has been a look of autonomy for the initial style to serve and transcribe, but under close inspection this autonomy is compromised. The initial style creates nearly as much as it records. It creates Stephen, and permits a central ambiguity in all Stephen's speculations on his entoilment in a web of determinism, caught as he is in Joyce's book where Joyce is composing his words though he often thinks (and we think) that he composes them. It creates Bloom, too, and if we think the style simply responds to Bloom as Bloom responds to the sensations of the morning— Bloom's mind an ironic surrogate for objectivity itself—we are mistaken to the extent (we cannot calibrate it) that Bloom, too, is a creation of words, which sometimes overlay and amend "his" words and are also sometimes shut off, as when he came through his front door and later could not remember what the words did not record, what he had done with his hat.

The poet, Aristotle thought, shows men in action, and in Homer a character is a doer of deeds; even a speech is a deed. The men of *Ulysses* are generally dwelt on by the poet when they are between such deeds as the day affords: rather reflecting than acting, and generating spoken or unspoken words which on the book's page are not wholly theirs. A character in *Ulysses* (in a city of talk) is an interference phenomenon between "his" language and language not his, sometimes other characters', sometimes the author's. The second half of *Ulysses* dissolves into "styles" the way all events in Dublin dissolve into gossip. From end to end *Finnegans Wake* is a mull of gossip.

Ulysses will also supply, in its second half, innumerable details which supplement, modify, sometimes contradict what we have come to suppose. Only after Bloom has angrily asserted his Jewish identity (12.1804) shall we learn that he is not circumcised (13.979), lacks a Jewish mother (15.281), and has undergone two valid Christian baptisms (17.540). Bloom, seemingly one of fiction's little men, will grow when we are apprised of his stature and his hidden fiscal assets. Stephen, whom we may once have thought was to be the book's hero, at any rate its focal consciousness, will lose his bright subjectivity, will be reduced to grunted replies, will be deprived (in part by drink, in part by narrative method) of his quick-darting faculties, and will eventually walk out of the Joyce universe altogether. Molly, at first a voice that grunted, "Mn" ("no") (4.57), then an impression of lazy sluttishness, then a glimpse of "a plump bare generous arm" (10.251), will turn into an unexpectedly realized character whose final word is Yes.

And linkage after linkage of plot will be supplied, commanding so much terrain of datable past that what seemed a single day's slice of inconsequence will become the chronicle, generations in extent, of an immigrant family in Ireland, that country whose citizens characteristically emigrate.[14] (The very potato that doomed Ireland in the 1840s will become in this odd family a good-luck charm, preservative against pestilence.)

So as the Arranger takes increasingly prominent charge, the ten-episode *Ulysses* of "objective" irony, the book that terminates with "Wandering Rocks," will turn into a different sort of book altogether. Still, there is no sharp break. The Arranger was there all the time, and the principles according to which he will now commence to alter *Ulysses* were potential from the start, latent, obeying an aesthetic of delay.

Notes

1. Joyce wrote to Harriet Weaver of "the initial style" (*Letters* I, 129) in a context that makes this phrase include the first ten episodes; he is defending "Siren," the first manifest departure. The most willful disruption of this style, the captions in "Aeolus," got added as late as August 1921, while the book was in press. Michael Groden, *"Ulysses" in Progress* (Princeton, N.J.: Princeton University Press, 1977) 105.

2. See *Letters* II, 190. Titles in the *Dubliners* mode—e.g., "Grace"—make simple ironic points. It is hard to see how much more Joyce could have intended in calling a short story "Ulysses."

3. Herbert Gorman, *James Joyce* (New York: Farrar & Rinehart, 1939), 224.

4. The famous anecdote is provided by Frank Budgen in *James Joyce and the Making of "Ulysses"* (London: Oxford University Press, 1972) 20.

5. Groden, 64–114.

6. *Letters* I, 114, where the main part of the book is to have only eleven episodes. See Groden, 33.

7. David Hayman, *"Ulysses": The Mechanics of Meaning* (Englewood Cliffs, N.J.: Prentice-Hall, Inc., 1970), 70: "I use the term 'arranger' to designate a figure who can be identified neither with the author nor with his narrators, but who exercises an increasing degree of overt control over his increasingly challenging materials."

8. Clive, Hart, "Wandering Rocks," in Clive Hart and David Hayman, *James Joyce's "Ulysses"* (Berkeley: University of California Press, 1974), 186.

9. Ibid., 190.

10. Conor Cruise O'Brien, *States of Ireland* (London: Hutchinson, 1974), 160, supplies the biographical information but does not notice the Arranger's reticence, and supposes that the date of Bloomsday is idealized. But not in this chapter.

11. Bloom had a Catholic baptism prior to his marriage with Molly, but has apparently never received communion, since he wonders (5.346) if the hosts are in water. "Non-Catholic" seems appropriate.

12. In "The Text of James Joyce's *A Portrait*," *Neuphilogische Mitteilungen* 65 (1964), Chester G. Anderson noted the frequency of this device. Since typists' eyes tended to skip from one repetition to another, it was a prime occasion for textual corruption.

13. See Hans Walter Gabler, "The Seven Lost Years of *A Portrait of the Artist as a Young Man*," in Thomas F. Staley and Bernard Benstock, eds.

Approaches to "Ulysses": Ten Essays (Pittsburgh: University of Pittsburgh Press, 1970).

14. In John Henry Raleigh's *A Chronicle of Leopold and Molly Bloom* (Berkeley: University of California Press, 1977), the earliest entries date from the eighteenth century.

Book of Many Turns

FRITZ SENN

✦ ✦ ✦

JOYCE'S WORKS CAN BE SEEN, with equal validity, either as one great whole or as a series of self-contained units. Seemingly contradictory statements can make good sense: Joyce kept reshaping the same material in more complex ways—he never repeated himself. The reiteration, even permutation, of some fundamentals is striking. We can trace the terminal actuality of *Finnegans Wake* from the germinal potentiality of *Dubliners*; but conversely we are also tempted to emphasize the unique whatness of every single work. Joyce kept repeating himself in metempsychotic succession—but if we highlight the individual incarnations, each of his major works is essentially and unpredictably different from its predecessors.

In coming to terms with Joyce's particular other world of words, we can choose between two different sets of terminology. Taking up Joyce's own, or Stephen Dedalus's, insistent metaphors, we can see literature as a process of conception and parturition. A quasi-biological vocabulary suggests itself which serves to describe an evolution of powerful, vital drives in a teeming world of luxuriant growth. In fact, such a monstrosity as the "Oxen of the Sun" chapter in *Ulysses* can be read as a hymn to fertility in its theme and by its very nature—a misbirth maybe, but the offshoot of some generative (perhaps too generative) force. If we were not trying to be so erudite about this chapter, we might be impressed by its sheer animal exuberance. It seems that all of Joyce's creations came into being through some analogous biological force and were subject to many changes during their prolonged periods of gestation. The works are not only separate, though related, but they all got out of hand in the workshop; they could not be contained within whatever original ground plan there was. They proliferated into something never imagined at the instant of conception.

Even the smallest elements in a literary universe, the letters of the alphabet, can be fertile. Long before Joyce thought of *Finnegans Wake*, he made one of the characters in his first short story reveal her ignorance with an illiterate "rheumatic wheels" (*D* 9). The life force, like everything else in the story, has gone wrong; it has been turned into decay. So, through a tiny change of two letters or one sound, an appropriate word "rheum" (suggesting a disease: natural development gone wrong) replaces another word.[1] In *Ulysses*, a typographical misbirth, which disfigures the funeral report in the newspaper, is called, with good reason, "a line of bitched type" (*U* 16.1263), bitches being proverbially and indiscriminately fertile. The simple letter *l*, whether superfluous as in "that other world" (*U* 5.245), or missing as in "L. Boom" (*U* 16.1262), has a pullulating force and invites speculation.

But then it is exactly such exuberant, freakish offshoots as the "Oxen of the Sun" chapter that can be demonstrated to be the disciplined, programmed, calculated, systematic completion of an elaborate plan by a meticulous artificer—perhaps an obsessed one. Chaos resolves itself into the painstakingly structured order of layered symmetry, of catalogs and charts, schemas, correspondences, and parallels. The jungle is also a garden. Much of our labor actually consists of exposing the manifold coordinates in the system. To some of us the existence of such a system amounts to the major justification of a work of literature. To others, Joyce has become too exclusively a cerebral constructor and callous arranger.

In *A Portrait*, the two aspects are clearly interfused. We have now been trained to see its rigid structure as a verbal and symbolic system. But to early readers sheer disorder seemed to prevail. Richard Ellmann, drawing on internal as well as biographical evidence, uses biological terms to characterize the novel as embryonic (*JJ*1 306–9).

I take my starting point from a different but related ambiguity. It is contained in the title of the novel, that oddly trailing, spiraling, threefold phrase: "A Portrait—of the Artist—as a Young Man." It looks like an attempt, pedantic and verbose, to fix the subject as accurately as possible. The incongruous effect is that the subject becomes all the more elusive. A less clumsily delimitative title might not have made us aware of the aim of portraiture to pinpoint quiddity in the way that those portraits adorning the walls of Clongowes Wood (*P* 46–47) preserve something unchangeable for all eternity.

The title implies, however, that there is no portrait as such, that a choice must be made. Out of a wide variety, only one phase or pose can be selected. So the implication is that there must be other poses or phases perhaps equally pertinent in the room of infinite possibilities. In the novel Joyce of course gives us a series of such poses and aspects, a chronological succession in which each phase extends and modifies the previous ones. Perhaps only in perpetual qualification can that quintessential quality be circumscribed which, in itself—as the title indicates— remains beyond our grasp. The specification "as a young man" is necessary to the nature of portraiture, but it also contradicts its concept.

In the title it is the unstressed but potent conjunctive particle "as" which seems to infuse the novel. This particle denotes, as the dictionary will tell us, something or someone "in the character, in the capacity," or "in the role" of something else. The *Portrait* is a sequence of such parts of character. Stephen, knowingly or unknowingly, assumes an amazing number of character roles as he grows up. Before he appears in the flesh, Stephen has already been transformed into a fairy tale character which is specifically glossed ("He was baby tuckoo" [*P* 5]). He soon learns to play some parts, often protective ones, with varying degrees of skill and success. Stephen learns to imitate and to pretend: on the second page he is already "feigning" to run. A number of roles are prescribed to him by the communities of family, school, church, and nation, and it takes some growing up to make him realize the reticular hazards involved. His reading provides a further set of models to be imitated. In the second chapter Stephen actually prepares for a stage performance in a school play, a take-off on one of his masters. He deliberately and, at times, histrionically rejects some roles, whereas he remains quite unaware of certain others. It is easier for us than it was for some earlier readers to recognize the stagey nature of some turning points in Stephen's career. Finally Stephen chooses to become an artist, that is, a creator of fictional roles. And in *Ulysses*, the same Stephen singles out, for a dazzling display of theorizing, the writer who probably created more roles than anyone else, Shakespeare (and Stephen is aware that Shakespeare also played real theatrical parts on the London stage). Stephen's artist is compared to "the God of the creation" (*P* 181), and this God is immediately epiphanized in one particular pose—"paring his fingernails."

Somehow Stephen, who enumerates with such gusto the chosen roles of his father: "a tenor, an amateur actor, a shouting politician . . . a taxgatherer, a bankrupt and at present a praiser of his own past" (*P* 203), is a chip off the old block, with a self-written scenario that is just a bit more *recherché*. A predominant role is preordained in the family name, Dedalus, which was taken, along with the motto of the novel, from an ancient book of roles and transformation scenes entitled *Metamorphoses*.

All of this is carried over into *Ulysses* and magnified there. The conjunctive potential of that word "as" permeates all of *Ulysses*. But Joyce need no longer plant it into his title. The title *Ulysses* proclaims a role, one Leopold Bloom *as* Odysseus, or Odysseus *as* modern man. And once we catch on to this new game of aliases or analogies, there is no holding back. *Ulysses* is Joyce's *Metamorphoses*, a book of roles and guises, a game of identities, of transsubstantiations. It is pantomimic in the sense of imitating everything. Molly Bloom tells us that her husband is "always imitating everybody" (U 18.1204). But even without Molly's corroboration it would be superfluous, after fifty years, to reiterate all the parts that all the characters play in the book.

It is sufficient, by way of recall, to mention the first appearance of a character in the novel. Joyce portrays a real Dubliner, Oliver St. John Gogarty, who was well known in Dublin and remains in Dublin memory just because he was able to carry off so many roles with impressive alacrity. In the book he immediately assumes one particular role, that of a priest, pretending to be a vicar of Christ and a follower of St. Peter. And one of Buck Mulligan's first mocking actions concerns the miraculous eucharistic metamorphosis of mundane into divine substance. He does it, profanely but tellingly, to the pretended accompaniment of slow music, as an *artiste* in the music hall sense, a conjurer. And by means of electric current, as magic trickery, cunning deceit. His subject, however, is transformation, and he keeps transforming himself according to whim or opportunity. A true panto-mime, he becomes, in skillful mimetic turn, a priest, a military commander, patron of an artist, friendly adviser, medical rationalist, and so on. His repertoire transcends the boundaries of sex or humanity: he can imitate Mother Grogan or become a bird or an ascending Christ. His observer, Stephen, projects yet other roles onto him, while behind or beyond or above his handiwork an increasingly conspicuous author dangles another assortment of analogies. All of this takes place within some twenty pages comprising the first chapter.

It is no wonder that Gogarty, who could successfully bring off so many roles as doctor, athlete, poet, and later on as nationalistic senator, aviator, and carouser with the British nobility (quite apart from his histrionic talent ad hoc), resented the perpetuation of some post-adolescent roles in fictional permanence. Joyce had obviously and maliciously encroached upon his own chosen territory, and Gogarty was only paying back in kind when he revealed (to an audience of would-be Joyce idolators) the real, as he maintained, meaning of the term "artist" in Dublin parlance, reducing, in intention, Joyce's and Stephen's roles to the limited one of poseurs.[2]

The simplest way of playing imitative roles is by repeating someone else's words: thus *Ulysses* opens with an explicit quotation. The first words spoken aloud, "*Introibo ad altare Dei*" (*U* 1.5), are not of that everyday common speech that Joyce could evoke so well; they are neither everyday English, nor even English, nor even speech. They are "intoned," in Latin, that dead tongue with which the Church until recently chose to transmit its messages. The stability of the ritual from which these words are taken contrasts of course with Mulligan's volatile flexibility and lack of principle. The words, in any case, are imitation, resounding for the millionth time, as prologue to the book whose characters play parts, whose actions often consist in acting, and many of whose words are quotation to an extent that the author never even attempted to single out individual quotes by customary typographical marks. A quotation also links the present occasion with a former one; it is a strandentwining chord back in time. So the first words uttered aloud in *Ulysses* take us even beyond the Roman Catholic Mass to the Hebrew Psalms of the Old Testament. They span several millennia.

One capsular reflection of the whole is this: the novel, whose Latin title suggests a Greek hero based (as Joyce believed) on Semitic tales, begins like a play, with stage directions in the first paragraph and an opening speech by an Irish character whose language is English and who, with a flair for imitation, intones a sentence from the Latin Mass, which is in itself a translation of a Hebrew Psalm. The ethnological and literary multiplicity is already present, while on the surface of it we never for a moment leave a simple, realistic story.

Joyce, who reveals the identity of Buck Mulligan at the outset, keeps the question of who and what he really is suspended throughout. We first witness mimicry, mummery, and mockery; the first voice we hear is put on, and it continues to change. It would be hard to determine exactly where Buck Mulligan drops all of his guises and pretenses and speaks in his own voice, if ever he does. I think that for all his imitative zeal we can feel the man's character behind the sequence of adornments. But it is interesting to note how much at variance all our feelings are once we try to bring them into the open. And so, it is no wonder that critics disagree in their assessment of Buck Mulligan; this is in keeping with mercurial Malachi cheerfully contradicting himself while manipulating his various personae.

Hence *Ulysses* appears, from the start, as a reapplication of a principle evolved in *A Portrait*. The artist is reportrayed as a slightly more disillusioned young man with some newly acquired roles. But the foreground is dominated by his mercurial counterpart, who condenses a whole portrait gallery of a vaudeville *artiste as* (to pick some more items from the script) a mocker, *as* St. Peter, *as* a sycophant, *as* Cranly, *as* a Homeric suitor, or, in the overall view, *as* a Shakespearean clown who sets the stage.

This stage will before long be occupied by Leopold Bloom, whose verbal and mimetic repertoire is much more limited. Mulligan's brilliance is set off against Bloom's lackluster commonness and common sense. Bloom's opening words could not possibly elicit the same sort of extended commentary that Mulligan's require. But with his trite "O, there you are" (*U* 4.17), Bloom at least reaches his speechless partner, the cat, and attains whatever contact is called for. His concern for that partner is unfeigned. And the cat immediately responds with "Mkgnao," and two variations of the same theme: "Mrkgnao!" and "Mrkrgnao!"

The first book begins on top of a tower with imitative words and divine reverberations. The second book begins below ground in Bloom's kitchen, with simple words and onomatopoeic animal noises. It is intriguing to follow one reader, the Italian translator of *Ulysses*, who claims that the consonantic structure of the cat's "Mrkrgnao" utterance is a covert evocation of Mercury.[3] This would introduce either the Homeric messenger Hermes appropriate to the chapter, or else constitute an animal echo of Mulligan's mercurial role in the parallel chapter. As the novel moves on, Mulligan's brilliance can hardly be increased, while Bloom's earthy wit and less ostentatious resourcefulness have a way of growing on most readers.

But then of course Bloom is accorded a great deal of scope.

Although he is remarkably awkward in acting out such roles as he might enjoy playing in real life, like Philip Beaufoy or Don Juan, he is unconsciously carrying a much greater load than all the other characters. Most roles (Mr. Bloom *as* Odysseus, Christ, Moses, Wandering Jew, and so on) have been well studied. I would like to single out a far less personal role. Within the totality of the novel, Bloom is also a part of speech. In purely grammatical terms, Bloom is also an all-round man. His name is taken through all the cases of the singular: "Bloom. Of Bloom. To Bloom. Bloom" (*U* 15.677), and he seems to have become a grammatical case history. On occasion he resembles a noun with a relative pronoun in various inflections like "Bloowho" (*U* 11.86), "Bloowhoose" (*U* 11.149), "Bloohimwhom" (*U* 11.309), in passages that seem to bring out Bloom's relativity. An inflated version is "puffing Poldy, blowing Bloohoom" (*U* 15.157). At times perhaps Bloom appears more like a verb than a noun, the *verbum* of Latin grammar or else of the Gospel of St. John. In the course of the novel he seems conjugated in all tenses, past, present, and future; in the active and the passive voice; in all the possible moods—indicative, imperative, subjunctive, optative—not to forget participial forms like "blooming." He becomes a universal paradigm of the school book; if we can parse him, we can parse humanity. Beyond grammar, he is anagrammatically transformed into "Old Ollebo, M. P." (*U* 17.409). And "POLDY" is the basis for an acrostic (*U* 17.412).

Bloom's nominal existence is diverse too. He has been translated from Hungarian *Virag*, and he is translating himself into such fictitious roles as Henry Flower, to which Molly adds, "Don Poldo de la Flora" (*U* 18.1428), and the author such variants as "Professor Luitpold Blumenduft" (*U* 12.468) or "Senhor Enrique Flor" (*U* 12.1288). Other transformations are geometrical, a concave distortion like "Booloohoom," or a convex "Jollypoldy the rixdix doldy" (*U* 15.149). Typography adds an insult, "L. Boom" (*U* 16.1262), to the catalog. Etymology extends the range further: Skeat's *Etymological Dictionary* relates "bloom" to "blood." Leopold Bloom does not read Skeat's by the hour, but he substitutes his own name for "Blood" in a throwaway (*U* 8.8), unaware of a momentary eucharistic function. No wonder there are Bloomites in the book, and that the hero is sartorially celebrated in "bloomers" and even citified into "Bloomusalem." Thus, on the merely nomenclatural level of this ominously cluttered novel, Bloom is awarded unprecedented scope as a paradigm.

We know that Joyce found in Homer's Odysseus the universal paradigm from myth that he needed. Hence, I would like to rephrase some of my remarks in the light of Homeric analogies. I have to admit first that I always thought these analogies meaningful, fruitful, and even helpful, even if some of our heavy-footed glosses may not be so. The Homeric ground plan provides another link with the past; it takes us back, as Joyce always tries to do, to first beginnings. Homer's epics are, for all practical purposes, the origins of Western literature. *Ulysses* comprises all literature from its Greek roots (as well as its Hebrew roots in the Old Testament) to its latest ramifications in Yeats and a just emerging Synge. In between, English literary history is amply documented, notably in "Scylla and Charybdis" and "Oxen of the Sun," and there are vestigial traits of Italian, French, and German literature throughout. Homer's highly finished art is a beginning for us, but it was in turn already the culmination of a long development now lost in obscurity. It is an end turned into a new beginning, which makes it all the more fitting for Joyce's purposes.

That the Homeric poems were not, originally, written down and read but passed on orally and recited with musical accompaniment moreover conveniently ties them to an oral tradition very much alive in Ireland. The art of storytelling was still practiced in Joyce's Dublin in those communities that had to be culturally self-sustaining.

Joyce preferred the *Odyssey* to the much more martial *Iliad*, not merely because of his pacifist inclinations nor because he needed more social relationships than a war report can provide, but also because the action of the *Iliad* is subsumed in its sequel. The *Odyssey* is wider in scope: temporal, topical, and simply human.

Even though the so-called Homeric parallels, the transpositions of characters and situations, have definite purposes, it is sometimes useful not to insist on the strictly parallel nature of the correspondences: the pattern is often a crisscross one, and similarities often go by contrast. Perhaps the most pervasive Homeric features in *Ulysses* are not the one-to-one relationships that Stuart Gilbert began to chart for us, but principles or motive forces—such as the Protean force of transformation in the third chapter. Homer and Joyce both had the ability to condense certain overall principles into concise verbal form. Joyce was fond of condensing the themes and techniques of his whole works into his opening words (as on the first page of *Ulysses*, which I have dwelt upon in the preceding pages). I believe that Joyce realized that the opening of the *Odyssey* is similarly fashioned, and that he was aware that Homer, much more pointedly and literally than Vergil, Milton, or Pope, put the subject of his poem right in front of us. The subject is Man. The *Odyssey* begins with that word— "*Andra*"—in the objective case, the central object, and Homer keeps it suspended over the first line. It is fortunate that Joyce, who knew little classical Greek (though a Zurich friend, Paul Ruggiero, taught him some modern Greek), recorded the first line of the *Odyssey* in the original, or very close to it. Ellmann implies that it was quoted from memory (*JJ*1 585). It is misquoted, of course, and we can explain Joyce's faulty accents as the result of understandable ignorance or, maybe, as a shift in emphasis. At any rate, Joyce knew by heart, and was ready to scribble beside the only authentic portrait of Mr. Bloom we have, the well-known line:

Andra moi énnepe, Mōusa, polýtropon, hòs mála pollà[4]

It happens, fortuitously, that in Greek the accusative noun can be placed before us without a definite article and with its defining adjective being cleverly withheld for a few beats. Thus "Man" is placed before us in his most universalized form before the focus narrows to one particular individual. This obviously suits Joyce's purpose.

In the Homeric text the second noun is "Troy, the holy city" (*Odyssey* I.2). So even here Joyce's favorite coupling of the individual and the community of the city seems anticipated. But the word that is especially emphasized in Homer's first line and which is skillfully introduced after a weighty pause, is the epitheton that accompanies "man"—"*polytropos.*" It has occupied commentators a good deal, and W. B. Stanford in his excellent study, *The Ulysses Theme,* devotes some pages to it.[5] Joyce could have found most of the glosses in reference books or in the standard Greek dictionaries that he was quite able to consult. Any Greek dictionary would have given him more or less the same information that Liddell and Scott provide: literally, *polytropos* means "much turned," "of many turns." It is taken to mean that Odysseus is a man much traveled, "much wandering." But the meaning was soon extended to suggest characteristic resourcefulness—"a man capable of turning many ways," a versatile character. It acquired a pejorative use too: it came to mean "shifty" or "wily" (in this sense the adjective is applied to Hermes, i.e., Mercury). It can mean "fickle" or just "changeable," or become a vague term for "various" and "manifold."

I submit that all of these potential meanings of the one word[6] are, literally or figuratively, transferred into *Ulysses.* When Joyce described an early plan of his novel to Stanislaus in 1915, he referred to the central section as "Ulysses Wandlungen."[7] Since Stanislaus at the time was interned by Austrian authorities, the postcard had to be written in German. What Joyce probably wanted to say was "Wanderungen"—wanderings—but he was either confused by the intricacies of the German vocabulary (where the verb *wandeln* can mean both "to wander" and "to change") and hit on *Wandlungen* (which means "changes" but not "wanderings"), or he was trying to entertain his brother by a double entendre. The result, in any case, is that "Ulysses Wanderungen" happens to be an excellent summing up of the novel and also of the two main meanings of Homer's adjective, stressing the hero's travels as well as his versatility.

But to return to the Greek dictionary. Its philological lore seems to appear, in part verbatim, throughout the book. "Wily," for example, is an epithet reserved for the voluble sailor in "Eumaeus," whose pseudo-Odyssean role we have known all along ("such a wily old customer" [*U* 16.625]). He pretends to be much traveled, and he is in fact a resourceful inventor of tales. Another adjective, "shifty," is applied by Bloom to such "crawthumpers" as one of the Carey brothers who plotted murder and then turned on his accomplices (the negative side of Odyssean changeability): "there's something shiftylooking about them" (*U* 5.383). The other adjective of the dictionary, "fickle," occurs in "Nausikaa." The boy whom Gerty MacDowell admires in vain seems to her a "Lighthearted deceiver and fickle like all his sex" (*U* 13.584). Actually Homer's hero had appeared in just such unfavorable light to some of the early unsympathetic commentators.[8] Now I am not sure how far Gerty's boyfriend qualifies for an Odyssean role of tertiary importance, but he is apparently capable of doing clever turns on his bicycle, and it is a nice touch that his name is Reggie *Wylie*. Since Joyce invites us to compare Odysseus with Leopold Bloom and since Gerty compares Bloom with Reggie Wylie, this may be a peripheral instance of Joyce's reserving some Odyssean versatility for minor characters as well.

Most editions of the *Odyssey* list, in their variant readings of *polytropos*, the different adjective *"polykrotos."* This is in fact usually the first textual note in the book. The meaning is generally given as "wily, sly, cunning" (which corresponds to *polytropos*), but originally it meant "ringing loud, resounding." Somehow this might contribute toward making L. Boom a noise in the street. Stanford's interpretation of the adjective as "knocked about"[9] would also apply to Mr. Bloom. But even if this philological spectrum were outside of Joyce's ken, it is worth noting that Homer's first emphasized adjective was soon changed, distorted, or parodied— the earliest anticipation perhaps of Joyce's technique of meaningfully distorted readings.

The translation of the *Odyssey* by Butcher and Lang, which Frank Budgen assured me Joyce had used and for which Phillip Herring found notebook evidence, renders the first epithet as "the man, so ready at need." I cannot help being amused, perhaps coincidentally, by Bloom's being described as "a man and ready," and rising to make for the "yard," contemplating on his way Greek goddesses yielding to Greek youths (*U* 8.933–35). Immediately afterward his elusiveness is commented upon. But this connection may merely be an instance of one reader's mind being polytropically affected.

Homer's Odysseus appealed to Joyce because of his universality and his encyclopedic turns. In him the two opposites, the individual and the universe (poles that appear throughout in Joyce's works, from Stephen's geography book in *A Portrait* to Shem's riddle of the universe), are combined. I cannot help but think that Joyce was conscious of a translation of *polytropos* into Latin, which would yield *multi-versus*, the exact anthetical correspondence to *uni-versus*.

Naturally it does not matter too much whether some general principle in either the *Odyssey* or *Ulysses* finds one particular verbal incarnation. But Joyce had a way of expressing in representative detail what is also present in the organic whole. The preceding philological digressions are justified, perhaps, simply because Joyce was a philologist, in the etymological sense of being a lover of words and also in the sense of being a commentator of Homer. He attributed the art Philology to the chapter devoted to change and Odyssean flexibility.

Diverging from Homer, Joyce does not start with an invocation stating his theme, but he puts the principle into action by putting the most conspicuously *polytropos* man in the novel right in front of us: Buck Mulligan, whose shifting roles can now be reinterpreted as Odyssean. Buck Mulligan does not know how much he is in fact hellenizing Ireland (*U* 1.158). Fairly early he uses the Homeric type of adjective himself, both in the hackneyed original "*epi oinopa ponton*" and in parodistic variation "the scrotumtightening sea" (*U* 1.78). His early Greek samples, incidentally, refer to the eminently changeable elements of water ("ponton," "thalatta") or wine.

Mulligan is resourceful and skillful in dealing with any situation at hand. But he also incorporates the qualities of trickery and deceit that the detractors of Odysseus had pointed out in antiquity. Again there is the tenuous possibility that Joyce had heard of one such detractor who claimed that Homer's account was a tissue of lies. Stanford goes on to say that this critic, whose "oration is bland, persuasive and superbly argued," is hardly trying "to do more than dazzle and astonish his audience," his aim being "to gain admiration for skill in rhetorical technique."[10] There is something very Mulliganesque in all this, but what makes the connection particularly intriguing is that the name of the critic was—Dio Chrysostomos.

We are on safer ground by taking Bloom's word for it that Buck Mulligan is an untrustworthy but "versatile allround man, by no means confined to medicine only" (*U* 16.288). "Versatile" is, of course, the standard definition of *polytropos*; "allroundman" echoes Lenehan's grudging concession of Bloom as "a cultured allroundman" (*U* 10.581). It echoes, moreover, Joyce's conversation with Frank Budgen in Zurich about Odysseus as a complete all-round character.[11] Lenehan, as it happens, is a little Odysseus in his own small cadging way, wandering and wily and versatile (in "Two Gallants" he is described as a "leech" and is performing an odyssey in a minor key). It is remarkable how frequently the Odyssean characters in *Ulysses* comment on each other, and often in Odyssean terms too: Lenehan comments on Bloom; Bloom on Buck Mulligan, Lenehan, Simon Dedalus, and on the Sailor; Simon Dedalus on Buck Mulligan ("a doubledyed ruffian," [*U* 6.64]); the Sailor on Simon Dedalus (his yarn presents Dedalus as *polytropos*, much-traveled: "He toured the wide world" [*U* 16.411–12]); Buck Mulligan on Bloom; and so on.

Our first glimpse of Buck Mulligan shows him literally and physically as a man of many turns. Within the first few pages he is choreographically living up to his polytropic nature: he faces about, bends toward Stephen, peers sideways, shows a shaven cheek over his right shoulder, hops down from his perch, mounts the parapet, and actually "turn[s] abruptly" (*U* 1.86).[12]

Polytropia in *Ulysses* then is not limited to any one feature, or level, or any one person—not even to persons. It is polytropically distributed and incarnated throughout. Animals too, like Stephen's protean dog on the beach or the dog following Bloom into the byways of "Circe," perform feats of amazing versatility. Even inanimate objects, such as Bloom's newspaper, his wandering soap, or Stephen's ashplant, are capable of transformation.

One whole chapter hinges on the volatile mutability of all things, the "Circe" episode. It is made up of all the previous roles in the novel and a number of new ones, a gigantic transformation scene in pantomime, where old roles are continually permuted. Among its polymorphic turns are the deviate turns of the psyche, with such authorities as Krafft-Ebing being responsible for parts of the script.

It is appropriate that Stephen comes to grief in this sequence, also because, for all the flexibility of his mind, he fails, or refuses, to be flexible enough to deal with a real situation and to evade a blunt danger. He is not trying to select a more opportune role, but rather continues a monologue that is unintelligible and must appear provoking to the soldiers, who of course are equally inflexible. The physical altercation in "Circe" is between characters who are rigid and might be called "monotropic." Stephen, in crucial moments, is scornful of such advice as Buck Mulligan has given him in the morning: "Humour her [his mother] till it's over" (*U* 1.212). Mulligan does a lot of opportunistic humoring, and Bloom is good-humoredly trying his best.

The culminations of "Circe" can be regarded as outgrowths of such mimetic features as are already present in the first chapter. "Circe" is made up almost entirely of Mulliganesque poses and projections. In the morning Buck Mulligan begins by quoting Latin from the mass. Near midnight Stephen enters the scene by actually responding to Mulligan's opening words: *"ad deam qui lae-tificat juventutem meam"* (*U* 15.122–23). His version contains one small change (*deam* for *Deum*), but it is an entire perversion, a wholly new and utterly Circean turn. The first sounds heard in "Circe" are the call and answers of the whistles (*U* 15.9) which are an echo of the first page. The first words spoken aloud, "Wait, my love," are a variant of Mulligan's "Yes, my love" (*U* 15.11, 1.48). With his conjuring imitation of the transubstantiation, Mulligan has also prepared us for the magic, the technique of the Circean transformations.

An interesting scene in the first chapter foreshadows many phenomena of "Circe." Mulligan, who has just challenged Stephen with "Why don't you play them as I do?" puts on some clothes with the remark that "we'll simply have to dress the character"—a dress rehearsal for the rapid costume changes in "Circe." Mulligan justifies the contradictions in his words and actions with a quotation from Whitman. In "Circe" all contradictions are staged. The paragraph in which Buck Mulligan is dressing (*U* 1.513–18) is, incidentally, the first in the book in which we cannot be certain which words are actually spoken by Mulligan and which are part of Stephen's thoughts. The distinction between speech and thought will make little sense in the hallucinations of "Circe." Thus we do not know whether "Mercurial Malachi" (*U* 1.518) is actually spoken by mercurial Mulligan or not, but Mercury, Hermes, the wily, roguish god, is also presiding over the "Circe" chapter just as he was instrumental in helping Odysseus.[13] Mercurial Malachi paves the way for the technique of "Circe."

In this view, then, an extravagant convolution like "Circe" is a polytropical reconjugation of familiar elements met before. Joyce manipulates his material in the most suitable manner. This technique—of adapting one's approach to the situation—is in itself an Odyssean one. Like Odysseus, Joyce chooses his speech, his role, and his narrative stance carefully and ruthlessly. Every style is a role adapted for some purpose. Part of our difficulty as readers is that we are too rigidly fixed to follow the abrupt turns, the changes of the stage, so that the verbal, situational, and narrative texture is too polytropic for our customary inertia.

Odysseus, as well as his presidential adviser, Athene, was not particularly scrupulous in the means he employed to attain a given end, and literal truth is not his overriding concern. Nor, in a way, is it Joyce's. He is not exclusively concerned with realistic verisimilitude and can depart from it entirely. The roles, the styles, the perspectives are chosen for optimal effect ad hoc.

Ulysses is Homerically polytropical. Voices change, characters are not fixed, language is versatile and polymorphous. The reader is puzzled by new turns. Where passages, or even chapters, are monotropic, their effect is parodistic, and they strike us by their inadequacy and incongruity; in their totality they add up to the most encyclopedic mosaic in literature.

In the "Wandering Rocks" chapter the many turns are those of a labyrinth, solidified into the bricks and stones of the city. "Aeolus," the first of those extravagant chapters in *Ulysses* which draw attention to their form, is made up of all the traditional rhetorical figures. It is literally composed of many turns, of tropes—all the preformed roles available in human speech. Language is intrinsically metaphorical. Part of the dynamism of Joyce's prose arises from the contrast of figurative to literal meaning, or the ironic unfittingness of a metaphor or a cliché fixed in some no longer congruous roles. Language, the most polytropic invention of the human mind, fascinated Joyce. Skeat's *Etymological Dictionary,* a catalog of the historical roles of words, makes us aware of morphological and semantic transformations. Joyce makes us aware, moreover, of the various roles that even the most ordinary and familiar words always play. Such a simple and seemingly unambiguous unit as "key," for example, is capable of amazing variety and change of identity. That it can refer to those domestic objects that Bloom and Stephen find themselves without, or to symbols of power (as with St. Peter), to musical notation in "Sirens," to a political institution (the House of Keys), to a name (Alexander Keyes), to connotations like a keyhole in "Circe," or else to a woman "properly keyed up," and so on, is all very commonplace and generally unnoticed, but belongs to the polytropic potential that Joyce found in everyday language.

Fortunately for him, the English language is particularly flexible. Its powers of assimilation, its wide and varied vocabulary, but above all its lack of determining inflection, allow Joyce the scope he needed. In English the miraculous fact that "A belt was also to give a fellow a belt" (*P* 7), which puzzles a young Stephen Dedalus, is easily possible—but perhaps only in English. Native English speakers may not realize, for example, what duplicity the simple title "The Dead" contains. A foreigner, especially if he wants to render it into his own language, may well wonder whether "Dead" is singular or plural. In the course of reading the story we could easily fluctuate in our view, at times taking the word in its more general sense until at one point it seems limited to Michael Furey before it is universalized again in the last paragraph. In other words, it seems to be a title that changes with our experience. Its flexibility is possible in English—in all other languages the meaning would probably remain fixed.

Bloom can beautifully make a trite phrase—"Another gone" (*U* 5.136)—do double duty, neatly referring, superficially, to Dignam's demise and internally to voyeuristic frustration. Once you try to do this in another language you will find that gender and inflection present some serious obstacles. Similarly, a "goal" scored in hockey cannot play the role of the great "goal" toward which all history moves (*U* 2.380–81) outside of the English language. English must be one of the most Odyssean languages; resourceful, pliant, homophonous, versatile, it allows Joyce to assume the voice appropriate for the occasion, multiple guises, mercurial transformations. Now the virtuoso performances of cunning and punning have appeared to some critics as questionable manipulations, forms of trickery. Interestingly enough, the two contradictory evaluations of Joyce's ways happen to reflect the two views held of the character of Odysseus—the superbly agile and ingenious hero, or else the artful, deceitful trickster. Not very surprisingly, the first one to take this negative view was the Homeric Cyclops, an early victim. It may be significant that his vision was troubled from the outset and worsened in the process. In his naiveté his one-track mind trusted words and names. For Polyphemus, at any rate, the pun on the name of Odysseus was a mean trick of some consequence, and it taught him the treacherous and potent nature of words. It taught him, one presumes, to trust no man and no man's words.

Language in the *Odyssey* and in *Ulysses* can be deceptive, elusive, often unreliable. "Sounds are impostures," says Stephen (*U* 16.362), and he says so in a chapter particularly suited to presenting the untrustworthy nature of all communication. The neatest instance is the funeral report in the newspaper. It contains untruths of two kinds. First the conventional hyperbolic formulas that have little relation to a real emotional involvement which they pretend to express: *"The deceased gentleman was a most popular and genial personality in city life and his demise . . . came as a great shock to citizens of all classes by whom he is deeply regretted"* (*U* 16.1250–53). This form of falsification is less conspicuous but more ubiquitous than such strident deviations from factual truth as the listing of mourners present like Stephen Dedalus, J. P. McCoy, L. Boom, and M'Intosh. The reader of the novel is contextually privileged, but readers of the *Evening Telegraph* would have been seriously misled. And the characters of *Ulysses* are being similarly taken in. Even the author himself at times assumes the pose of trusting speech and language naively, by pedantically transforming, in one case, a glib and bibulous and next-to-meaningless "God bless all here" into a prolonged scene depicting a ceremonial benediction (*U* 12.1673–1750), one example of the rigid belief in the literal meaning of powerful words. This happens in the "Cyclops" chapter, which shows the clash of the unifocality of view with the multivocality of language.

The reader, as against the more shortsighted of the characters involved, has enough information at hand to adjust his views. But even today it does take a reader with at least a minimum of Odyssean agility. After a half century of *Ulysses* we have learned to regard any information provided within the novel with skeptical, in fact Bloomian, reserve. On the other hand, we invest the words of the text with unusual trust. We know that "L. Boom" is, on the realistic surface of it, simply a piece of misinformation. But we tend to rely on the assumption that the distortion means something, and usually more than just one thing. A principle of obverse truth seems to pervade the novel: somehow, "Boom" is literally true and relevant; its incongruity serves intricate purposes.

And perhaps the Latin phrase from the Mass that is irreverently quoted at the beginning of "Telemachus" also indicates that the book is also perversely like the Mass. Not only because it deals with transubstantiations, significant changes, but also because in it, as in the liturgy, every detail—gesture, word, vestment, and so on—is meaningful, a product of a process of condensation and accretion, and generally overdetermined.

So language as a means of communication in *Ulysses* cannot be trusted and at the same time justifies unusual trust, within a hierarchy of potential contexts. An ignorant rendering of "metempsychosis" as "met him pike hoses" is plainly erroneous in one context, but it is appropriate, word for word, to the character who enunciates it and to some major themes of the novel. Bloom's innocent statement "I was going to throw it away" (*U* 5.537) is met with distrust, and its unambiguous everyday meaning is disregarded. Bantam Lyons, a particularly biased person, considers it *purely* allusive and is even willing to back his trust in it as an allusion with hard cash. Reality then turns the initial error into unexpected truth, and the reader can rely on some further nonrealistic relevance. Sounds are tricky, but even their trickiness has a communicative value.

In the episode in which a false Odysseus tells obvious falsehoods, in which the novel's real Odysseus warns Stephen against trusting the novel's preparatory Odysseus, and in which Stephen declares sounds to be impostures, the language of even the tritest of clichés has an odd way of sidelighting some truths. I have had occasion to stress some similarities between Leopold Bloom and Buck Mulligan (they concerned me for the present purposes more than their patent dissimilarities). The two form an uneven pair each with Stephen in the respective chapters of book I and book III. Now, besides some parallels already mentioned and others easy to work out, I think a few different ones are potentially contained as homonymous asides in the first sentence of the "Eumaeus" chapter:

> Preparatory to anything else Mr Bloom *brushed* off the greater bulk of the *shavings* and handed Stephen the hat and ashplant and *bucked* him up generally. (*U* 16.1–3)

I have italicized "brushed," "shavings," and "bucked" because to me they echo, unassumingly, a-semantically, and in-significantly, the first scene in which Buck wields his brush to shave himself. A few sentences later a connection is further made with Stephen's handkerchief "having done yeoman service in the shaving line." These frail links do not contribute much to the passage, but they do bring out, once more and in a different guise, the principle of the same elements being reshuffled within the novel, and here the elements are partly phonetic. The tiny point is that those signs singled out here are not *only* impostures. They contain a measure of oblique truth. (Incidentally, the vowel sounds of "sh*a*vings," "br*u*shed," and "b*u*cked" are the same as of "Stately, plump Buck.")

Or perhaps, to improve on my phrasing, these words and sounds are, literally and etymologically,[14] impostures, being imposed upon the text as an additional layer of gratuitous correspondence, ironic contrast, deviate reliability, or polytropical pertinence.

The novel's versatile and occasionally tricky resilience then can be accounted for as a quality that Homer ascribed to his hero. Joyce went on to write an even more *polytropos* novel with an entirely pantropical hero; also, among countless other things, an Irish Ulysses: "Hibernska Ulitzas" (*FW* 551.32). Because of its polytropic nature, *Ulysses* is capable of meeting us all on our own terms, or on any other terms we may think of. Strangely enough, we still tend to forget the lesson we might have learned and to fall back on monotropical statements of the form "*Ulysses* is basically this or that," and we can only do so by emphasizing one of the potentially multiple turns in our own Cyclopean fashion.

If there is any quintessential formula for *Ulysses*, I do not think it will be contained in a resounding, world-embracing *yes*, nor in an equally reductive nihilistic *no* and rejection of our time, but in a modest, persistent, skeptical, Bloomian "Yes but."

Notes

1. Fritz Senn, " 'He Was Too Scrupulous Always': Joyce's 'The Sisters.' " *James Joyce Quarterly* 2 (Winter 1965): 70–71.

2. "In Dublin an 'artist' is a merry droll, a player of hoaxes," said Oliver St. John Gogarty in "They Think They Know Joyce," *Saturday Review of Literature* 33 (Mar. 18, 1950), 70.

3. "Notice that the first time [the cat's meow] is spelled with Mk, the second time with Mrk, the third with Mrkr. . . . That's the Greek spelling of Mercury. The cat is Mercury." Sidney Alexander, quoting Giulio de Angelis, in "Bloomsday in Italy," *Reporter* 24 (Apr. 13, 1961), 42.

4. Joyce's version, as reproduced by Ellmann, *JJ*1 facing p. 433, is faulty and has here been substituted by the transcription of the standard Greek text.

5. *The Ulysses Theme: A Study in the Adaptability of a Traditional Hero* (1954; reprint, Ann Arbor: University of Michigan Press, 1968).

6. A selection of phrases with which translators of Homer tried to come to terms with *polytropos* is revealing: the hero fated to roam; who roamed the world over; who drew his changeful course through wanderings; that Great Traveler who wandered far and wide; an adventurous man who wandered far; of craft-renown that hero wandering; man of many changes; that sagacious man; resourceful; so wary and wise; various-minded; skilled in all ways of contending; steadfast, skillful and strong; for wisdom's various arts renown'd; who was never at a loss; ready at need; ingenious hero; the shifty; famous for cleverness of schemes he devised.

7. Reproduced in "Album Joyciano," p. 39, in Stelio Crise, *Epiphanies & Phadographs: Joyce & Trieste* (Milano: All' Insegna del Pesce D'Oro, 1967); it is also in the Frankfurt edition of Joyce: *Werke 5, Briefe I, 1900–1916* (Frankfurt: Suhrkamp Verlag, 1969), 574. The postcard is dated June 16, 1915.

8. "The Grandson of Autolycus," in W. B. Stanford, *The Ulysses Theme: A Study in the Adaptability of a Traditional Hero*, 2nd ed. (Ann Arbor: University of Michigan Press, 1968).

9. Ibid., 260–61.

10. Ibid., 148.

11. Frank Budgen, *James Joyce and the Making of "Ulysses"* (1934; reprint, London: Oxford University Press, 1972), 15ff; see "Conversations with Joyce" in this volume.

12. After this paper was read in Tulsa a member of the audience suggested that "plump," second word in the book, also somehow means "all-round."

13. "Moly is the gift of Hermes, god of public ways. . . . Hermes is the god of signposts: i.e. he is, specially for a traveller like Ulysses, the point at which roads parallel merge and roads contrary also. He is an accident of providence" (*Letters* I, 147–48).

14. Relying on etymological potential is a form of circuitous trust.

Art and Life, Nature and Culture, *Ulysses*

CHERYL HERR

❖   ❖   ❖

> It was life but was it fair? It was free but was it
> art?
>
> (*FW* 94.9–10)

I N   A   R E F L E X   F R O M   I T S   O W N   E N E R G Y ,   *Ulysses* has
moved its readers down many critical paths. In the early 1920s
Valery Larbaud and company sought the clue to *Ulysses* in the
work's Odyssean and other schematic structures. During the New
Critical heyday, the key was thought by some to be, among other
things, the one that Bloom leaves behind him and seeks all day
along alley and, yes, quay. Readers fruitfully charted images and
triangulated motifs in order to reveal the designs-upon-designs
upon which the meaning of the work was assumed to rest. More
recently we have seen a poststructuralist concern with disembod-
ying voice and locating aporias, with reflexivity and the self-
consciousness of Joyce's fiction. And in recent work, Freud / Lacan
and Marx have begun to receive articulation with Joyce's writing.
The fact is that Joyce's great narrative has made the critical enterprise into a simulacrum of the travels of the legendary Wandering Jew whose footsore angst Leopold Bloom emulates and
whose worldweariness formed an unmistakable part of Joyce's
own experience of Europe between the two wars. Legend composing art composing life composing art composing response to
life and art—something like this vacillating sequence maps out
a territory that is not contained within the covers of the "usy-
lessly unreadable Blue Book of Eccles" (*FW* 179.26–27). What I

propose to offer here is not a compact reading of the narrative but a positioning of it; I want to identify the key to *Ulysses* not with a theme nor even with the roads along which the narrative has guided us but with what the narrative does, not with the action in the work but with the work enacted on the borderline between art and life.

I chart my course in this way partly because, like the literalist preachers of my youth, I have discovered that Joyce's synoptic scripture, as the author knew, interacts alchemically with life. Like most if not all great works of art, *Ulysses* changes with the reader[1] and unlike many merely interesting pieces of literature, keeps pace with (or perhaps even paces) the reader's experience of life. At first, the reader finds in *Ulysses* the grand themes of Western literature: the son's search for the father, the father's search for the child he can never truly know to be his offspring, the artist's struggle for recognition and cash, the quest for romantic love, the often unsatisfying domestication of that love, the acceptance of death, the human battle with betrayal and despair. Visiting Ireland, the same reader may become convinced that the narrative must be understood in context; it is a book about a writer's vexed relationship to a land plagued with poverty, dominated by an oppressive foreign government, and hostile to its own prophets. Later, our reader may tire of travel or politics and turn to aesthetics. By these new lights, *Ulysses* becomes a multiply reflexive work; style is the subject as well as the medium of this metafiction. Or the work may turn forward another of its prismatic faces and lure the reader into a study of metaphysics, theosophy, epistemology, psychoanalysis, or syntax. In contrast, the philosophical and psychological colors may fade along with the technical and archetypal, casting into relief the personal dimension of the work. Hence, it may dawn on our representative reader that *Ulysses* is *really* about the effort to return home and the difficulties of getting there, or it may seem that the novel centers on whether Bloom, at day's end, will go upstairs and join his unfaithful Penelope in bed.

But I do not want to be misunderstood as merely voicing the platitude that *Ulysses* is a great and various fiction that grows with the reader. Rather than view Joyce's first epic as being about the topics and ideas traditionally put forward as explaining or unlocking the work, it seems more enlightening altogether to view such material as the stuff through which Joyce posed his challenge to the received relationship of art and life. Without a doubt, that confrontation is in *Ulysses* raised to a power higher than is characteristic of any other work canonized in most American colleges and universities. The challenge emerges from the fact that the narrative is a masterpiece of semiotic pseudocomprehensiveness; it is a model of cultural processes and materials. And it is the nature of this model, what it encompasses and what it marginalizes or excludes, that occupies me when I consider not this or that aspect of *Ulysses* but the work as a tenuous and vexing whole. Certainly, a margin—in addition to being a popular spot in critical discourse today—is the appropriate area for examination when studying the whole, not least because it defines a dialectical relationship between what is inside and what is regarded as external. As I read it, *Ulysses* calls into being a boundary that it challenges in order to reveal the formulaic nature of both life and art—and to evoke something not contained by the specific formulas it repeats. That "something" I will later label, in echo of Fredric Jameson's work, the "cultural unconscious" of *Ulysses*; it is the complex nostalgia that the work's probing of both mind and society centers on.

But first, to underscore the peculiar relationship of *ars* and *vita* that *Ulysses* explores, I must return to a day not long ago that I spent in the National Library of Ireland. While doing some research into Irish censorship, I ran across an open letter written in 1885 by a Mr. Frederick J. Gregg to the *Dublin University Review*. Mr. Gregg claimed to have overheard an attendant at the National Library tell a reader "that Walt Whitman's poems had been suppressed." Gregg asked about this matter and was informed that the librarian, William Archer, had in fact banned or withheld the volume from circulation. Gregg then proceeded to defend *Leaves of Grass* as a great book, which he found, despite the objections of some critics, not "indelicate." In fact, he calculated that only 80 of its 9,000 lines could be considered objectionable.[2] In a letter of response printed the following month, Archer denied having suppressed Whitman, but what caught my eye in this controversy was the cited address of the open-minded Gregg: 6, Eccles Street, Dublin. Delighted at the possibility that Gregg was Leopold Bloom's next-door neighbor, I was playfully pulled at once in two directions. First, I wanted to check Thom's Directory to see how long Mr. Gregg had resided on Eccles Street; was he there in 1903 when the Blooms "moved in"?[3] At the same time, I thought of the ironies of Stephen Dedalus's disappointing conversation with the intelligentsia at the National Library. Whether or not Archer's defense was any more accurate than Gregg's accusation, it is woefully appropriate that after having his place at the Tower usurped by Haines, Stephen should find no better reception in the library than was apparently accorded to Whitman. In another corner of my mind, I wondered in which room of the current library the conversation of Stephen, Mulligan, A.E., Eglinton, Best, and company "took place." Clearly, there are problems involved in such speculation, not the least of which is punctuation; are quotation marks (like those I've used above) the appropriate markers for verbs that refer to the projected-as-real actions of Joyce's characters? A similar difficulty plagued Richard Best, who, having been absorbed into the world of *Ulysses*, felt that he had to defend his status as a nonfictional person.[4] He had to fight against the quotation marks that forever surrounded his name once it was used in *Ulysses*.

At this point in the history of *Ulysses* criticism, it is not necessary to document in detail the curious effect that the novel creates from its reference to an overwhelming number of details from the real Dublin. Nor need we linger long over the book's own oblique comments upon its narrative practice. It may be sufficient to note that "Scylla and Charybdis," the episode in which Stephen devotes extensive theoretical ingenuity to elaborating his theory that Shakespeare wrote his life into his art, begins with words that comically highlight the literary uses of life:

> Urbane, to comfort them, the quaker librarian purred:
> —And we have, have we not, those priceless pages of *Wilhelm*

Meister. A great poet on a great brother poet. A hestitating soul taking arms against a sea of troubles, torn by conflicting doubts, as one sees in real life.

He came a step a sinkapace forward on neatsleather creaking and a step backward a sinkapace on the solemn floor.

A noiseless attendant setting open the door but slightly made him a noiseless beck.

—Directly, said he, creaking to go, albeit lingering. The beautiful ineffectual dreamer who comes to grief against hard facts. One always feels that Goethe's judgments are so true. True in the larger analysis.

Twicreakingly analysis he corantoed off. (*U* 9.1–12)

The librarian measures art by its echoing of "real life," but his words and actions as *Ulysses* presents them echo the works he has read and are narrated to us in a self-consciously artificial style. In the brief passage quoted above, we find not only that the librarian's romantic notion of literary truth relies on Goethe but also that the texture of his "life" blends phrases from *Wilhelm Meister's Apprenticeship, Hamlet, Twelfth Night, Julius Caesar,* and the *Essays in Criticism: Second Series* of Matthew Arnold.⁵ Clearly figuring the process by which texts make our reality, Joyce continually quotes both other works and his own, extending the reflexive gesture of his fiction to include all of the life that the tradition of Western fiction has created.

The significance of Joyce's varied and insistent mingling of art and life is not exhausted when we merely cite his idiosyncratic attachment in the narrative to the facts of his experience of Dublin. At least two aspects of *Ulysses* come to mind as germane to our understanding of this narrative practice. The first is Joyce's well-advertised narrative "innovation" in *Ulysses*—one that attracted much of the initial attention to the text. I refer to Joyce's use of the interior monologue and stream-of-consciousness techniques. A second relevant matter is the rough adherence of the book's design to the encyclopedic schemata that Joyce circulated to Carlo Linati, Stuart Gilbert, and Herbert Gorman. I want to discuss here the persistence with which *Ulysses* looks and moves in both directions—interior and schematic—at once. With its

attention to the supposed workings of the mind and the revelation of the inner identity of Western man, the stream-of-
consciousness technique appeals to our sense of what is natural—
to the life, particularly the unconscious life, that we seem to
share. With its attention to many of the categories by which the
Westen world knows itself, this schematic book directs us toward
a concept of culture, toward the domain of art. Life and art,
nature and culture—on these grand dichotomies *Ulysses* is constructed, and to the exploration of these oppositions as such the
fiction is dedicated. From this process of assertion and challenge,
which describes what *Ulysses* does at its margins, comes, I believe,
the force of the narrative for a surprisingly diverse community
of readers.

Stream of Consciousness: "Nature It Is"
(*U* 18.1563)?

Arthur Power tells us of an intriguing conversation in which
Joyce maintained that *Ulysses* explored parts of the psyche that
had never before been treated in fiction. "The modern theme,"
Joyce argued, "is the subterranean forces, those hidden tides
which govern everything and run humanity counter to the apparent flood: those poisonous subtleties which envelop the soul,
the ascending fumes of sex."[6] The means of this revelation have
long been discussed,[7] the techniques employed by Joyce including
third-person narration attuned to the speech mannerisms and
thought patterns of the character under attention, direct dialogue, interior monologue, and seeming transcription of thoughts
in sentence or fragment form. There's no question that Joyce's
approximation of the flow of consciousness, although dependent
on at least fragments of words, represents a significant experimental attempt to portray the movements of the mind; hence,
quite early in the presentations of Stephen, Bloom, and Molly,
the narrative begins to employ this crucial modernist technique.
By the fourth page of the book, we find ourselves eased from

narration per se into Stephen's first fully presented thought, "As he and others see me. Who chose this face for me? This dogsbody to rid of vermin. It asks me too" (*U* 1.136–37). Elegaic, measured, rhetorical—these few comments introduce us to Stephen's mind and set the tone for much of his moody self-assessment on June 16, 1904. Similarly, by the eleventh line of "Calypso," the episode in which we meet Leopold Bloom, we find fragments of directly "reported" thought punctuating the third-person narration:

> Another slice of bread and butter: three, four: right. She didn't like her plate full. Right. He turned from the tray, lifted the kettle off the hob and set it sideways on the fire. It sat there, dull and squat, its spout stuck out. Cup of tea soon. Good. Mouth dry. (*U* 4.11–14)

Likewise, from the first word of "Penelope," Molly may be regarded as speaking, or rather thinking, her mind.

In one sense, then, *Ulysses* constantly and with ever-greater fervor moves us close to life not only by signaling about certain word-units, "These are an individual's most personal thoughts," but also by directing those thoughts toward a wide range of topics, including many subjects obviously unsuitable for polite conversation in Joyce's Dublin. For instance, Bloom recalls his lovemaking with Molly on Howth and ponders Milly's budding sexuality; he thinks that he might masturbate in the bath; he considers Gerty's serviceable underwear. Stephen rejects both the corpse-chewing God of his imagination and the ghost of his mother; he broods over his social usurpation by medicine man and conqueror; he probes the mysteries of sex and birth. Molly thinks of Boylan, Bloom, Mulvey, Stephen, Rudy, Milly, and a host of other people; she appreciates her soft thighs and firm breasts; she remembers with joy various sexual experiences; she declares her belief in her own powers of seduction. *Ulysses* asks us to view these passages as reporting the kinds of things that most real people think even if they do not always say them, and readers generally go along with the game, many of them marveling, as Carl Jung did, at Joyce's psychological acumen. That is, the narrative asks for our tacit agreement that the art of *Ulysses* mirrors life.

But in addition, we are asked to agree that life is like art, that our own thoughts emerge just as spontaneously as those of Joyce's characters not out of a void of preverbal desire but out of the fictive discourses and received ideas among and through which we live. Consider Stephen as he walks along Sandymount Strand: freed from friends and foes alike, he occupies himself with speculations on God, fatherhood, consubstantiality, aesthetics, sensation, women, language, library slips, and his own rotting teeth. Although "Nestor" ends with the supposed comment of a supposed omniscient narrator ("On his wise shoulders through the checkerwork of leaves the sun flung spangles, dancing coins" [*U* 2.448–49]), "Proteus" begins by confronting us immediately with the language of Stephen's thoughts: "Ineluctable modality of the visible: at least that if no more, thought through my eyes. Signatures of all things I am here to read" (*U* 3.1–2). The entire first paragraph presents part of Stephen's somber/witty meditation on vision, knowledge, and the reality of the external world. From these thoughts, we learn that the young Dubliner, supposed by Homeric design to be in search of his father / Father, is wondering how he will know him if he meets him, with the emphasis on *how*. The process of knowing and the perils of that process occupy Stephen's interior experience as he defines for himself the bottom line of cognitive possibility ("at least that if no more, thought through my eyes") and accepts the challenge of living as he sees it (not to be able to say with Mr. Deasy, "*I paid my way*" [*U* 2.251] but to read the "Signatures of all things"). Stephen's thoughts here, as Weldon Thornton, John Killham, Hugh Kenner, and others have documented,[8] are mainly derived from philosophic or mystic masters like Aristotle, Aquinas, and Boehme. The precision and inventiveness with which Stephen weaves together bits and pieces from their texts are his own, of course, but it is the implied presence of such texts that structures his thinking.

Possibly Stephen's awareness of the claustrophic hovering of Western cultural tradition both outside and within his mind accounts in part for his nostalgic search for a nonreceived language of gesture. As he drunkenly describes the project to Lynch in "Circe," he wants to transcend derivation from intermediary texts and to speak the "structural rhythm" of things. To create or use such a "universal language" would be to find "the gift of tongues rendering visible not the lay sense but the first entelechy" (*U* 15.106–7). Hours after his walk on the strand, Stephen returns to the question of the visible and his hope that he can both read the language of nature and learn to speak it. Alas, Stephen's illustrative gestures allude to "the loaf and jug of bread or wine in Omar" (*U* 15.117); the *Rubaiyat* is for the moment the dominant work, although not the only one giving contextual significance to Stephen's gestures. One of the things that Joyce's insistent alluding makes clear is that thinking, the streaming of consciousness, the content of interior monologue, the very shape of the self are woven from the materials of one's culture. *Fair Tyrants* joins the *Odyssey* and a host of other books in accounting for the contours of individual experience in the narrative; such works ensure that whatever the stream of consciousness accomplishes in terms of artistic technique, it does not provide even the shadow of an access to a mythical human nature within or behind or beyond or above those informing texts. The art that seems to bring us closer to life seems to show us that art constitutes life and that nature as we can know it is always only culture. This conclusion, though familiar enough in contemporary thought, had its own radical charm in Joyce's day; it clearly fascinated Joyce enough for him to devote years to charting its implications.

A similar point might be made in our consideration of Molly's thoughts as they are rendered in "Penelope." Even without knowing Joyce's famous description of her chapter as "perfectly sane full amoral fertilisable untrustworthy engaging shrew limited prudent indifferent 'Weib,' "[9] readers would have identified Molly with nature. Her ready acceptance of sexual difference and of different sexualities, her flowing speech and overt desiring, her maternity and menstruation, all mark Molly's Gea-Tellus status and distinguish her from the more intellectual Stephen and Bloom. This assessment of Molly recurs throughout Joyce criticism. And yet, however fundamentally unreflective she may appear to be, Molly's "thoughts" exhibit as much of the reflexive quality of language as do Stephen's. For example, the almost continuous pressure of syntactic ambiguity in her monologue ("the german Emperor is it yes imagine Im him think of him can you feel him trying to make a whore of me" [*U* 18.95–96]) urges on the reader the constructedness of that prose and its attention to itself as language. Similarly, the eight "sentences" of "Penelope" and the "8 big poppies because mine was the 8th" (*U* 18.329–30), like her reference to other books that have Mollys in them, nudge the reader into seeing *Ulysses* as a world of ambiguous and constantly shifting signs.[10] Like the "Circe" episode, which pretends to be a descent into the unconscious but constantly cycles out into the comedy of received ideas, "Penelope" paints the mind almost exclusively as the site on which convention and cliché register. And yet, perhaps because of Molly's own enthusiastic embracing of the natural ("God of heaven theres nothing like nature" [*U* 18.1558–59]), or because of the convention by which women are construed to be closer to nature than men,[11] readers have often coded her as the Flesh or Nature or Life that Stephen must embrace before he can become an artist. Elaine Unkeless directly attacks this view in her essay "The Conventional Molly Bloom," in which she argues that Joyce's portrait mostly restricts Molly to "preconceived ideas of the way a woman thinks and behaves."[12] Hence, our response to Molly as Earth Mother is based on our conventional notions of what constitutes naturalness. Drawing that artificial nature into the text, Molly's interior monologue is not unshaped thought but idea and self-image structured by society. The episode conveys at best a nostalgia for primal authenticity voiced from within the heart of culture. This voice echoes Stephen's sense that the "self" is "ineluctably preconditioned to become" what it is (*U* 15.2120–21); such conditioning, as we see it in *Ulysses*, is largely social.

The ersatz quality of nature in *Ulysses* is perhaps most pointedly conveyed when Joyce's Dubliners go on or think about going on holiday outside of Dublin. Miss Kennedy and Miss Douce vacation at a seaside of music-hall clichés; Bloom recalls a "High School excursion" (*U* 15.3308) to the falls at Poulaphouca, the most typical of tourist day trips from the city. In "Eumaeus," the narrative portrays Bloom as pompously and hilariously holding forth on the value of such trips; "the man in the street," he feels, "merited a radical change of *venue* after the grind of city life in the summertime for choice when Dame Nature is at her spectacular best constituting nothing short of a new lease of life." Bloom cites Poulaphouca, Wicklow, "the wilds of Donegal," and Howth as suitable spots in which to become attuned to nature (*U* 16.551, 552–54, 557). Similarly, Simon Dedalus seems able to conceive of nothing farther outside Dublin than the fifty-mile-away Mourne mountains: "—By Jove, he mused, I often wanted to see the Mourne mountains" (*U* 11.219). Significantly, in "Sirens" that wish becomes part of the linguistic play of that extraordinarily reflexive episode: he speaks and drinks with "faraway mourning mountain eye" (*U* 11.273).

Even when *Ulysses* deals with animals, natural behavior is subsumed by cultural vision. Consider Bloom's conversation with his cat:

—Milk for the pussens, he said.

—Mrkgnao! the cat cried.

They call them stupid. They understand what we say better than we understand them. She understands all she wants to. Vindictive too. Cruel. Her nature. Curious mice never squeal. Seem to like it. Wonder what I look like to her. Height of a tower? No, she can jump me.

—Afraid of the chickens she is, he said mockingly. Afraid of the chookchooks. I never saw such a stupid pussens as the pussens.

—Mrkrgnao! the cat said loudly.

She blinked up out of her avid shameclosing eyes, mewing plaintively and long, showing him her milkwhite teeth. He watched the dark eyeslits narrowing with greed till her eyes were green stones. Then he went to the dresser, took the jug Hanlon's milkman had just filled for him, poured warmbubbled milk on a saucer and set it slowly on the floor.

—Gurrhr! she cried, running to lap.

He watched the bristles shining wirily in the weak light as she tipped three times and licked lightly. Wonder is it true if you clip them they can't mouse after. Why? They shine in the dark, perhaps, the tips. Or kind of feelers in the dark, perhaps. (*U* 4.24–42)

Bloom's early morning interchange with Molly parallels this scene. Molly's twice-repeated "Poldy" and insistence that he hurry with the tea are forms of mild anxious, aggressive purring. Bloom "calmly" gazes at Molly's "large soft bubs, sloping within her nightdress like a shegoat's udder" (*U* 4.304–5), much as he observes the cat's whiskers and sheen: "Mr Bloom watched curiously, kindly the lithe black form. Clean to see: the gloss of her sleek hide, the white button under the butt of her tail, the green flashing eyes" (*U* 4.21–23). Molly drinks her tea with a degree of self-absorption also found in the milk-lapping "pussens." Of course, the cat does not question Bloom on the meaning of metempsychosis, but the narrative does suggest that the feline and the female share a quality that the book is working hard to capture.

Again, many readers have taken this kind of connection at face value and have asserted that Molly is not only artless; she is nature itself. But we need only return to the description of the cat to be aware of the nonobjective rendering of experience in *Ulysses*. On the one hand, it is the subjective Bloom who sees cruelty as natural to a cat and masochism as natural to mice. On the other hand, for the narrative to portray a cat as having "avid shameclosing eyes" that are "narrowing with greed" is not even to pretend to a neutral description; animal "nature" is indistinguishable from imposed interpretation. To be sure, there is much about cats that Bloom does not know: he is unsure of how he looks from the cat's perspective; he thinks its feelers might "shine in the dark." But to observe these gaps in his knowledge, especially the latter, is only to recognize that this modern Odysseus has merely blundered about in his culture's encyclopedia of texts and has emerged from his brief schooling with his facts awry. Bloom's view of what is natural and his quest to understand the essence of things lead only to conventional wisdom and comically fractured received ideas.

In portraying the unreflective and animal, the text undoes our belief in the natural by circling us back to the social and to a language that purposefully confuses nature and culture. Despite the narrative's evident desire to uncover "subterranean forces" in the mind, the presentation of minds in progress remains a combination of old materials in new ways. In general, the primal unconscious mind, unknowable in words, is evoked—only to be blocked or even denied by the strategies, styles, and content of the fiction. And yet, there is the occasional exception to this statement. For example, Stephen's description of the self, which I mentioned above (the "self" is "ineluctably preconditioned to become" what it is), suggests a contradiction—that the self is culturally conditioned to assume a certain shape, *and* that identity is conditioned by certain unnamed inevitabilities. These ineluctable forces seem to have, because of their sheer predetermination, the status of natural forces. What intrigues me here is the summoning up of an unknown sphere of inevitability and instinct, which appears to counter the recurrently asserted constructedness of all conditioning forces and the reflexively self-contained quality of *Ulysses*.

The Schema: Encyclopedism and the Unknown

Ulysses produces within the terms of its own artistry an illusion of unmediated mind, of unstructured consciousness. At the same time, the narrative announces the dominion of culture over nature. In tandem with his ambivalent approach to the unknown unconscious, Joyce explored what in his notes for "Ithaca" he calls the "as yet unknown."[13] This negative space within and outside the text is suggested by the known, the disciplines that make up Western culture and on which Joyce drew for his many allusions. From that body of knowledge, *Ulysses* generates problems of heuristics, epistemology, ontology, and aesthetics; it also produces lacunae, ambiguities, and our sense of what I have alluded to as the "cultural unconscious" (a concept discussed below by way of conclusion). One efficient way to deal with this version of the enigmatic while developing an argument about Joyce's portrayal of consciousness is to explore Joyce's own abstracts of *Ulysses*, the schemata that he prepared for his friends as aids to textual explication.[14] Certainly, the schemata cannot be considered authoritative guides to the fiction, for they are themselves only Joyce's fictions about *Ulysses*. Nonetheless, they continue to be reprinted, drawn on for clues, and distributed as hard classroom guides to the book. David Hayman's widely used study, *"Ulysses": The Mechanics of Meaning*, includes a version of the charts. Similarly, Richard Ellmann's now classic *Ulysses on the Liffey* and Don Gifford and Robert J. Seidman's *Notes for Joyce* both liberally incorporate schemata information as readily as do many Joyce scholars when they want to emphasize this or that point of interpretation. Hence, although no one would grant the charts a sacrosanct status, very few readers, scholars, and teachers of Joyce have eschewed their use altogether.

The Linati-Gorman-Gilbert charts have long puzzled those readers who seek in them the keys to the work or a simplified model of its meanings. In fact, the lists of places, times, organs, arts and sciences, colors, symbols, stylistic techniques, and Homeric correspondences tend to muddy the waters. Attempting to take the charts seriously, we often pose more questions than answers. Some questions involve the seeming overexplicitness of the charts; for example, what relationship does the "technic" of "tumescence / detumescence" have to the meaning of "Nausikaa" beyond underscoring the already obvious sexual encounter of Bloom and Gerty MacDowell? Why, amid the Homeric citations of the Correspondences, is it necessary to mention that the Stephen of "Telemachus" is like Hamlet? Other questions probe strategy. Why do episodes such as "Lestrygonians," "Eumaeus," and "Ithaca" lack designated colors? What accounts for the choice of listed organs? (Why, for instance, is there no episode for the gall bladder? Why are both muscle and flesh given space?) Still other questions involve relationships among parts of the schema or the interpretation of individual items. How much do Homeric details control, for instance, the problems of organicity mentioned above? Does the art of "Calypso," in Stuart Gilbert's version designated as "economics," suggest or include, as has been argued, "home economics"? Any reader of the charts could supply a sizable list of queries.

Yet surely to pose such questions is to seek significance without first attending to the very process of categorization. Certainly, each column suggests a body of knowledge or a frame of reference in a way that highlights the conventionalities of Western culture. Like a university displaying in its catalog its arbitrary division into what used to be regarded as self-evidently coherent "disciplines," Joyce's charts accept and even seem to authorize a divide-and-conquer mentality; they signify atomization as much as the encyclopedic wholeness that, following Joyce's lead, we often assume to be the point of the schematization.[15]

Hence, it is important that the bodily organs, the symbols, the colors—all the columns—are made analogous or homologous to the arts and sciences, the disciplines through which our culture marshals and imposes the information it generates. Music, medicine, and mechanics, like theology and magic, are in *Ulysses* the categories by which a social status quo is maintained. Similarly, the many "scenes" that Joyce's schemata list and that his narrative describes are the typical points of political and socioeconomic domination. School, house, graveyard, newspaper office, library, streets, tavern, hospital, brothel, cabman's shelter, house, and bed—the cityscape is broken down into its institutional components, and these elements redefine as a cultural site the "natural" strand along which both Bloom and Stephen walk during their shared day. That Joyce was able to find in Ireland many a comic and many a serious parallel for the details of the society Homer portrays in the *Odyssey* reinforces our sense that Joyce's text reproduces the traditional organization of Western culture. The categories dividing and ruling the Dublin of 1904, including male and female, young and old, potent and impotent, rich and poor, country and city, science and theology, heart and loins, citizens and revolutionaries, are all implied by the terms of the schemata. They form a statement about what Joyce shows us in *Ulysses*, the swallowing up of the instinctual and unprogrammed by a form of highly organized urban culture that assimilates all experience. They represent the impossibility of conceiving of the self and of exploring nature, human and otherwise, except through this or a similar conceptual paradigm.

To summarize, both from within and from without *Ulysses* announces its approximation to a nature that is in fact absent from the work. The stream-of-consciousness technique, which seems to transcribe real thoughts and their typical patterns of association, may be more accurately described as documenting the emergence of what appear to be personal thoughts from an impersonal environment of conventions and texts. The schemata, which have long been used as external but reasonably reliable abstracts of *Ulysses*, must be recognized as signifying a wholeness or encyclopedism that they in fact undermine from within as they present more lacunae and differentiations than clues to coherence.

This external evidence from Joyce's charts provides suggestions that are borne out in the narrative. For instance, *Ulysses* is a book of divisions more insistent than those divisions of economic convenience, the Victorian novel's "parts," or even than those units of mnemonic and pedagogical convenience, novelistic chapters. Eschewing such conventions, the narrative refuses to divide itself using titles, numbers, or asterisks. On the other hand, the movement from one episode to another becomes increasingly clear in *Ulysses* owing to the changes in point of view and style. Like the analytic schemata, the narrative achieves through these unpredictable shiftings not only a quasi-encyclopedic scope but also a content that refuses at many points to compose a seamless whole.

In addition, just as the schemata do not make self-evident the logic behind the selection of arts and sciences they list, so Joyce's book fails to provide an *Ur*-rationale for all of the varied philosophical, philological, historical, mythical, literary, scientific, mathematical, and other information put to use in the narrative. Instead, the text seems to ground the information used in the story in the minds of its characters and to suggest that somehow Bloom, Stephen, and Molly directly or indirectly access their culture's most spiritually valuable knowledge. Certainly, one might argue that the controlling aim of Stephen's agonized self-examination is to engineer from the cultural material at his disposal an intuitive knowledge of some unifying code system or other means of establishing connections among divine and human, person and person, philosophic theory and poetic lyric; this and more he appears to signify in the phrase "that word known to all men" (*U* 3.435). Further, as already noted, Stephen's drunken entrance into Nighttown, during which he declares to Lynch his desire for a universal "language of gesture," recalls his morning's contemplation of the confluence of and perhaps potent parallels among natural process, linguistic variety, and primal matter. For all of his Aristotelianism, Stephen is also attracted to Giordano Bruno's Neoplatonic quest for grand design and substantial unity; he wants to connect the language of culture to the perhaps mystic vocabulary of nature and divinity. But the most that Stephen achieves is his morning's ironic restatement of Western humanity's chain of being: "God becomes man becomes fish becomes barnacle goose becomes featherbed mountain" (*U* 3.477–79). Like Bloom, who repeatedly puzzles over the exact wording of various scientific principles as well as over their meaning ("Black conducts, reflects, [refracts is it?], the heat" [*U* 4.79–80]; "what's parallax?" [*U* 8.578]), Stephen has access to only a part—and arguably a marginal part—of human knowledge. Despite the frequently cited suggestion that Stephen represents Art and Bloom Science ("What two temperaments did they individually represent? The scientific. The artistic" [*U* 17.559–60]), their interaction in "Ithaca" does not encourage the view that together they form a "whole" person with "complete" knowledge, or even that they together possess an epistemologically sound and comprehensive approach to human experience.

Hence, the extraordinarily diverse body of information alluded to in *Ulysses* defines an encyclopedism that is at best hollow; it serves to emphasize the distinctions which the schemata present in abstract—not wholeness but discrete sets that defy and thwart holism, terms for the deployment of institutional power. Given this framework, the more details Joyce added to typescript, galley, and proofsheet, the more he signified in his practice the futility of the encyclopedic enterprise: he could never include all of even the culturally selected information at his disposal. Yet ironically, as Joyce embroidered into *Ulysses* the names of flowers, references to science, Homeric allusions, and the like, the text did take on a "life" of its own. That is, it engaged with the energy of Western culture in absorbing into its organizational and conceptual paradigms any raw material exposed to it. But this process, by which facts become ideology, is a hegemonic activity, whether in a society or in a work like *Ulysses* that reiterates its social environment. Hence, more than representing unity and completeness, Joyce's fictional encyclopedism reproduces and critiques the dominating divisions at the heart of the Irish life that he shows us.

Finally, like the schemata, the narrative prompts many questions and cannot help revealing many gaps, especially in the sphere of characterization. Like the schemata's list of "organs," the text's references to organs, added together, would not form a whole individual, but only a textualized and scattered Osiris. Like the "technics," which may appear to imply voices but actually include only such substitutes as "narrative (mature)" and "catechism (impersonal)," the narrative's voices are less personal than cultural. Above, I have tried to establish the sense in which *Ulysses* pretends to reveal identities but in fact undermines our traditional concept of mind by clearly deriving the content of consciousness from existing texts and conventions. As *Ulysses* has it, individuals conceive the truth of their selfhood to rest not in the enclosing culture but in an unspecifiable and largely inaccessible personal unconscious. Yet the derived discourses of *Ulysses* create a different sense of what it is to be a person in Joyce's world: one lives within a stream of consciousness that is finally not distinct from other discursive streams; one can never fully know the external imperatives that shape desire and condition action. In *Ulysses*, then, the signifiers of nature and individuality are indistinguishable from those of culture and conventionality.

A fiction often read as struggling to present the unified complexity of consciousness,[16] *Ulysses* thus produces characters largely reduced to compilations of received fictions enacting a life that at best recalls the natural by arguing the narrative's nostalgia for it. As a fragmented product, the narrative ultimately signifies something other than itself, a kind of "cultural unconscious" that can never be known except through the styles and strategies of the narrative, which transmit restricted ideological practices and stylized versions of lived experience. The enclosing culture does not know but substitutes for a nature that is never trapped in discourse, for what is missing from *Ulysses*—the living tissue of consciousness and a Gestalt that exceeds the mechanically charted—is missing as well from the society Joyce shows us; at the very least, the "cultural unconscious" that *Ulysses* evokes is perpetually chased, never grasped.

The result of Joyce's carefully engineered intersection of the social and the narrative is his exposing the insufficiency of our knowledge of self and society. For fifty years, readers have explained to one another what Stephen, Bloom, and Molly are really like, have unearthed the real reasons for Stephen's brooding inactivity, for Bloom's similar paralysis, for Molly's adultery. *Ulysses* has thrown the seeker after causes from Bruno to Vico to Aristotle to Jacob Boehme to Gaelic etymology to topographical study to Krafft-Ebing to Richmal Mangnall to the study of Joyce's school records. In these and in many other sources, valuable information has been discovered; we have enlarged our knowledge of what Joyce did know or could have known. We have understood more about the impact of life on art, even while the absorption of the first into the second demonstrated the artifice within both nature and culture. That is, Joyce's stream of consciousness is a gathering of discursive fragments from culture, and the schemata denote only an engineered unity that the novel partly produces and partly rejects—the unity of philosophic systems, the merely logical internal coherence of a cultural system or paradigm. The unconscious and the unknown are the same absent figures for both *Ulysses* and life, for nature and for a culture which cannot know themselves fully.

The Cultural Unconscious

Above, the term "cultural unconscious" referred to something unrepresented in *Ulysses*, whose reality is nonetheless affirmed, or at least desired, by the narrative. *Ulysses*, that is, may be read as nostalgically yearning to embody discursively the nature that it posits as desirable and necessary for truly gratifying human experience. To this end, *Ulysses* asserts its status as an encyclopedic book, as a work so comprehensive that it implies or can even capture glimpses of raw motivation, nonideological concept, and uninstitutionalized experience. Bloom's thoughts, however continuously impinged upon and shaped by the city through which he moves, appear to offer the possibility of connection to uncensored impulse and unconditioned emotion. Especially when Bloom drifts off to sleep after his remote encounter on the beach with Gerty MacDowell, we seem to enter a gentle drift of uncontrolled ideas, and this event seems to promise deep revelation when the reader gets to "Circe." But the expectation is never fulfilled. In its place, the narrative provides a cycling through one cultural proposition after another. The minds that we see in *Ulysses* are very much the products of their environment, and tracking down the things alluded to in those minds has consistently driven scholars to the world external to the text. The book's cultural unconscious remains an inaccessible force which motivates the various searches by character, author, and reader for the chemical that will transform charted fragments into luminous certitudes about consubstantiality, the incorruptibility of the soul, and the meaning of experience.

In *The Political Unconscious* (1981), Fredric Jameson uses a term similar to "cultural unconscious," and clearly my own phrase alludes to his; in fact, the line of reasoning that Jameson follows in his exciting introduction and problematic conclusion must be partly rehearsed here if I am to round out my sense of the work enacted in *Ulysses*. Early in his study, Jameson states his belief that a chief task of the narrative analyst is to see every story as part

of the "single great collective story" of, as Marx and Engels would
have it, "oppressor and oppressed."[17] Jameson contends, "It is in
detecting the traces of that uninterrupted narrative, in restoring
to the surface of the text the repressed and buried reality of this
fundamental history, that the doctrine of a political unconscious
finds its function and its necessity."

Whereas Jameson sees the "political unconscious" as a "master-
narrative" of historical struggle which is inscribed in various ways
into every literary work, I find that in addition *Ulysses* has inscribed into it also a cultural master-narrative (no doubt specific
to the social formation in and through which the work was written) of human connection with primal instinct and authentic
wholeness. This vision, what Jacques Derrida and others might
subsume into a myth of plenitude, might also be viewed as the
logical outcome of bourgeois reality in a world of increasing social
fragmentation, reification, alienation, and commodification. By
this line of reasoning, nature is construed as transcendent or at
least as a good to be sought outside of or in the usually unex-
amined folds of culture. The cultural unconscious is thus a narrative of nature which emerges from the pressure of modern
society, though it has obvious affinities with the pastoral vision
of earlier centuries and with various countercultural ("back-to-
nature") movements of the postmodern decades. A Lacanian
might argue additionally that this cultural unconscious, however
much it may be a social construct, nonetheless functions as a
motivating Other, a nature that speaks culture. Thus, nature is
less a place or an ideal than it is a discourse whose themes are
wholeness and psychological or even spiritual integrity. The measure of Bloom's and Stephen's inevitable defeat by a manipulative
society is their steady inability to procure imaginative access to
this extracultural language. The measure of the narrative's affirmation of this discourse's potency is the constant stream of coincidence that textures the fiction and tempts us always to discern
within difference the presence of consubstantiality, connection,
and communication. The nature in question here is quite other
than the ideological construct that marks Molly as Gea-Tellus

and as earthily polyphiloprogenitive; the latter marks only desire in submission to convention, while the former "exists" in the negative space outside the text.

One of Jameson's aims in *The Political Unconscious* is to broaden Marxist theory from its well-known concern with demystification to a recognition that "all literature must read as a symbolic meditation on the destiny of community."[18] To be sure, *Ulysses* itself accomplishes many kinds of demystification; the narrative's exploration of selfhood, gender distinctions, family relations, the social order, and Anglo-Irish interaction vigorously exposes the ideological practices shaping these concepts and dominating much of the life in Joyce's city.[19] However, *Ulysses* also addresses the issue of community, both by demonstrating the absence of the communal in the Dublin of 1904 and by emphasizing the events, actions, thoughts, and dreams linking meandering Stephen and wandering Bloom. In a city marked by clerical, patriarchal, economic, and political domination, Joyce signifies a consubstantiality of characters which, liberated from the theological doctrine that Stephen brings to the coding of coincidence, alludes to the many varieties of collectivity that the narrative aggressively lacks. Thus to contribute here my own coding of the characters' experience is neither sheer fabrication nor mere figure. Rather, to do so is to extrapolate the desire for community (as a version of nature) from the kinds of anomie experienced by Bloom, Stephen, and Molly; from the recurrent critical efforts to account for the novel's odd blend of depressing details and exuberant wit; and from Joyce's persistent interest in social forms and theories.[20]

One place in which theories abound is the penultimate episode of *Ulysses*, and it is from this site of rationalization that the cultural unconscious asserts its discourse of nature and community. In fact, it is the contradiction between culture and unconscious that accounts for the mixed readings of that chapter. Many critics have argued that despite the pseudo-scientific perspective, the narrative allows, via the good offices of Epps's Cocoa, a symbolic communion of father and son. Other readers maintain that even to suggest a meeting of minds is to indulge

in the novelistic sentimentality that Joyce abhorred. But I de-
tect in the Blephen-Stoom encounter the same voice of desire
for nature that shapes the consensus perception of Molly as
Earth Mother. It is not just by convention that readers have
found Molly to be natural; such a reading also emerges from
the dialectic between the culture and its unconscious. Strictly
speaking, of course, we can never *know* the difference between
these two terms; certainly, those of us who are caught within
Western language and logic can conceive of the cultural unconscious only by analogy to our thoroughly conventional experience. What we can know, as Vico proclaimed and Joyce un-
doubtedly noted, is the "world of civil society" (what Vico also
calls the world of the "gentiles"), which "has certainly been
made by men." Vico strictly distinguishes the human sphere
from "the world of nature, which, since God made it, He alone
knows."[21] Given the predilection for etymological study that
Vico and Joyce shared, it is of interest that the word "nature"
has affinities with the Indo-European root *gene-*, from which
"gentile" derives; that is, "nature" contains Vico's world of culture. On the other hand, as anyone with an *American Heritage
Dictionary* can determine, the word "culture" shares its Indo-
European root *kwel-* with "entelechy," the Aristotelian term that
Stephen seems in "Circe" to associate with the *quidditas* of an
object. Perhaps because nature and culture write themselves in
each other, Joyce's fiction nostalgically projects wholeness despite the undeniable fragmentation in the work and its framing
world.

Less positive assessments of Joyce's fiction have, of course, always been made. Early readers of *Ulysses* emphasized the "waste
land" of Dublin life as portrayed by Joyce, and shades of that
reaction color many different readings of the narrative, from
Hugh Kenner's *Dublin's Joyce* (1956) to Franco Moretti's "The Long
Goodbye." Moretti's argument about *Ulysses*, which appears in his
very instructive *Signs Taken for Wonders* (1983), interests me because
he argues unequivocally for Joyce's portrait of a Dublin caught
in the "crisis of liberal capitalism," a "negative utopia" informed
by the author's "consummate scepticism." Moretti grounds this

view in the notion that the specific Irish context of the narrative is far less important than is the pressure of English economic history.[22] That is, the essay screens out the very details that *Ulysses* uses (the life it absorbs into art) to strike a balance between dystopia and community. Such a detail occurs in "Aeolus," in which the stalled trams call to mind not only the celebrated paralysis of Dublin life as Joyce portrayed it in his short stories but also the 1913 Dublin Lock-Out.[23] That the Lock-Out was a brutally effective management strategy only highlights its equal success in generating some measure of class consciousness. Such solidarity Jameson links to the utopian desire for a communal society which he discerns in many literary works. Joyce's own text claims both less and more through its portrayal of the stalled trams, for swirling around those few paralyzed machines is the ongoing life of the city of words in which Irish laborers pursue their tasks, an Irish dilettante named Dedalus ponders consubstantiality, an Irish canvasser named Bloom seeks community, and the discourses of modern social life force us to recognize the significance of what is not said. It is at the margins of Joyce's discourse, where life and art entangle, that the dialectic of nature and culture enacts the work, in both senses, that we call *Ulysses*.

Notes

1. An excellent commentary on this phenomenon occurs in Fritz Senn's "Righting *Ulysses*," in *James Joyce: New Perspectives*, ed. Colin MacCabe (Sussex: Harvester Press; and Bloomington: Indiana University Press, 1982), 3–28.

2. "The National Library of Ireland *versus* Walt Whitman," *Dublin University Review* 1 (May 1885): 97–98. It is likely that this or a similar story of censorship reached Joyce's ears. In *Finnegans Wake*, Jaun includes in his sermon some comments on censorship and mentions that "William Archer's a rompan good cathalogue and he'll give you a riser on the route to our nazional labronry" (*FW* 440.3–5).

3. See John Henry Raleigh's *The Chronicle of Leopold and Molly Bloom: "Ulysses" as Narrative* (Berkeley and Los Angeles: University of California

Press, 1977), 179–81. Raleigh finds 1903 to be the most likely date for the Blooms' move to Eccles Street.

4. For an account of Best's well-known defense of his extraliterary reality, see Richard Ellmann, *JJ*2, 363–64. Ellmann speaks at some length of the peculiar relationship between Joyce's life and art, addressing an issue that recurs throughout the criticism as well as in Joyce's own theorizing about art.

5. Weldon Thornton, *Allusions in "Ulysses"* (New York: Simon and Schuster, 1973), 151–52.

6. Arthur Power, *Conversations with James Joyce*, ed. Clive Hart (London: Millington, 1974), 54.

7. Most thoroughly perhaps by Erwin R. Steinberg in his *The Stream of Consciousness and Beyond in "Ulysses"* (Pittsburgh, Pa.: University of Pittsburgh Press, 1973). Also of interest in this discussion are Hugh Kenner's *Joyce's Voices* (Berkeley and Los Angeles: University of California Press, 1978) and Karen Lawrence's *The Odyssey of Style in "Ulysses"* (Princeton, N.J.: Princeton University Press, 1981).

8. See Thornton, 41.

9. Joyce to Frank Budgen, August 16, 1921 *SL* 285.

10. For a discussion of reflexivity in *Ulysses*, see Brook Thomas, *James Joyce's "Ulysses": A Book of Many Happy Returns* (Baton Rouge: Louisiana University Press, 1982). Thomas argues that each episode destabilizes its own reality and the authority of all the others, an effect that the reader further complicates by interpretively acceding to the reflexive contours of the text.

11. A study of the conventional link between women and nature may be found in Carolyn Merchant's *The Death of Nature: Women, Ecology, and the Scientific Revolution* (San Francisco, Calif.: Harper & Row, 1980).

12. *Women in Joyce*, ed. Suzette Henke and Elaine Unkeless (Urbana: University of Illinois Press, 1982), 165. Cf. Bonnie Kime Scott's *Joyce and Feminism* (Bloomington: Indiana University Press; and Sussex: Harvester Press, 1984), 156–83.

13. Phillip F. Herring, ed., *Joyce's "Ulysses": Notesheets in the British Museum* (Charlottesville: University Press of Virginia, 1972), 455.

14. There was, of course, more than one version of the schema, Joyce having given somewhat different charts to Carlo Linati, Herbert Gorman, Stuart Gilbert, and others. My comments here on the schemata refer to the composite version printed in the appendix to Richard Ellmann's *Ulysses on the Liffey* (New York: Oxford University Press, 1972). [See Appendix.]

15. Joyce wrote of *Ulysses* to Carlo Linati on September 21, 1920: "È una specie di enciclopedia anche" (*SL* 271).

16. For example, see James H. Maddox, Jr., *Joyce's "Ulysses" and the Assault upon Character* (New Brunswick, N.J.: Rutgers University Press, 1978).

17. Fredric Jameson, *The Political Unconscious: Narrative as a Socially Symbolic Act* (Ithaca, N.Y.: Cornell University Press, 1981), 19–20. Jameson cites Karl Marx and Friedrich Engels, "The Communist Manifesto," in Marx, *On Revolution*, ed. and trans. S. K. Padover (New York: McGraw-Hill, 1971), 81. Below, I quote from Jameson, 20.

18. Jameson, 70.

19. See Cheryl Herr, *Joyce's Anatomy of Culture* (Urbana and Chicago: University of Illinois Press, 1986).

20. For discussion of the last, we must turn to Dominic Manganiello's *Joyce and Politics* (London: Routledge and Kegan Paul, 1980); Manganiello comments (98–114) on the "vision" in *Ulysses* "of a classless, humanitarian, pacifist and co-operative society." Raymond Williams's *The Country and the City* (New York: Oxford University Press, 1973) also devotes attention to the question of community in *Ulysses*. Williams speaks of Bloom, Stephen, and Molly primarily as isolated figures whose internal experience—their unspoken streams of consciousness—not only is richer than their social interaction but also implies the reality of a "collective" mind: "In and through the intense subjectivities a metaphysical or psychological 'community' is assumed, and characteristically, if only in abstract structures, it is universal; the middle terms of actual societies are excluded as ephemeral, superficial or at best contingent and secondary." It is the community of the collective consciousness—or, as Williams notes, of what Jung called the "collective unconscious"—that *Ulysses* calls forth. Finally and most important, Williams discerns in Joyce a "community of speech" (245–46). It is likely that Williams might see my notion of the "cultural unconscious" as identical to what he calls "rhetorical projections of connection or community or belief," but I find the multivalent nature sought in and through *Ulysses* to be less conventional than, strictly speaking, unsayable. Thus the largest effect of Joyce's use of the strategies of Menippean satire is to build by suggestion a sense of the extent and significance of what the text can never tell us, the nature of nature.

21. *The New Science of Giambattista Vico*, ed. and trans. Thomas Goddard Bergin and Max Harold Fisch (Ithaca, N.Y.: Cornell University Press, 1968), 96.

22. *Signs Taken for Wonders: Essays in the Sociology of Literary Forms*, trans.

Susan Fischer, David Forgacs, and David Miller (London: Verso-NLB, 1983), 201, 189–91. For Moretti's comments on stream of consciousness, which partly align with my own, see 194–98.

23. Cf. Colin MacCabe, *James Joyce and the Revolution of the Word* (New York: Barnes & Noble, 1979), 140.

The Ghosts of *Ulysses*

MAUD ELLMANN

✦   ✦   ✦

The Sheeted Mirror

In the film *Ghost Dance*, directed by Ken MacMullen, Jacques Derrida is interviewed by an ethereal young woman who asks him if he believes in ghosts. "That's a hard question," he smiles, "because, you see, I *am* a ghost."[1] Eerily, this reply turned out to be prophetic, not for Derrida (who is no deader than the rest of us), but for the questioner herself, who died before the movie was released and her image was set loose to haunt the screen. Yet in the film itself, the living man is just as insubstantial as his dead inquisitor, for both have been dispatched into the afterlife, translated into bodiless projections. Through the photographic image we survive the grave but also die before our death, disenfleshed before our hearts have ceased to beat. To be or not to be is no longer the question.

What could be blinder than refusing to believe in ghosts? Our ghost-free civilization is based upon the myth that presence is superior to absence, and that absence is a lack of presence rather than an independent power. Although most of us have grown embarrassed by racism, sexism, homophobia, and all the other violent exclusions which reveal the sacrificial logic of the modern state, we persevere in *vivacentrism*, the fiercest and perhaps the founding bigotry of all: the illusion that the living may eradicate the dead through burial, cremation, and forgetfulness. It is to protect the living from the dead that our culture insists upon their opposition, policing those extravagant and erring spirits who refuse to be confined to either realm.

Shakespeare knew better than to underestimate the vigor of the dead, or the irrepressible activities of emptiness. The very task of poetry, he said, was to give to airy nothing a local habitation and a name—thus curtailing its insidious meanderings. In Shakespeare's drama, it is usually women who are obliged to speak and represent the truth of nothing: just as Molly Bloom becomes the prophet of "omission" in Penelope.[2] Gertrude, for example, sees nothing and hears nothing when Hamlet thinks he sees his father's ghost, who being cuckolded, dethroned, and dead is three times nothing (*Hamlet* III.iv.123, 144). Ophelia, on the other hand, professes to think nothing: "a fair thought to lie between maids' legs," Hamlet bawdily retorts, in an unconvincing effort to relegate the nothing that patrols the night to its local habitation as castration (III.ii.116–17). And of course there is Cordelia, who knows that she can only meet her father's absolute demand for love by yielding him the nothing of desire: "Nothing, my lord" (*Lear* I.i.86). However, Lear is not content with *having* nothing unless he can *be* nothing, too, and his daughter's answer guides him through his odyssey of destitution toward a vision of the rapture of unbeing.

This "nothing," therefore, cannot be confined to women, although it circumambulates between the injured daughter and the guilty queen, because it always seems to come to rest in the ghostly figure of the father. "The King is a thing. . . . Of nothing," Hamlet says (IV.iii.27–29). It is significant that he could be referring either to the king that's dead or to the king of shreds and patches who has seized his throne, because he knows that both are nothing, specter and impostor (I.i.44; III.iv.103). The king is a thing of nothing. How can you murder nothing? This is the question that paralyzes Hamlet, who fears moreover that by killing nothing he would be obliged to take its place, to be *and* not to be, by playing father. The true father, in Stephen Dedalus's words, is necessarily a "ghost by absence" or a "ghost by death," and those who take his role are always player kings (*U* 9.175–76). In the case of *Hamlet*, the father's murder has occurred before the tragedy begins, unwitnessed and unverifiable. Yet this death, which never literally *takes place*, is *represented* time and again, by the dumb show and the mousetrap, by the testimony of the ghost, and by the carnage which completes the tragedy: "Nine lives are taken off for his father's one," as Stephen says (*U* 9.132). Thus it is telling that Hamlet exults in the success of the play-within-the-play as if he had already murdered Claudius by staging the destruction of a king: for he can only conquer theater with more theater, compelled to reenact the uncorroborable death which institutes the order of paternity.[3]

What is a ghost? It is Stephen Dedalus who poses this question in "Scylla and Charybdis," and his own answer is curiously undefinitive. A ghost, he says, is "One who has faded into impalpability through death, through absence, through change of manners" (*U* 9.147–49). Stephen is well aware that one can be transformed into a ghost without the bother of an actual demise, since every absence is a dress rehearsal of one's death, and even a change of manners may precipitate one's obsolescence. Odysseus, for instance, visited the Phaiakians in disguise and heard the story of his own adventures from the mouths of strangers, thus learning that his legend had already usurped his life and reduced him to the phantom of his name. As Tennyson's Ulysses says, "I am become a name," which is another way of saying that he has become a ghost before his time. For the name is the ghost bequeathed to each of us at birth, insofar as it prolongs our subjectivity beyond our death. The name survives its owner, and therefore it foreshadows his extinction in the very moment that it calls him into being. To sign one's name, moreover, is to manufacture one's own ghost, one's own extravagant and erring spirit: for writing may be iterated anywhere, by anyone, independent of the life of its creator. Accordingly, Stephen's task in *Ulysses* is to reduce his father to a ghost in order to unleash the symbolic power of his name.

In *Totem and Taboo*, Freud argues that ghosts are compromise-formations which embody both reverence and horror toward the dead. He says that primitive societies first acknowledged death when they invented ghosts, yet this is also when they first denied it by asserting that the dead return (Freud 1913: 25, 61). The ghost, then, could be seen as the first pure symbol in that it bespeaks the absence rather than the presence of its referent, just as language recreates its objects in their absence, both affirming and denying their propensity to disappear. In this sense, words are the ghosts of things, their chattering afterlife. The very term "ghost" confuses categories, insofar as it can either mean the spark of life or the disembodied emanation of the dead. To "give up the ghost," for instance, is to lose one's life but also to unleash one's vengeful shade. Ghosts are almost always hungry, and they are usually angry too, for "ghost," as the *Oxford English Dictionary* informs us, derives from the Teutonic word for "fury." A "ghost" in optics is a bright spot, like a livid mole, produced by the reflection of a lens. It is, in other words, a mark of mediation, and people who see ghosts, like Hamlet or Macbeth, know better than to overlook the blind spots embedded in the visible.

In theatrical slang, "the ghost walks" means that the treasury is full and that the wages will be paid. That this perambulating spirit represents the actors' very livelihood implies a bond between the theater and the resurrection of the dead, a bond affirmed in the dramatic chapters of *Ulysses*. For *Ulysses* is a book about mourning: about the death of love and its return as fury; about the ghosts who vampirize the ego like the famished specters of the underworld. In "Mourning and Melancholia," Freud describes how the ego incorporates the objects that it mourns in order to preserve them from oblivion, populating itself with their phantoms. But these objects, once instated, feed upon the ego until the latter is "totally impoverished" (Freud 1917: 243–58). Mourning, therefore, is the struggle to release the ego from the very ghosts that it is trying to revive.[4] Whenever this struggle comes to a climax in *Ulysses*, the theater invades the narrative, and words give way to figures, thought to reenactment. First, in "Scylla and Charybdis," *Hamlet* provides the imaginary stage where Stephen hallucinates his parricide, for he disposes of his living father through the figure of the murdered king. If his living father is dead, however, his dead mother is very much alive, demonically vital. It is in "Circe," the theater of the dream, that he banishes her ghoulish specter. Two theaters, then, the first for parricide, the last for matricide. Yet in the enclosed world of the stage there is no room for the true death—as the Greeks acknowledged by restricting murder to the wings and purging the theater of event. In another sense, however, death *is* theater, since it is always represented, never *lived*, and the drama in its turn could be regarded as the art of vicarious unbeing.

What *is* the theater, that ghosts should find it so enticing? In particular, why should the theater conjure up *parental* ghosts? André Green (1979: 2–8) suggests that in the family the child witnesses the daily drama of his parents' romance, and it is in the theater that he rediscovers the fascination of spectatorship. The stillness of the audience recalls the speechless passivity of infancy, while the darkness recreates the state of sleep, when the unheeded wishes of the day return in the dramatics of the mind. For the dream is the theater of desire. Freud argues that in dreams, desires are performed rather than thought: words become deeds, fears become monsters. This is what happens in "Circe," the dream theater of *Ulysses*, which stages the apocalypse of Bloom's unconscious: for his desires are replaced by their embodiments, and his ego is dispersed among the ghosts of its libidinal positions. When he becomes a woman, we know that he has longed for subjugation; when he creates Bloomusalem, we know that he has also lusted after power; and when he is accused of a dizzying spectrum of perversions, we know that his desires speak in his accusers' tongues, together with the added frisson of chastisement. According to Yeats (1959: 341), such dreams arise because "the passions, when . . . they cannot find fulfilment, become vision." In the visionary stage of "Circe," unconscious impulses are acted out, theatralized, and the unspeakable erupts into phantasmagoria.

So ghosts have an affinity to theater, as theater has to dream, since each in different ways embodies language in the form of visions. Hegel (1977: 443) argues that drama consists of picture-thoughts which take the place of verbal narrative, just as Freud says that pictures take the place of wishes in the dream. Similarly, ghosts are the visions which arise when words have failed to purge the agony of loss. Moreover, a theatrical performance is a text incarnate which embodies written words in living voices. As Artaud has suggested (1958: 117, 89), the word is made flesh and the dead letter is restored to life, resurrected from its mortuary in the alphabet. To perform a play is therefore to revive the dead, since every actor is the phantom of a script, as each performance is the afterlife of writing.

Drama originates in ritual, and for this reason it preserves the magical power to *present* rather than *explain*. In the immediacy of the theater, representation masquerades as presence, afterward as now. As Hegel says (1977: 443–44), "the language ceases to be narrative because it enters into the content," and the "hero is himself the speaker," rather than the object of the speech. Lévi-Strauss, however, criticizes ritual as a regression, contrasting it to the creative alterity of myth. In the final volume of *Mythologiques* he argues that myth is superior to ritual because it is "essentially transformative," a narrative modified by each retelling. Ritual, by contrast, denies difference, surrendering the metamorphic power of the myth to the stupefying incandescence of the spectacle. According to Lévi-Strauss, ritual is a futile attempt "to re-establish the unbrokenness of a reality dismantled by the schematism which mythic speculation has substituted for it."[5] Rituals *act out* what myths *remember*, and Lévi-Strauss agrees with Freud that psychic maturity depends upon converting reenactment into memory.[6] Artaud, on the contrary, celebrates the specious immediacy of the theater as revolutionary rather than regressive. "If theater is as bloody and inhuman as dreams," he writes, "it is . . . to demonstrate and to confirm in us beyond all forgetting the idea of a perpetual conflict, and of a spasm where life is cut through at every moment; where the whole of creation rises up against our state as finished being."[7] This is the kind of theater that Joyce creates in "Circe," where he exploits the regressive elements of ritual but only to undo the perilous coherence of the daytime self by unleashing the nightmare of its history. The barrier of the unrepeatable is broken and the past erupts into the present, dismantling narrative in a carnival of secular and sacred rites.

In "Scylla and Charybdis," Stephen seems to be defending Lévi-Strauss's point of view, because he uses "dialectic," the technic of the chapter, to hold the world of ritual at bay.[8] But the style of the prose constantly breaks out of his control, making *scenes* as fast as he makes *sense*, as if the theater were subverting the linear progression of the narrative, transfixing it with ritual and reenactment. Lacan (1982:39), in an essay on *Hamlet*, argues that it is dangerous to deny the realm of ritual because it irritates the dead out of their graves. Ghosts, he says, arise out of "the gap left by the omission of a significant rite." The ghost of Hamlet's father, for example, rises from the grave "unhousel'd, disappointed, unanel'd," because he died without receiving the last rites (I.v.77). Stephen, on the other hand, refused to perform the ritual that would have kept his mother quiet in her tomb. As Mulligan mocks, "—You could have knelt down, damn it, Kinch, when your dying mother asked you . . . to think of your mother begging you with her last breath to kneel down and pray for her. And you refused. There is something sinister in you" (*U* 1.91–94). In the place of this omitted rite, this unsaid prayer, the ghost of Stephen's mother rises to demand her obsequies in "Circe," and she brings with her the denigrated principle of ritual which Stephen has been trying to subdue with dialectic.

The Mole and the Molecule

It is the father's ghost who dominates the stage in "Scylla and Charybdis," where Stephen pontificates on *Hamlet*. At one point in this chapter Stephen is debating whether to excuse himself from paying back the pound he owes to AE (the mystic acronym of George Russell) by claiming that his molecules have all been overhauled: "Wait. Five months. Molecules all change. I am other

I now. Other I got pound." However, alarmed by this vision of
his own unraveling, he bethinks himself that "I . . . am I by memory." If the body changes every moment, weaving and unweaving
its own substance, memory alone ensures that the I who borrows
is the I who owes. History, Stephen finds, is rather an expensive
luxury: "A.E.I.O.U.," he admits at last (*U* 9.204–5, 208, 213). But
because he would rather be indebted than unselved he opts for
memory and stakes the mole against the molecules:

> —As we, or mother Dana, weave and unweave our bodies,
> Stephen said, from day to day, their molecules shuttled to and
> fro, so does the artist weave and unweave his image. And as
> the mole on my right breast is where it was when I was born,
> though all my body has been woven of new stuff time after
> time, so through the ghost of the unquiet father the image of
> the unliving son looks forth. (*U* 9.376–81)

Stephen is saying that despite the deconstruction of the body the
mole reprints itself afresh and thus affirms the continuity of
memory. Yet the term "mole" also alludes to the ghost of Hamlet's father, whose son addresses him as "old mole" (I.v.170). Stephen is punning on this epithet when he associates the mole on
his right breast with the ghost of the unquiet father. The "ghost
of the unliving son" is Hamnet, Shakespeare's son who died in
childhood. With the death of Hamnet, the "son of his body,"
Shakespeare's name can only survive him in his words, and Stephen sees his opus as the mausoleum of the patronym (*U* 9.172).
It is true that a malaise about the father's name pervades the
tragedy of *Hamlet* from the start, when the ghost arises instead of
a name and as the emblem of the namelessness of Shakespeare's
lineage. The tragedy opens with the words "Who's there?"—and
everyone who witnesses the father's ghost is struck with an apha-
sia about his name, resorting to such euphemisms like "this
thing," "this dreaded sight," "this apparition," or Hamlet's antic
epithets, "true-penny" and "old mole." In the end, Hamlet *fils* is
sacrificed for Hamlet *père*, thus erasing both the name and its
descendance (*U* 9.1034). Shakespeare, who played the specter at

the Globe, employed the tragedy to fantasize the murder of his
father and his son, and to taste his own death, too, in a symbolic
murder of himself. As Stephen says:

> —The play begins. A player comes on under the shadow, made
> up in the castoff mail of a court buck, a wellset man with a
> bass voice. It is the ghost, the king, a king and no king, and
> the player is Shakespeare who has studied *Hamlet* all the years
> of his life which were not vanity in order to play the part of
> the spectre. (*U* 9.163–67)

If the mole, then, stands for both the undead father and the
unliving son, it marks the spot where death irrupts in life, where
the ghosts of the future and the past look forth from the mo-
lecular decomposition of the present. It corresponds to the function of the *name* of Hamlet, in which Shakespeare's life converges
with his art. For the molecules of Ham*n*et, "the son of his body,"
were transfigured into the artifact of Ham*l*et, "son of his soul"
(*U* 9.171). As Stephen puts it, Hamnet Shakespeare died at Strat-
ford so that "his *namesake* may live for ever" (*U* 9.173; my emphasis). In the play, it is the name which has survived the dissolution of the father's molecules, and it only comes into its full
symbolic force when he is dead. "That mole," Stephen laughs, is
"the last to go" (*U* 9.391); and here the mole may either mean
the burrowing beast, the blemish on the breast, or the "vicious
mole of nature" in the soul. Most important, however, Stephen
means the father's *ghost* ("old mole"), which is the ectoplasmic
version of his *name*.[9]

Since the mole is associated with the name of the father, it
seems to represent the triumph of paternity, the transcendence
of the father's word over the mother's flesh. But Joyce subjects
the mole to the paronomasia that undercuts all of the master
signifiers of his text. Acoustically the mole is related to the "moly"
which preserves Odysseus's manhood when he walks among the
swine in Circe's den. In Joyce's version of the Circe episode, Bloom
surrenders his potato—the Irish equivalent of moly—and
thereby forfeits his virility to Bella Cohen. "I should not have

parted with my talisman," he laments (*U* 15.2794). Bella becomes Bello and Bloom becomes a woman until he has retrieved his potato from the prostitutes. Greedy for emasculation, Bloom has also forfeited another form of moly, *Molly*, to the gallantries of Blazes Boylan. Thus Bloom's manhood depends upon possessing moly, or possessing Molly; but since both these charms show an alarming tendency to circulate his potency is constantly in threat. Stephen, on the other hand, alludes to the mole of Imogen in *Cymbeline*, which also represents the threat of cuckoldry. Imogen's husband Posthumus mistakenly believes she has betrayed him because his rival reports that he has seen the mole beneath her breast: "Imogen's breast, bare, with its mole cinquespotted" as Stephen says (*U* 9.474).[10] Though Imogen's honor is salvaged in the end, the mole has come to represent the ineradicable possibility of her adultery.

Always the binarist, Stephen ignores the emasculating implications of the mole to relegate the mother to the molecules. As Penelope wove her web, so Mother Dana weaves the flesh, unraveling its molecules incessantly. The mole is where the father's name transcends the mother's metamorphic flesh, just as the "mole of boulders" in Proteus provides a point of fixity in Stephen's decomposing universe of sand and sea (*U* 3.356). His equation of the mother with the dying body and the father with the deathless word (the name) scarcely amounts to an original theology, but Stephen insists upon it doggedly. In his famous disquisition on paternity, he argues that the mother's role in parturition is self-evident, whereas the father's role is hypothetical, since he can never guarantee his offspring as his own. "Fatherhood, in the sense of conscious begetting, is unknown to man," he declares (*U* 9.837–38). A ghost by absence from the act of birth, the father is always potentially a ghost by death as well (*U* 9.174–75). It is only through the "legal fiction" of the name that he can reclaim his dubious paternity (*U* 9.844).

It is at this point of Stephen's analysis of *Hamlet* that the parricidal motives of literary criticism are unmasked. Yet if the father is as dead as Stephen says he is, it is strange that he discusses it so imperturbably. He elaborates his theory in the library, amidst his cozy if competitive fraternity, and neither Stephen nor his audience seems to be ruffled by his dreams of murder, incest, and adultery. What has happened to the agony of mourning, the rage, the guilt, and the garrulity—"Words, words, words," as Hamlet says (II.ii.192)—which hollow themselves out with their own petulance? Stephen himself admits that he does not believe in his own theory (*U* 9.1065–67). His abjuration of the father is a decoy, a displacement of his more insidious negation of the mother, and the whole theory serves as "the creation he has piled up to hide him from himself" and in particular to blind him to his matricide (*U* 9.475). Indeed, he only denies the father's actuality in order to affirm the "mystery" of paternity. For it is on "that mystery and not on the madonna which the cunning Italian intellect flung to the mob of Europe [that] the church is founded and founded irremovably because founded, like the world, macro and microcosm, upon the void. Upon incertitude, upon unlikelihood" (*U* 9.839–42). This theory implies that what the father loses in the real he regains in the symbolic, in which the "legal fiction" (*U* 9.844) of paternity overrides the *fact* of motherhood. "Loss is his gain," as Stephen says (*U* 9.476).

Ernest Jones (1951: 358–73) argues that another phantom, the Holy Ghost, arose out of the same desire to erase the mother in the guise of a denial of the father.[11] According to Jones, the Christian Trinity is the only holy family in mythology in which the mother has been ousted by a masculine progenitor, that is, by "the mysterious figure of the Holy Ghost." The myth of virgin birth expresses a desire to repudiate the father's role in reproduction, but also to atone for this emasculating wish by granting him stupendous potency. For God impregnates Mary with a word, a breath, a thought, and he does not even have to move an inch. The Holy Ghost takes care of everything. This spirit, Jones thinks, derives from infantile fantasies about the fecundating power of another kind of breath or *spiritus*, that is, the gaseous exhalations of the anus. In other words, behind the myth of virgin birth lurks the belief that Mary was inseminated by a cosmic fart. This theory of flatulent conception disavows the father's sexual possession of the mother and thereby frees her for the child's own incestuous imaginings.

However, Jones goes on to argue that the story of religion represents the never-ending struggle to overcome desire for the mother and to achieve atonement with the father. This is why Christianity has concocted an all-male family for the savior, demoting the mother goddess to a mortal woman who merely incubates the father's procreative breath. While the Holy Ghost usurps the position of the mother in the Trinity, the priests appropriate the mother's role within the church, since it is they who feed the congregation with the blood and body of the savior, a masculine substitute for mother's milk. Indeed, they even dress like women, and by assuming the emblems of castration—the robes, the shaved heads, and the celibacy—they assert that women are no longer needed even to represent men's lack. In this way a religion which began as a denial of the father has ended up with the obliteration of maternity.

"Himself his own father," Stephen also tries to disavow the mother and to rebeget himself in the eared womb of his own brain.[12] Yet he has not murdered his mother sufficiently to rid his mind of the tormenting image of her wasting flesh. It is in "Circe" that the mother he has tried to murder, first with silence, then with words, rises up to teach him *amor matris* and remind him of love's bitter mystery (*U* 9.843, 15.4190). To borrow Molly's malapropism, it is his "omission" of the mother in his analysis of *Hamlet* that causes her "emission" in the dream of "Circe" (*U* 18.1170). For this reason it is significant that Ernest Jones (1971: 92–100) interprets *Hamlet* as a *matricidal* rather than a merely parricidal tragedy. Margaret Ferguson (1985: 292–309) has also pointed out that *Hamlet* abounds with allusions to maternity: Shakespeare uses the word "matter" twenty-six times, more than in any of his other plays, typically twinning it with "mother" to suggest a pun on the Latin *mater*. Hamlet's opening gambit in the closet scene is a good example: "Now, mother, what's the matter?" (*Hamlet* III.iv.7). In "Circe," matter and maternity are also interlinked in that Stephen's denial of the mother bespeaks a denial of the matter of the body and also a denial of the written or acoustic *matter* of the word. It is this matter that returns to haunt him in "Circe," the substance rather than the sense of words. A swarm of half-remembered words assails him, wrenched out of the daytime chapters of the book and deformed by the compulsions of the dream. It is the contrast between the logic of the day and the madness of the night which gives the second coming of these traces its uncanniness. If the father's ghost assumes the form of a disembodied spirit in *Ulysses*, the mother's ghost returns as the body of the word evacuated by the spirit of its meaning.

The matter and the meaning of the word have also parted company before, and taken off on separate odysseys, like the HELY'S sandwichmen who wander off in "Lestrygonians," each "scarlet letter" wending its own way, or the literary flotsam that meanders down the Liffey into the alphabet soup of the sea (*U* 8.126–28). In "Circe," however, matter takes command, and surface takes the place of depth in word and flesh. Everything is *on show* in this chapter: the veil is rent which hides the inner workings of the mind or the inner significance of words. Indeed, this whole theology of meaning explodes into theatrics. The subject who *knows* is ousted by the subject who *shows*, that is, the subject of hysteria, possessed by memories that he enacts but cannot know.

At the beginning of the episode Stephen speaks of a language of "gesture" which would render visible "not the lay sense but . . . the structural rhythm" (*U* 15.105–7). "Circe" itself is written in the language of gesture, for discourse is embodied as performance, and it is the rude and epileptic rhythm of the words that matters, rather than their "lay sense," their vulgar meaning. This rhythm is diagnosed by the prostitutes as "locomotor ataxy": a disease which involves the inability to coordinate the voluntary movements, or constitutional unsteadiness in the use of limbs (*U* 15.2592). Not only are the characters ataxic or convulsive but the very body of the text is wracked with cramps. "The stiff walk," Bloom declares, referring both to his own ataxic movements and to the "stiffs" who walk the night, the corpses of the dead. Bloom is attacked by spasms, stitches, tics, and palpitations; the ghost of

Shakespeare is afflicted with a facial palsy; and Stephen, who scarcely bears a body, jerks and gabbles, whirls and totters, drops his cigarette, and stammers parapraxes.[13] Here, symptoms speak instead of words, and even the ratiocinative Stephen is reduced to the theatrics of hysteria.

Lurking behind "Circe" is the legend that hysteria originates in a wandering womb, a uterine version of the odyssey. For Bloom admits to menstrual cramps at the very outset of his nightmare: "Bit light in the head. Monthly or effect of the other," he complains (*U* 15.210). Indeed, the heroes cannot keep their femininity at bay: Bloom forfeits his potato-talisman and turns into a woman, while Stephen is beleaguered by the mother who wombed him in sin darkness. Like Lear, he must subdue the mother in order to be cured of his hysteria, so that he may speak in language rather than convulsions: "O! how this mother swells up toward my heart; / *Hysterica passio!* down, thou climbing sorrow!" (*Lear* II.iv.54–55). In "Circe" it is by crying "*Nothung!*" and by brandishing his ashplant sword that Stephen overcomes the wandering womb, dispatching the castrating figure of his mother to the darkness (*U* 15.4241–45). And it is not until he sends his mother back to hell that he is freed from the delirium of matter. At this point, the beasts become men again, having mastered and externalized the feminine, and to certify their triumph the police return. The ghosts disperse, and the bedrock of the present reemerges from the flood of that which was.

If Stephen is a ghost-buster, Bloom the advertising canvasser facilitates the transmigration of commodities and souls, ferrying them across the Styx of "civic finance" (*U* 17.983–84). The reason that he relishes the inner organs of beasts and fowls, or envisages the human body as a bunch of pumps, is that he functions as intestine to the world of commerce, transforming and dispersing its consumer goods. Less interested in ineluctable modalities than in the metempsychoses of the large intestine, he flushes words and flesh into their afterlife. Joyce complained that Stephen had a shape that could not be changed, but Bloom, by contrast, represents the shape-changing wizardry of commerce (R. Ellmann 1972: Appendix). In *Faust*, Goethe draws attention to the link be-

tween the world of commerce and the world of phantoms by
punning on the word for banknote (*Geldschein*) and the word for
ghost (*Gespenst*).[14] Money is a ghost because it has no body of its
own but is constantly reincarnated in the bodies of commodities.
Moreover, money *wanders*, and for this reason it resembles both
the "extravagant and erring spirit" of the father and the odyssean
wanderlust of Bloom. Joyce hints at these analogies in "Ithaca,"
where we learn that Bloom once launched a florin on a mercan-
tile odyssey. Having "marked a florin (2/–) with three notches on
the milled edge," he gave it to the grocer "for possible, circuitous
or direct, return." The text demands, "Had Bloom's coin returned?" and the implacable riposte is "Never" (*U* 17.981–88). Like
the florin, Bloom himself is sent into diaspora, destined for dissemination rather than return.

Though Bloom does return to the Ithaca of 7 Eccles Street it
is only to discover that Molly's bed is thronged with the ghosts
of other men. He surrenders to these spectral lovers, much as
Gabriel Conroy surrenders to the ghost of Michael Fury in "The
Dead" ("ghost" being derived from the Teutonic word for "fury").
But it is precisely by renouncing carnal love that Bloom defeats
the suitors in "Penelope," because he leaves his body on a distant
shore in search of a symbolic consummation in the seas of Molly's
reverie. In this chapter it is his name which wins the day. For
Molly concludes her monologue with the wild dissemination of
her husband's name in a torrent of *blooms*, an ocean of flowers:[15]

> I love flowers Id love to have the whole place swimming in
> roses ... flowers all sorts of shapes and smells and colours
> springing up even out of the ditches primroses and violets ...
> and O that awful deepdown torrent O and the sea the sea
> crimson sometimes like fire ... and the rosegardens and the
> jessamine and geraniums.... (*U* 18.1557–58, 1562–63, 1597–
> 1601)

In the "Lotus Eaters" episode, Bloom assumes the name of Henry
Flower, and he concludes the chapter gazing at the "languid floating flower" of his penis in the bath: "limp father of thousands"

(*U* 5.571–72). Like the mole, however, the image of the flower cannot be reduced into a phallic symbol. Joyce knew that the Earl of Rochester used "flowers" to mean menstruation, thus identifying them with the *female* blood which Molly consecrates in her apocalyptic image of the crimson sea. It is also important that *flowers* mean figures of rhetoric. Since Bloom associates the "flow" of water with the "flow" of poetry in "Lestrygonians," the flow of flowers which concludes the novel seems to represent the infinite fecundity of figuration. Molly's rhapsody plunges "deepdown" into the matrix of the language, in which the myths of gender and identity dissolve into the "flowers" of the rhetoric where they originate. In this ecstatic surge of floral imagery she relinquishes Bloom's presence for his name, and thus bequeaths him with his ghostdom and his passport to eternity.

Agenbite of Inwit

Peter Underwood (1986: 16–37), the president of the British Ghost Club, has discovered a dozen different kinds of ghost, including cyclic ghosts, poltergeists, ghosts of animals, haunted objects, and ghosts of the living, and for those who plan to take up ghost watching, he has also written a handy guide to gear. However, *Oedipus* and *Hamlet* show that the theater is the place to look for the vindictive phantoms of paternity. Like a dream, the theater embodies the unspeakable, replacing words with deeds, wishes with apparitions. Indeed, the theater is a dream turned inside out, the outer image of the oneiric stagecraft of the mind. If Western drama has been dominated by the father's spirit, though, the theater of *Ulysses* is besieged by the mother's unpropitiated flesh. In "Circe" as in the unconscious, the corpse of language reasserts its obstinate materiality, like the white corpuscles in Buck Mulligan's mock eucharist which stubbornly resist the transubstantiation of his shaving lather (*U* 1.1–29). Milan Kundera (1986: 123) has observed, "Death has two faces. One is nonbeing; the other is the terrifying material being of the corpse." It is the second face of death which is invoked in the unstageable delirium of "Circe." By denying the matter associated with the mother, the father establishes his ghostly kingdom; thus the flesh is made word. In "Circe," on the contrary, word becomes flesh in the savage hieroglyphics of hysteria and the return of the maternal corpse of language.

Notes

1. My translation is condensed and approximate. A longer version of "The Ghosts of *Ulysses*" was published in Martin 1990: 193–227. This essay was first delivered as the Richard Ellmann Memorial Address at the Eleventh International James Joyce Symposium, Venice, June 1988.

2. Molly uses "omission" for "emission" throughout "Penelope," and the malapropism suggests that the role of woman in the text is to emit omissions or breed absences: "how much is that doctor one guinea please and asking me had I frequent omissions where do those old fellows get all the words they have omissions with his shortsighted eyes on me cocked sideways" (*U* 18.1169–71).

3. For Freud's theory of the murder of the primal father by his sons, see *Totem and Taboo* (Freud 1913: 141–60). Ernest Jones, in *Hamlet and Oedipus* (Jones 1951: 89) cites Otto Rank's argument that the play-within-the-play, in which a nephew kills his uncle and in which there is no talk of adultery or incest, is in Hamlet's imagination the equivalent for fulfilling his task.

4. See also Leo Bersani's discussion of the "moribund nature of the ego, . . . its status as a kind of cemetery of decathected object-choices" (Bersani 1986: 93–100).

5. Cited from *L'homme nu* in Trotter 1984: 37.

6. See Freud 1914: 150: "the patient does not *remember* anything of what he has forgotten or repressed, but *acts* it out. . . . He *repeats* it, without . . . knowing that he is repeating it."

7. Cited in Green 1979: 10; a less elegant translation may be found in Artaud 1958: 93.

8. See Joyce's schemata for *Ulysses* in Richard Ellmann 1972: Appendix (n.p.). "Dialectic" is the technic in the Linati scheme; the Gilbert/Gorman scheme designates "whirlpools" as the technic and "two-edged dilemma" as the sense. [See also the appendix in this volume.]

9. Hamlet's speech about the "vicious mole of nature" which can undermine the goodness of the soul occurs in I.v.24.

10. Posthumus uses the ring that Imogen has given him to bet that

she could never be unfaithful. But by pressing her gift into his rival's hands he symbolically exchanges Imogen as well, suggesting an unconscious desire for betrayal. It is curious, moreover, that Posthumus should give a love token to the very man who means to cuckold him, because it hints that Imogen is being used to establish an erotic bond between the men. The mole, like the ring, becomes the currency of this unconscious intercourse.

11. Ernest Jones, "A Psycho-Analytic Study of the Holy Ghost Concept," *Essays in Applied Psychoanalysis* 2: 358–73.

12. Stephen speaks of "uneared wombs" in "Scylla and Charybdis" (*U* 9.664).

13. See *U* 15.163, 183, 3822, 3881, 4151–52, 3641, 2091–92. Joyce indicated in the Gilbert/Gorman scheme for *Ulysses* that Stephen (Telemachus) does not yet bear a body in the first three chapters of the novel. [See Appendix.]

14. Marc Shell discusses this pun in *Money, Language, and Thought* (Shell 1982: 6n., 84–130).

15. I am indebted here to Jean-Michel Rabaté's brilliant analysis of the flower motif in *James Joyce: Portrait de l'auteur en autre lecteur* (Rabaté 1984: 86–87).

References

Artaud, Antonin. 1958. *The Theatre and Its Double*, trans. Mary Caroline Richards. New York: Grove.

Bersani, Leo. 1986. *The Freudian Body: Psychoanalysis and Art*. New York: Columbia University Press.

Ellmann, Richard. 1972. *Ulysses on the Liffey*. New York: Oxford University Press.

Ferguson, Margaret W. 1985. "*Hamlet*: Letters and Spirits." In *Shakespeare and the Question of Theory*, ed. Patricia Parker and Geoffrey Hartman, 292–309. New York: Methuen.

Freud, Sigmund. 1913. *Totem and Taboo*. In Strachey 1953–1974. 8:1–162.

———. 1914. "Remembering, Repeating and Working Through (Further Recommendations on the Technique of Psycho-Analysis II." In Strachey 1953–1974. 12: 145–56.

———. 1917. "Mourning and Melancholia." In Strachey 1953–1974. 14: 237–58.

Green, André. 1979. *The Tragic Effect: The Oedipus Complex in Tragedy*, trans. Alan Sheridan. Cambridge: Cambridge University Press.

Hegel, Georg Wilhelm Friedrich. 1977. *The Phenomenology of Spirit,* trans. A. V. Miller. New York: Oxford University Press.

Jones, Ernest. 1951. *Essays in Applied Psychoanalysis.* London: Hogarth.

Kundera, Milan. 1986. *The Art of the Novel,* trans. Linda Asher. New York: Harper.

Lacan, Jacques. 1982. "Desire and the Interpretation of Desire in *Hamlet.*" In *Literature and Psychoanalysis: The Question of Reading: Otherwise,* ed. Shoshana Felman, 11–52. Baltimore, Md.: Johns Hopkins University Press.

Martin, Augustine, ed. 1990. *James Joyce: The Artist and the Labyrinth.* London: Ryan.

Rabaté, Jean-Michel. 1984. *James Joyce: Portrait de l'auteur en autre lecteur.* Petit-Roueulx, Belgique: Cistre.

Shakespeare, William. 1992. *King Lear,* ed. Kenneth Muir. London: Methuen.

———. 1982. *Hamlet,* ed. Harold Jenkins. London: Methuen.

Shell, Marc. 1982. *Money, Language, and Thought.* Berkeley: University of California Press.

Strachey, James, ed. 1953–1974. *The Standard Edition of the Complete Psychological Works of Sigmund Freud.* 24 vols. London: Hogarth.

Trotter, David. 1984. *The Making of the Reader: Language and Subjectivity in Modern American, English and Irish Poetry.* London: Macmillan.

Underwood, Peter. 1986. *The Ghost Hunter's Guide.* London: Javelin.

Yeats, William Butler. 1959. *Mythologies.* New York: Macmillan.

The Female Body, Technology, and Memory in "Penelope"

EWA ZIAREK

◆ ◆ ◆

M Y READING OF THE FEMALE body in "Penelope" starts in fact with the last, unanswered, question of "Ithaca": "Where?" Providing a transition of sorts to Molly's monologue, this suspended question problematizes the discursive location of the female body. Indeed, where is she when she is at home—seemingly in the most familiar and intimate space? Where is the meaning of the female body, and by extension, of sexual difference to be found? In what discursive space? An inquiry into the discursive position of the female body in the context of modernity involves rethinking not only the public and private distinction but also the problem of a specific rhetoric through which this distinction is expressed. My reading of "Penelope" focuses on the contrast between the private space, intertwined with the pronounced rhetoric of organicism, and the public space, associated with the equally compelling, though much less frequently discussed, rhetoric of mechanical reproduction. Consider, for instance, the sharp difference between Molly's fantasy of extramarital sex on the train and her *memory* of Bloom's proposal:

O I love jaunting in a train or a car with lovely soft cushions
I wonder will he take a 1st class for me he might want to do
it in the train by tipping the guard . . . 1 or 2 tunnels perhaps
then you have to look out of the window all the nicer then
coming back suppose I never came back what would they say
eloped with him (18.366–75)

O that awful deepdown torrent O and the sea the sea crimson
sometimes like fire and the glorious sunsets and the figtrees in
the Alameda gardens . . . and the rosegardens and the jessamine
and geraniums and cactuses and Gibraltar as a girl where I was
a Flower of the mountain . . . and how he kissed me under the
Moorish wall and I thought well as well him as another and
then I asked him with my eyes to ask again yes and then he
asked me would I yes to say yes my mountain flower (18.1597–
1606)

The contrast between these two passages implies that the dynam-
ics of female desire can be articulated in two very different discourses. Obviously synchronized with the movement of the machine in the first passage, female desire circulates in the public
and cultural space, which, at the turn of the century, undergoes
increasing technologization. Assimilated to the organic torrents
of the sea and the blossoming of flowers in the second quotation,
female desire retreats to the private and natural space. Producing
a strange bifurcation of female desire, these oppositions between
technology and organicism, between the public and the private,
suggest not only a certain nostalgia for "natural" sexual identity
but also a promise that the organic female body might be a site
of resistance to the mechanization of public life.

Such nostalgia is implied in the way these two kinds of desire
are valorized: if the passion incited by the onward movement of
the machine is associated with Molly's infidelity, the passion in
harmony with nature stands for her faithfulness and marital
union. In contrast to deception, duplicity, and pretense associated
with the sex on the train ("then you have to look out of the
window all the nicer"), the celebrated erotic union among the

rhododendrons conveys the authenticity of experience, preserved and recuperated by erotic memory: "the day we were lying among the rhododendrons on the Howth . . . it was leapyear like now yes 16 years ago" (18.1572–75). Thus, by retreating to the natural and private space, the union of eroticism and memory promises the possibility of an authentic subjective experience—experience which seems to be increasingly endangered in the technologized public sphere.

By contrasting the rhetoric of organicism with mechanical reproduction on the one hand, and the public and the private spheres on the other, female desire in "Penelope" performs two very different functions. When assimilated to the inner work of memory, the movement of female desire recuperates the authenticity of experience, subjective identity, and the temporal continuity of life, dissipating in this way the modern anxiety about the effects of technology. Yet, on the other hand, when associated with technological and public means of transport, such a desire intensifies the deceitful play of appearances, discontinuity of experience, and the possibility of a radical break from the past. It is not by accident that the fantasy of sex on the train, intertwined with speculation about elopement, takes Molly to a point almost beyond return: "suppose I never came back." The recuperation of experience by female erotic memory is no doubt nourishing, even if excessively so; however, the motif of the breast milk, or sharing of the famous seedcake, is ironically juxtaposed with the nervous spilling of the soup on the platform, with antifat ads, or most drastically, with the motif of poison administered by an unfaithful wife. In contrast to the rhetoric of life, the unfaithful female desire displays the threatening effects of technology in terms of nonsatisfaction, privation, and finally, death.

What the rhetoric of organicism consistently implies is a singular and private form of enunciation, based on the unity of voice, experience, and erotic memory. This subjective identity in turn suggests that the truth of female sexuality is to be found in the natural body.[1] Because the rhetoric of organicism consolidates desire with memory on the one hand, and sexuality with nature on the other, such a desire bears the mark of "fidelity." Consider, for instance, that Molly does not even have to articulate her desire to Bloom—it is enough that she "asks" with her eyes. What this scene suggests is that the authentic female passion communicates immediately, without the slightest detour of voice, without any mediation of the artifice of language. Consequently, only memory could preserve the immediacy and authenticity of such a wordless experience. I would like to suggest that this profound complicity between a singular form of private enunciation and a "naturalized" sexual identity constitutes the paradigm of Molly's fidelity in the text. In contrast, the convergence of mechanical reproduction and female sexuality intensifies the effects of infidelity and inauthenticity. Taken as a rhetorical figure, "infidelity" indicates not only a breakdown of the epistemological unity of memory, experience, and voice, not only the dissolution of sexual identity, but also the disturbance of the distinction between the public and the private. The trope of infidelity questions, therefore, both the role of the subject as the origin of signification *and* the role of the body as the location of sexual truth. From this perspective, I would like to raise the performative aspect of Molly's monologue and to examine it from the discursive rather than the subjective angle. That is, what interests me here is the question of performance exceeding the function of the subject, that is, performance as an effect of the overlapping discourses in a textual "machinery."

In order to elucidate further why Molly's infidelity is linked both with a dissolution of sexual identity and with a mode of enunciation under the conditions of mechanical reproduction, I would like to refer to Walter Benjamin's two famous essays "The Work of Art in the Age of Mechanical Reproduction" and "On Some Motifs in Baudelaire." As one of the first theorists of modernity, Benjamin not only emphasizes the theme of technology in modern literature but also underscores the impact of mechanical reproduction on the structure of the work of art and on subjective experience. By exploring some of the familiar tropes of modernity, which Joyce also deploys and elaborates in *Ulysses*,[2] like the crowds of passersby, gambling, new means of public transportation, newspaper headlines, printing techniques, advertising, telephone communication, and photography, Benjamin calls our attention to the technologization of the public sphere and to the subsequent fragmentation of subjective experience. No longer a neutral tool of domination over nature, modern technology transforms both social relations in the public sphere and subjective experience in the private sphere.[3] In his "Civilization and Its Discontents," Freud speaks in a similar way about the effects of the technologization of the body: "man has, as it were, become a kind of prosthetic God" (38–39). Freud suggests that the supposedly neutral technological tools function in fact as prosthetic devices, reshaping and destabilizing the contours and the significance of the body.

As Benjamin argues, modernity represents first of all an epistemological shift from the familiar philosophical model of experience rooted in memory to the technological conditions of mechanical reproduction (most evident in film or photography).[4] The consequences of this shift can be seen in the destruction of the uniqueness of the text, the autonomy of the subject, and the self-evidence of the real. By supplanting memory (which preserves individual experience) or tradition (which preserves collective experience), mechanical reproduction shatters the authority of the original, and consequently, destroys the authenticity of the work of art—or what Benjamin calls its *aura*. In contrast to memory's faithful recreation of the past, mechanical reproduction obliterates the authenticity of experience not only because it substitutes mechanically produced copies for the original, but also because its technological apparatus penetrates into the very structure of reality, fragments it, and then reassembles it under its own technological laws. In this context, the anxiety linked to the modes of mechanical reproduction, in particular to photography, indicates a certain crisis of the real.

Similarly, the conditions of mechanical reproduction penetrate into the structure of subjective experience, causing the fragmentation of the subject. This change is evident in the erosion of memory by shock, which Benjamin describes as a breakdown of the protective shield of consciousness under the pressure of the mechanisms of the urban life. If memory allows the subject to recover both the individual and the collective past, shock merely discloses an interruption of the mental life which assigns "to an incident a precise point in time in consciousness at the cost of the integrity of its contents" (163). Such fragmentation of the subject makes him or her even more dependent on the resources of mechanical reproduction to preserve the past. Consequently, shock destroys the autonomy of the subject and connects it to a larger social mechanism: pedestrians in the crowd, workers at the assembly line, and even crowds in the amusement parks "act as if they had adapted themselves to the machines and could express themselves only automatically" (176). "They live their lives as automatons and resemble Bergson's fictitious characters who *have completely liquidated their memories*" (178; emphasis added). Thus, the figure of shock blurs the boundaries between private and public, inner and outer, natural and technological, subjective and collective. As a mode of enunciation, the figure of shock indicates that the decentered subject is included in the larger, external mechanisms of signification, whose operations it can no longer control or contain.

The emblems of this disintegration of the public sphere and subjective experience abound in the iconography of modernism— the modern metropolis, the shock effect, and finally and above all, the image of the urban crowd replacing a rational critical public. What is characteristic about the urban crowd, according to Benjamin, is the erasure of intersubjectivity. If the crowd appears uncanny, inanimate, and inhuman, it is because the mutual interdependence of its members is achieved by an efficient regulation of the social apparatus and not by the communicative consensus of the subjects themselves. What Benjamin emphasizes in his account of modernity is a different subject position in the modern public: no longer a rational agent acting in a community of debate, the modern subject is placed alongside the machine and subjected to its regulatory power. In a similar way, Jürgen Habermas argues that the effects of the disintegration of the public sphere can be seen in the decreased importance of the two major social roles—the worker and the citizen: the role of the worker is taken over by the consumer, that of the citizen by the client of the state bureaucracies.

Benjamin's account of the modern subject alongside the machine is still motivated by a nostalgia for the authentic structure of inner experience based on memory. Such nostalgia is conspicuously absent in postmodern views of textuality, which regard the text itself as a discursive machinery. Take, for instance, Derrida's discussion of "the gramophone effect" in *Ulysses*. Although Derrida's metaphor of the text as a gramophone develops Benjamin's insight that mechanical reproduction penetrates into the structure, production, and reception of the work of art, it provides a more positive view of these changes.[5] No longer preoccupied solely with the intentionality or memory of the subject, Derrida's interpretation of *Ulysses* focuses instead on the performative effect of the text itself. Such performance never assumes a singular form of enunciation—that is, textual production does not refer back to its point of origin in the subject—but is irreducibly linked to external signifying mechanisms, to other discourses, to other recorded voices. Derrida describes this polyphonic form of enunciation as a "gramophone effect." A certain telephonic *techné* not only destroys the intimacy of voice, but also mediates between the self and the other. In this context, Derrida juxtaposes a singular mode of enunciation of Molly's final "yes" with the figure of Bloom speaking at the telephone. Displacing the rhetoric of organicism, such "gramophonic enunciation" exposes the subject addressing itself to the adventures of repetition, difference, and technological networks of communication (256–309).

By interpreting "Penelope" in the context of Benjamin's or Derrida's approaches to modernity, we are confronted first of all with the question of the significance of the female body in the age of mechanical reproduction. As the example of *Ulysses* makes clear, the discourse of modernity defines femininity in contradictory ways: on the one hand, femininity promises an illusory escape from the technologization of the public space, but on the other hand, it dramatizes the effects of mechanical reproduction at the very core of inner subjective experience.[6] As Mary Ann Doane, for instance, argues, the anxiety about mechanical reproduction is often displaced onto the female body and reinterpreted within a more familiar framework of castration threat ("Technophilia" 163–75). Although this is not the place for a detailed discussion, I would like to suggest briefly why this displacement from mechanical reproduction to female sexuality is possible in the first place. The interrelation between mechanical reproduction and female sexuality once again returns us to the psychoanalytic construction of femininity as masquerade. What Benjamin's discussion of mechanical reproduction and the psychoanalytic account of female sexuality have in common, therefore, is the erasure of authenticity and the authority of the real. In psychoanalytic theory, in particular in its Lacanian version, the woman masquerading as the phallus both confirms the power of the paternal signifier and reduces it to the order of appearances (Lacan 290). As Judith Butler argues, we can interpret female masquerade either as a loss of authentic femininity or as a disclosure that all forms of being, including male and female subjects, belong to the order of appearances (43–57). The complicity between mechanical reproduction and female masquerade, therefore, threatens to invalidate the fundamental notions of authenticity, originality, and identity. Instead of securing the hierarchy of the original and the copy, mechanical reproduction and female masquerade postulate that origin is only a performative effect of discursive operations.

At the same time, however, femininity, defined in opposition to mechanical reproduction, seems to provide an imaginary means of escape from the increasing technologization of the public life. Because of the materiality of the body and its possible link to natural reproduction, and because of the historical exclusion of women from the public sphere, female sexuality seems to limit the negative effects of technology and to promise the epistemic security of origins. As Stephen claims in "Scylla and Charybdis," paternity may be "a legal fiction" but the maternal body remains the only true thing in life, immune to the impact of technology. We could say that femininity replenishes the aura, that is, authenticity and uniqueness, destroyed by mechanical reproduction.[7] By positing femininity between natural and mechanical reproduction, "Penelope" simultaneously secures the stability of origins and subverts any claims to authentic experience.

Interpreting "Penelope" in the double context of female sexuality and mechanical reproduction, rather than female sexuality alone, we are in a better position to understand why Molly is both faithful and unfaithful, and why the episode as a whole is both conventional and subversive. Whether interpreted as affirmative, subversive, or regressive,[8] the episode has often been taken as a retreat from the technological conditions of urban life. Because of the sexist ideology linking femininity with nature, and because of the historical exclusion of women from the public life, Joyce imagines a retreat from the threat of mechanical reproduction only through the mediation of female eroticism. As an alternative site of male self-elaboration, the female body could appease the modernist nostalgia for a more authentic way of being and for the structure of experience rooted in memory. It is not surprising, therefore, that critics like Karen Lawrence, who appreciate the adventures of textuality in *Ulysses*,[9] are clearly disappointed with this function of femininity: "The 'Penelope' chapter seems to me to be regressive, to present something denied by the rest of the book (the authority of consciousness). If Molly's monologue contains the truth or resolution, hasn't the book implicitly suggested that we cannot trust messages or any version of the truth?" (*Odyssey* 206). With such a reversal, the finale of *Ulysses* seems to stress the affirmation of life rather than technology, the origin rather than reproduction of meaning, memory rather than the heterogeneous operations of discourse.[10] Yet, as Lawrence argues, this simplification of textuality offers something in return—the episode provides a sense of emotional relief after the ordeal of reading more "depersonalized" episodes: "After the stark abstractions and cold 'precision' of 'Ithaca,' the breakdown of grammatical and syntactic categories into lush, emotional rhythms provides *a release of tension* in the narrative, soothing to the beleaguered reader" (205, emphasis added).

According to Lawrence's interpretation, Molly's monologue

dissipates the anxieties connected with "the cold impersonality" of the mechanically reproducible discourse and secures a retreat to a more personal, more "emotional" language, based on the authority of experience and memory. I would like to suggest that this reading of "Penelope," prepared in advance by the composition of previous episodes, is in fact an extension of male desires, expressed so straightforwardly by Bloom earlier in the text: "Be near her ample bedwarmed flesh. Yes, yes" (4.238–39). Not to mention that the calming effect of Molly's "large soft bubs, sloping within her nightdress like a shegoat's udder" (4.304–5) rescues Bloom from the bleak moments of despair and emptiness. Secluded in the privacy of home or situated in proximity to nature, Molly's "bedwarmed" body alone can replenish the humanity of the modern Odysseus—an advertising agent—after his exhausting peregrinations through the modern urban landscape. Not surprisingly, Molly's memory of Bloom's proposal mirrors faithfully his fantasy of her body: "I put my arms around him yes and drew him down to me so he could feel my breasts all perfume yes and his heart was going like mad and yes I said yes I will Yes" (18.1606–9). By reflecting Bloom's desires so closely, Molly's final words seem to restore his personality, as if to compensate for a dissolution of his identity in "Ithaca." In all of these examples, the performative effect of femininity in *Ulysses* bridges the gaps among memory, affectivity, and the economy of mechanical reproduction. In all of them Molly becomes a textual device that nostalgically recovers memory ("its just like yesterday to me"), emotional rhythms ("yes because I felt lovely") underlying language, and the authority of inner subjective experience.

However, the episode promises us the pleasure of recovery only when we accept this male fantasy of the female body—that is, only when we already "understood or felt what a woman is": "we are flowers all a womans body" (18.1576–79). As Annette Shandler Levitt suggests, the pleasure of the text depends on accepting the proffered flower as an emblem of diffuse female sexuality which partakes both in the abundance of the natural world and the richness of female language (507–17). Such pleasure, I argue, springs from the notion of Molly's language as preserving an immediate link to bodily experiences and female memory. Rich and alive, such language would be free not only from cultural mediation, but also from any sense of arbitrariness, discontinuity, or artificiality:

> I love flowers Id love to have the whole place swimming in roses God of heaven theres nothing like nature the wild mountains then the sea and the waves rushing then the beautiful country with the fields of oats and wheat and all kinds of things . . . that would do your heart to see rivers and lakes and flowers all sorts of shapes and smells and colors springing up even out of the ditches (18.1557–63)

This passage shows us why Molly's flowers are so exciting: by grounding female language and body in the rhetoric of organicism, the text suggests that it is possible to integrate language, memory, and the natural body into one flow and to protect it from the impact of technology. In this natural landscape the human body seems to be immune from technologization: it would be difficult to imagine in this passage a human heart as an "old rusty pump" (6.675). Unlike Molly's empty letters, the rhetoric of organicism consistently implies a singular form of enunciation, based on the unity of language, experience, and erotic memory. As I have suggested, this singular form of enunciation, in complicity with the natural truth of sexual difference, constitutes the paradigm of Molly's fidelity. And the only additional form of pleasure that such fidelity would allow for is female narcissism: a spectacle of a woman addressing herself, caressing herself, gathering herself in the rich flow of her memories and her pleasures.

In this context, it is not surprising that the critics' defense of Molly's fidelity is often intertwined with admiration for her memory, which, according to Hayman, preserves both "the texture of an experience" and the unity of time as "one continuous erotic present" (127). It is as if Molly's memory itself constitutes a sufficient "proof" of her fidelity. Molly's memory is seen as faithful to the structure of experience insofar as it is posited as unreflective and involuntary, preserving and itself preserved by the immediacy of sensations. This unity of memory and experience—the paradigm of epistemological fidelity in the episode—precludes any external ordering, either by technology, culture, discourse, or even intellect. Seemingly unmediated sense impressions, smells, sounds, and sights in the episode—"the smell of the sea excited me of course"—provide a sense of continuity among the past, present, and future without any "omissions." In the economy of unmediated memory nothing seems to be lost, especially not the authenticity and intensity of erotic experience.

And yet "omissions" trouble Molly, and not only gaps in her memories, but paradoxically, even omissions in the closed circle of her auto-affection.[11] And even though "emissions" of memory function for Molly as an extension of masturbation,[12] always bringing her into a close intimacy with herself, she is perturbed by a sense of emptiness she would like to "fill up." In spite of her vivid recollections, Molly is not satisfied with memories and sex alone and wishes for more clothes, gifts, love letters, and even for sensational publicity in newspapers, which would finally "fill up your whole day and life." This void that even memories cannot fill up is, not surprisingly, represented as a castrated female body. Despite all the joy that Molly can find in the admiration of her body, and despite all the pragmatic value of her natural charms, Molly complains: "I never in all my life felt anyone had one the size of that *to make you feel full up* . . . whats the idea making us like that *with a big hole in the middle of us*" (18.149–51; emphasis added). Like the empty letters that Molly posts to herself, the erotic memory closes the circle of narcissism only by covering over the omission, the void, represented by female sexuality.

Although Molly's "bedwarmed flesh" and her "large soft bubs" might dissipate anxieties concerning technology and mechanical reproduction (it is as if sexual pleasure were the last vestige of authenticity in the urban landscape),[13] the female body proves to be a disorderly figure in its own way. The early history of the reception of "Penelope" analyzed by Kathleen McCormick seems only to confirm the anxiety associated with female sexuality. It shows that Joyce's construction of femininity has been anything but soothing to his critics. In her discussion of the excesses, extremes, and exaggerations in the critical responses to Molly, Mc-Cormick demonstrates that the episode has tended precisely to beleaguer and shock, rather than to soothe Joyce's readers. By provoking a simultaneous reaction of "titillation and fear," Molly's explicit display of female sexuality parallels closely the effects of mechanical reproduction and shows that the Benjaminian notion of shock could be transferred to the sphere of sexuality. It was not until the impact of feminist and poststructuralist critics, like Cixous, Kristeva, Boheemen-Saaf, Henke, Scott, or McGee, that female sexuality in *Ulysses* could be linked to the subversive effects of writing, since both disturb rather than consolidate the mastery of male authorship.[14] However, by locating the unsettling or subversive effects of "Penelope" in female sexuality and language, these interpretations risk avoiding the social context of technology and mechanical reproduction altogether. We may wonder in fact whether the effects of mechanical reproduction, in particular its fragmentation of subjective identity, are not once again displaced onto the female body and reinterpreted through the tropes of subversive sexuality.

The strategy of displacement from technology to sexuality is particularly evident in the mythical approaches to "Penelope." I would argue that mythical interpretations of Molly have been so productive in Joyce criticism because they dissipate both the shock of technology *and* the fear of female sexuality. In a famous misreading of *Ulysses* ("*Ulysses*, Order, and Myth," 1923), T. S. Eliot postulates myth as an aesthetic ordering principle, capable of bracketing "the anarchy and chaos" of contemporary history (177). By placing the work of art outside the chaos of history, and by securing its "timeless organic unity," these mythical interpretations of *Ulysses* separate modern aesthetics from the impact of technology and mechanical reproduction. In fact, to use Benjamin's term again, the function of mythical interpretations is to restore the decayed aura of the work of art. However, as Kristeva reminds us in "Women's Time," such transformation of historical time into timeless myth, or the "organic spatial form," is invariably carried on along the traditional gender lines. The implicit connection between the nostalgia for myth and nature or, more precisely, for the myth of nature, presupposes the gendering of linear historical time as paternal (time as project, departure, arrival, as well as technological progress) and cyclical natural time as maternal (time of gestation and biological rhythms). Therefore, the escape from history to myth not only restores the aura of the work of art, but sooner or later evokes a "belief in the omnipotence of an archaic, full, total englobing mother with no frustration, no separation, with no break-producing symbolism (with no castration, in other words)" (205). Kristeva's critique of the myth of the archaic mother can be fruitfully extended to the "timeless, archaic Gea-Tellus" interpretation of Molly Bloom. The function of the Gea-Tellus myth is to replace mechanical reproduction with maternal reproduction. By translating the anxiety of technology as yet another symptom of castration anxiety, the myth of the archaic mother eventually provides the means for appeasing both.

Bearing in mind this function of myth, let us turn to a more witty discourse—to jokes. Jokes might reveal to us the historical and discursive function of femininity that the myth of the archaic mother tries to cover over.[15] In place of the Gea-Tellus myth, let us then consider the riddle of female sexuality in the light of the following joke from the "Aeolus" episode:

> What opera is like a railwayline?
> —Opera? Mr O'Madden Burke's sphinx face reriddled.
> Lenehan announced gladly:
> —*The Rose of Castile.* See the wheeze? Rows of cast steel. Gee! (7.588–91)

Restaging the Oedipal drama (the sphinx, the riddle) within the technological space, the joke parodies the rhetoric of organicism associated with sexual difference. Its performative effect collapses the boundaries between the binary oppositions on which the logic of the myth of the archaic mother depends: between art (opera) and technology (railway), nature (rose) and culture, body and the machine, and, as we shall see, between the circulation of female desire and the technological means of traffic. As a result of this performative force of the joke, which is explicitly about performance itself, an exotic discourse of music, romantic love, and organicism appears as an effect of the impersonal operation of technology.

Yet, this overt anxiety about the technologization of both art (opera) and the female body is expressed once again in terms of female infidelity. Taking a hint from Freud, we might suspect that this linguistic punning articulates both hostility and attraction to an unfaithful woman. After all, "The Rose of Castile" refers not only to the title of the opera but also to the name of its main heroine—a beautiful but false woman (Elvira, Rose of Castile)—who chooses "rank and empire" over her lover, in other words, social power over authentic erotic experience. In order to deflate the exotic charms of unstable female sexuality, the joke compares this "unnatural" and unfaithful circulation of female desire to a different sort of traffic—to technological means of transport. As the punning of the joke implies, the interplay between technology and treacherous female sexuality not only reduces authenticity to the order of appearances but also destabilizes the binary oppositions, such as nature and culture, art and technology, the male and the female.

If I pay more attention to jokes than to myths, it is because jokes both articulate *and* perform different aspects of infidelity in *Ulysses* associated with the motifs of femininity, language, and mechanical reproduction. It is not by accident that this particular joke is embedded in the chapter of *Ulysses* that explicitly experiments with new forms of mechanical reproduction and the circulation of discourse, like printing techniques and newspaper headlines. Advertising various forms of writing and rhetoric divorced from the authority of experience and memory,[16] "Aeolus" as a whole dramatizes both anonymity and the contingency of signifying effects. At the same time, however, it consistently returns to another, somewhat less joyful, mode of circulation and betrayal, that is, adultery: "—Onehandled adulterer, he said smiling grimly. That tickles me, I must say" (7.1072–73).

By condensing the effects of language, mechanical reproduction, and female sexuality, the "Rose of Castile" joke articulates in fact some of the main concerns of "Penelope": it brings to our attention the fact that Molly's explicit preoccupation with flowers, nature, and sexuality cannot be separated from the pervasive technologization of the body and the public sphere. It is as if the coda of *Ulysses* replays the joke in reverse and converts the textual web of "rows of cast steel" into a seductive and exotic "Rose of Castile," or—as Molly is fond of calling herself—"a flower of the mountain." A strange flower of rhetoric unfolding at the intersection of sexuality and technology, Molly seems to offer us "excitement like a rose." But "Penelope" returns to the rhetoric of organicism and to the immediacy of experience preserved by memory only to disrupt it by quite a different tonality—by the train whistle, which provides instrumental music for Molly's nocturnal concert. Although we do not know its point of departure or destination, we can take this distant train as a synecdoche for the pervasive effects of mechanical reproduction displayed not only in the previous episodes of *Ulysses* but in "Penelope" itself. Ranging from the circulation of photos (all kinds of photos, including "smutty" ones), ads, newspapers, and mass-produced clothes to the circulation of new sex objects—girls on bicycles—the examples of mechanical reproduction in Molly's monologue are in fact as numerous as the figures of flowers. The repetition of the mechanical noise in Molly's monologue has a double function: on the one hand, it points to a technologization of the female body and subjective experience, but, on the other hand, it demystifies the rhetoric of organicism and shows that such rhetoric—like the flowers on the wallpaper Molly so fondly remembers—is itself an effect of mechanical reproduction.

Even though "Penelope" capitalizes so much on the function of female erotic memory, the episode equally forcefully suggests its extension and replacement through photography, which for Benjamin constitutes the paradigm of mechanical reproduction par excellence. As a mechanical extension of memory, photography "fills up" the "omissions" in human recollections. However, if memory makes the original experience alive again, photography seems to freeze the moment and to replace the original through its representation. As Benjamin shows in "The Work of Art in the Age of Mechanical Reproduction," photography precisely undermines our notions of the original experience, immediacy, and authenticity. Similarly, whenever photography replaces erotic memory in "Penelope," it "denaturalizes" desire itself, connecting it with pornography, prostitution, and commodity. We remember, for instance, Bloom's suggestion that Molly should pose for nude pictures in the time of economic hardship, a suggestion which triggers Molly's imitations of other photographic representations of women. Even though Molly burns the semipornographic Photo Bits, her memory is sustained and mediated by photographic images and stock representations of femininity in popular culture: "would I be like that bath of the nymph with my hair down yes only shes younger or Im a little like that dirty bitch in that Spanish photo" (18.562–64). In this context it is significant that Milly, coming to terms with her adolescent sexuality, no longer relies on the maternal resources of erotic memory but studies photography.

If photography mediates the flow of Molly's memories, the noise of the train interferes with the seductive power of her voice. The train's whistle merges most often with the sentimental songs from Molly's repertoire, as if to disrupt the natural unity of voice and memory, of hearing and seeing: "that was Gardner yes I can see his face clean shaven Frseeeeeeeeeeeeeeeeeeeeeefrong that train again weeping tone once in the dear deaead days beyondre call close my eyes breath my lips forward kiss sad look eyes open piano ere oer the world the mists began I hate that istsbeg comes loves sweet soooooooooooong Ill let that out full when I get in front of the footlights again" (18.873–78). The distant noise of the engine not only provides a strange accompaniment to the popular sentimental songs from Molly's repertoire, but is explicitly compared to them: at one point, the noise of the engine appears "like the end of Loves old sweeetsonnnng." As its last stanza suggests ("Footsteps may falter, weary grow the way,/Still we can hear it, at the close of the day;/So till the end, when life's dim shadows fall,/Love will be found the sweetest song of all"),[17] "the sweetest song of all" expresses simultaneously a nostalgia for the past and the pathos of memory and voice, which can withstand the passage of time. Such unity of voice, memory, and love restores the shadows to life, the past to the presence of consciousness. With a touch of perversity, however, Joyce interrupts this seductive unity of voice, song, and memory with the noise of the machine. The intrusion of a purely mechanical noise into the melody of the song reminds me of Joyce's description of his authorship in a letter to Miss Weaver: "I am really one of the greatest engineers, if not the greatest, in the world besides being a musicmaker, philosophist and heaps of other things. All the engines I know are wrong. Simplicity. I am making an engine with only one wheel" (*Letters* I; 251).[18] Although this description refers to the composition of *Finnegans Wake*, even in the most organic chapter of *Ulysses*, Joyce the musicmaker joins hands with the great engineer over the "bedwarmed" female body.

But what would this conjunction of music and engineering mean in "Penelope"? In one sense Molly's entire monologue is like "loves sweet song"—an expression of faith that the unity of memory, art, and voice can revive "dear deaead days beyondre call," withstand the passage of time, and bring the past erotic experience back to the subject. As the words of the song suggest, forgetting and omissions are deadly. Yet, maybe because Molly experiences some trouble performing to the full capacity of her voice and her memory, because "letting that out full" is increasingly more difficult for her, this vocal deficiency reveals another, and equally compelling, aspect of this episode: the mediation of textual technique even within the most intimate recesses of body and voice. By supplanting the function of memory and voice, textual machinery interrupts the immediacy of experience and reinserts a sense of distance, artificiality, and exteriority. And here again, what is revealing is the contrast between Molly the singer, who desires to recover the fullness of voice, with Molly the letter writer, who either dispatches the empty letters or else reproduces clichés with spelling mistakes: "your sad bereavement symphathy I always make that mistake and newphew with 2 double yous" (18.729–31). Unlike recollections which always come from oneself to oneself, the mechanical noise—just as the mute graphics of the text—implies a movement from an unknown origin to an obscure destination. As a synecdoche for mechanical reproduction (but a synecdoche that fails to command the entirety of its effects), the train signals a possibility of nonrecuperation: the circle of memory is broken by the onward movement of the engine, the "weeping tone" of the lyrical song by the purely mechanical whistle, the performance of the singer by the performance of the machine.

In contrast to the end of the episode, Molly's figuration of desire, her "heat" of passion, and even her admiration for male and female bodies quite consistently fuse the rhetoric of organicism and technology. At the great finale of Molly's performance, voice, memory, and the rhetoric of organicism are intertwined not only to secure the singular form of enunciation but also to restore the "natural" gender difference and, it must be added, their "natural" hierarchy as well. The closure of the episode reveals a profound complicity between the affirmation of voice and the affirmation of the "natural" sexual difference. Ironically, it is the technologization of the body that reveals the fluidity of sexual difference and disarticulates its natural order:

> the savage brute Thursday Friday one Saturday two Sunday three O Lord I cant wait till Monday.
>   frseeeeeeeefronnnng train somewhere whistling *the strength those engines have in them like big giants* and the water rolling all over and out of them all sides like the end of Loves old sweeeetsonnnng the poor men that have to be out all the night from their wives and families in those roasting engines (18.594–600; emphasis added)

Molly's recollection and impatient anticipation of intercourse with Boylan turns into the paradoxical image of men trapped inside "those roasting" machines and separated from their wives. Molly not only reminds us of the role technology has played in the male conquering of nature but also stresses the effects of the machine on "the poor men." Given this image of the male romance with technology turned sour, we would expect at this point some vision of the organic body as a source of resistance to male domination. However, this is not the case—the passage neither deplores technological power as domination nor mystifies nature as a source of resistance. On the contrary, it is by acknowledging technologization of the body and desire that Molly feels empowered to rewrite the story of sexual difference. By implicitly rejecting the notions that the truth of female sexuality resides in nature or in the privacy of experience, Molly produces an androgynous fantasy, in which machine occupies both masculine and feminine positions. Clearly supplanting natural reproduction, Molly's phantasmatic machine becomes on the one hand a sort of technological womb, trapping men in its interior. I would like to suggest that this image of entrapment parodies the male myth of Gea-Tellus receiving "the childman weary" into her womb. But on the other hand, the machine also assumes the attributes of phallic power ("the strength those engines have") similar to the potency of "the savage brute." It even reproduces the intensity of male and female desire—"all fire" that Molly feels inside her is articulated in this passage as an unbearable heat inside the engine. Furthermore, Molly's description of the engine deploys the tropes reserved for the Gibraltar rock ("like big giants") and for the oceanic torrents ("the water rolling all over"), which so frequently function as a metaphor for the "flow" of her erotic memories. Needless to say, Molly's fantasy is conspicuous for its refusal (or "failure") to reproduce the binary gender roles faithfully. Usurping the rhetoric of organicism, Molly's androgynous machine disarticulates the binary gender opposition and demonstrates that the nature of sexual difference is in fact constructed by discursive operations.

Because of these consistent intersections with mechanical reproduction, feminine sexuality in "Penelope" participates in two contradictory economies of signification. On the one hand, the female body facilitates a retreat from the technologized public space into a singular form of enunciation and the privacy of subjective experience. As I have been arguing, this authority of subjectivity in the production of meaning is emphasized by the rhetoric of organicism, which restores not only the unity of voice, experience, and memory, but also the "natural" gender hierarchy.

These qualities of Molly's monologue qualify it as a *faithful* site of male self-elaboration. On the other hand, the technologization of the female body reveals it as a site of diverse cultural inscriptions, which cannot be unified into a singular form of enunciation. Moreover, the female body no longer reproduces those inscriptions faithfully. Whereas the faithfulness of "Penelope" is orchestrated as a recuperative movement of erotic memory, her infidelity indicates a breakdown of the singular form of enunciation and, even more important, a re-vision of gender differences.

My reading of "Penelope" has concentrated on the points of interruptions of the female voice, indeed, on the moments when technology seems to intrude upon the work of female memory. These moments of discord (rather than Molly's inner contradictions) disclose how the pressure of technology redefines the function of femininity and the epistemological and social stakes attached to it. The overlapping discourses of sexuality, memory, and mechanical reproduction in the coda of *Ulysses* disclose two performative effects of femininity. On the one hand, Joyce's display of female sexuality, no matter how audacious or subversive for his times, betrays a certain nostalgia for a more traditional paradigm of experience based on memory and for a more "natural" sense of gender difference. It is as if Joyce could imagine the female sexual body as the last remnant of authenticity in the increasingly technologized social space. On the other hand, however, the trope of female infidelity not only divulges a complicity between female masquerade and mechanical reproduction but also indicates that this unity of language, memory, and natural sexual identity has been irreparably broken. Consequently, in the last act of the textual performance, Molly's body functions as an alternative stage where paradigmatic shifts of modernity could be once again reenacted but their "shocking" effects immediately dissipated.[19]

Notes

1. No doubt, this interpretation has been invited by Joyce's frequently quoted description of the episode: "It begins and ends with the female

word *Yes*. It turns like the huge earthball slowly surely and evenly round and round spinning. Its four cardinal points being the female breasts, arse, womb and ... cunt expressed by the words *because, bottom* (in all senses, bottom, button, bottom of the glass, bottom of the sea, bottom of his heart) *woman, yes*. Though probably more obscene than any preceding episode it seems to me to be perfectly sane full amoral fertilisable untrustworthy engaging shrewd limited prudent indifferent *Weib*" (*Letters* I, 170). For a discussion of this description from a feminist point of view, see for instance, Bonnie Kime Scott (119).

2. This deliberate inclusion of the elements of urban experience in *Ulysses* has been very well documented in Joyce criticism, which often pays tribute to Joyce's ambition to render the cultural phenomenon of a modern metropolis: "If I can get to the heart of Dublin I can get to the heart of all the cities in the world" (*JJ* 2, 505). For a discussion of the city in *Ulysses* see among others, Fredric Jameson (173–88), Hugh Kenner (4–6), and Christopher Butler (269–70). For a general discussion of modernity and technology, see Astradur Eysteinsson (18–22).

3. For a discussion of the impact of technology on the social relations in modernity, see for instance, Herbert Marcuse (138–63) and Jürgen Habermas.

4. Walter Benjamin articulates this paradigm of modernity primarily in his two essays "On Some Motifs in Baudelaire" (155–200) and "The Work of Art in the Age of Mechanical Reproduction" (217–51.

5. For another discussion of the text as machinery, see Gilles Deleuze and Félix Guattari (81–88).

6. For postmodern approaches to this question see, for instance, Donna Haraway, "A Manifesto for Cyborgs: Science, Technology, and Social Feminism in the 1980," and a series of responses to this paper in Elizabeth Weed's *Coming to Terms*. See also Theresa de Lauretis's *Technologies of Gender*.

7. For a discussion of femininity in the context of Benjamin's concept of aura, see for instance, Mary Ann Doane's *The Desire to Desire* (29–33).

8. According to Jameson, for instance, "Penelope" collapses into "vitalist ideology" (188).

9. In a similar manner, Derek Attridge castigates critics, especially feminist critics, for overemphasizing the stylistic complexity of the episode and turning it into an example of subversive *écriture féminine* (543–64).

10. See also in this context Jean-Michel Rabaté, who sees "Penelope" as "an unexpected return to oral discourse" (*James Joyce* 105). A more

positive evaluation of textuality in "Penelope" as the staging of otherness can be found in Patrick McGee (170–72).

11. Derrida explains the term *auto-affection* as the basic trope of the mastery of the subject: "The lure of the I, of consciousness as hearing-oneself-speak would consist in ... transforming hetero-affection into auto-affection" (*Margins of Philosophy* 297).

12. For a critique of the representation of Molly as a conventional narcissistic woman, see Elaine Unkeless (150–68).

13. As Mary Ann Doane eloquently points out in her response to Foucault, "the unified and coherent bourgeois subject, threatened increasingly by a fragmentation imposed from without, finds its heaven in a sexualized, orgasmic body" ("Commentary" 70–71).

14. See for instance, Hélène Cixous (15–30), Julia Kristeva (*Powers of Horror* 22–23), Christine Van Boheemen-Saaf (29–36), Suzette A. Henke (126–63), Bonnie Kime Scott (107–27), Patrick McGee (37–68, 150–81), and Ewa Ziarek (51–60). For a good discussion of feminist readings of Joyce, see Karen Lawrence ("Joyce and Feminism" 241).

15. As Freud suggests, the pleasure of the joke depends on evading the restraints of logic and cultural censorship. The first source of pleasure is purely linguistic—we delight in throwing off the constraints of rational discourse and enjoy the linguistic play characteristic of the primary process. The second source of pleasure comes from a release of the unconscious hostile or sexual thought, that is, a release from inhibitions and moral censorship (117–39).

16. For an excellent discussion of this episode, see Karen Lawrence (*The Odyssey of Style* 63–67).

17. The text of the song is reproduced in Don Gifford and Robert J. Seidman (56–57).

18. For a discussion of Joyce's "triple profession" and an interpretation of the text as a machine in the context of *Finnegans Wake*, see Jean-Michel Rabaté ("Lapsus ex machina" 80).

19. Some ideas that went into the preparation of this essay were initially suggested by Nancy Armstrong's lectures "The Work of Art in the Age of Sexual Reproduction" and "High Culture, Savage Art, and the Uses of Pornography" delivered at the University of Notre Dame on April 9 and 11, 1981, and the informal exchange after the lectures. Also, I would like to express my gratitude to my colleagues Theresa Krier and Richard Pearce, whose attentive reading and generous comments strengthened my argument.

Works Cited

Attridge, Derek. "Molly's Flow: The Writing of 'Penelope' and the Question of Women's Language." *Modern Fiction Studies* 35 (1989): 543–65.

Benjamin, Walter. *Illuminations.* Ed. Hannah Arendt. Trans. Harry Zohn. New York: Schocken, 1969.

Boheemen-Saaf, Christine Van. "Deconstruction after Joyce." In *New Alliances in Joyce Studies.* Ed. Bonnie Kime Scott. Newark: University of Delaware Press, 1988. 29–36.

Butler, Christopher. "Joyce, Modernism, Post-modernism." In *The Cambridge Companion to James Joyce.* Ed. Derek Attridge. New York: Cambridge University Press, 1990. 259–88.

Butler, Judith. *Gender Trouble: Feminism and the Subversion of Identity.* New York: Routledge, 1990.

Cixous, Hélène. "Joyce: The (R)use of Writing." In *Post-structuralist Joyce: Essays from the French.* Ed. Derek Attridge and Daniel Ferrer. Cambridge: Cambridge University Press, 1984. 15–30.

Deleuze, Gilles, and Félix Guattari. *Kafka: Toward a Minor Literature.* Trans. Dana Polan. Minneapolis: University of Minnesota Press, 1986.

Derrida, Jacques. *Margins of Philosophy.* Trans. Alan Bass. Chicago, Ill.: University of Chicago Press, 1982.

———. "Ulysses Gramophone: Hear Say Yes in Joyce." In *Acts of Literature.* Ed. Derek Attridge. New York: Routledge, 1992. 253–309.

Doane, Mary Ann. "Commentary: Post-Utopian Difference." In Weed, *Coming to Terms,* 70–78.

———. *The Desire to Desire: The Woman's Film in the 1940s.* Bloomington: Indiana University Press, 1987.

———. "Technophilia: Technology, Representation, and the Feminine." In *Body/Politics: Women and the Discourses of Science.* Ed. Mary Jacobus, Evelyn Fox Keller, and Sally Shuttleworth. New York: Routledge, 1990. 163–75.

Eliot, T. S. *Selected Prose of T. S. Eliot.* Ed. Frank Kermode. New York: Harcourt Brace Jovanovich, 1975.

Eysteinsson, Astradur. *The Concept of Modernism.* Ithaca, N.Y.: Cornell University Press, 1990.

Freud, Sigmund. *Civilization and Its Discontents.* Trans. James Strachey. New York: Norton, 1961.

———. *Jokes and Their Relation to the Unconscious.* Trans. James Strachey. London: Routledge and Kegan Paul, 1966.

Gifford, Don, and Robert J. Seidman. *Notes for Joyce: An Annotation of James Joyce's "Ulysses."* New York: Dutton, 1974.

Habermas, Jürgen. *The Structural Transformation of the Public Sphere: An Inquiry into a Category of Bourgeois Society.* Trans. Thomas Burger. Cambridge, Mass.: MIT Press, 1989.

Hayman, David. "The Empirical Molly." In *Approaches to "Ulysses": Ten Essays.* Ed. Thomas F. Staley and Bernard Benstock. Pittsburgh, Pa.: University of Pittsburgh Press, 1970. 103–35.

Henke, Suzette A. *James Joyce and the Politics of Desire.* New York: Routledge, 1990.

Jameson, Fredric. "*Ulysses* in History." In *James Joyce.* Ed. Harold Bloom. New York: Chelsea, 1986. 173–88.

Kenner, Hugh. "Notes toward an Anatomy of 'Modernism.' " In *A Starchamber Quiry: A James Joyce Centennial Volume, 1882–1982.* Ed. E. L. Epstein. London: Methuen, 1982. 3–42.

Kristeva, Julia. *Powers of Horror: An Essay on Abjection.* Trans. Leon S. Roudiez. New York: Columbia University Press, 1982.

———. "Women's Time." Trans. Alice Jardine and Harry Blake. In *The Kristeva Reader.* Ed. Toril Moi. New York: Columbia University Press, 1986. 188–213.

Lacan, Jacques. *Écrits: A Selection.* Trans. Alan Sheridan. New York: Norton, 1977.

Lauretis, Theresa de. *Technologies of Gender: Essays on Theory, Film and Fiction.* Bloomington: Indiana University Press, 1987.

Lawrence, Karen. "Joyce and Feminism." In *The Cambridge Companion to James Joyce.* Ed. Derek Attridge. Cambridge: Cambridge University Press, 1990. 237–58.

———. *The Odyssey of Style in "Ulysses."* Princeton, N.J.: Princeton University Press, 1981.

Levitt, Annette Shandler. "The Pattern Out of the Wallpaper: Luce Irigaray and Molly Bloom." *Modern Fiction Studies* 35 (1989): 507–16.

Marcuse, Herbert. "Some Social Implications of Modern Technology." In *The Essential Frankfurt Reader.* Ed. Andrew Arato and Eike Gerhardt. New York: Urizen, 1978. 138–62.

McCormick, Kathleen. "Reproducing Molly Bloom: A Revisionist History of the Reception of 'Penelope,' 1922–1970." In *Molly Blooms: A Polylogue on "Penelope" and Cultural Studies.* Ed. Richard Pearce. Madison: University of Wisconsin Press, 1994. 17–39.

McGee, Patrick. *Paperspace: Style as Ideology in Joyce's "Ulysses."* Lincoln: University of Nebraska Press, 1989.

Rabaté, Jean-Michel. *James Joyce: Authorized Reader.* Trans. Jean-Michel Rabaté. Baltimore, Md.: Johns Hopkins University Press, 1991.

————. "Lapsus ex machina." In *Post-structuralist Joyce: Essays from the French.* Ed. Derek Attridge and Daniel Ferrer. Cambridge: Cambridge University Press, 1990. 79–102.

Scott, Bonnie Kime. *James Joyce.* Atlantic Highlands, N.J.: Humanities Press International, 1987.

Unkeless, Elaine. "The Conventional Molly Bloom." In *Women in Joyce.* Ed. Suzette Henke and Elaine Unkeless. Urbana: University of Illinois Press, 1982. 150–68.

Weed, Elizabeth, ed. *Coming to Terms: Feminism, Theory, Politics.* New York: Routledge, 1989.

Ziarek, Ewa. " 'Circe': Joyce's *Argumentum ad Feminam.*" *James Joyce Quarterly* 30 (1992): 51–68.

Reading *Ulysses*

Agency, Ideology, and the Novel

MARK A. WOLLAEGER

❖ ❖ ❖

JUST BEFORE HE IS DECKED (or "crowned") by a bellig-
erent British soldier in "Circe," Stephen Dedalus unwisely characterizes his desired relation to Ireland's reigning institutional authorities with a Blakean aphorism: "in here it is," he says, tapping
his brow, "I must kill the priest and the king" (*U* 15.4436–37).
The self-confessed "servant of two masters," Stephen wishes to
undo the internalization of authority that renders him, as he
dourly observes in "Telemachus," the political subject of "the
imperial British state" and the religious subject of "the holy Roman catholic and apostolic church" (*U* 1.643–44). Stephen's early
morning complaint is framed, courtesy of Haines, by a stark di-
chotomy. "I should think you are able to free yourself," says the
genially obtuse Englishman. "You are your own master." Retreating before Stephen's cynicism, however, Haines quickly reconsid-
ers: "An Irishman must think like that, I dare say. . . . It seems
history is to blame" (*U* 1.636–37, 647–49). Pivoting on the relation
between individual and nation, Haines's binary opposition between absolute autonomy and utter subjection elides the very

question posed in Stephen's attempt to negate priest and king in "Circe": Is the subject, confronted with ideological pressure, necessarily subjected?

The question asked of Stephen may also be asked of the reader, and in some ways the issue of what a novel "does" to its reader is an old one: Dr. Johnson worried over it in 1750, arguing that because novels are addressed to impressionable minds—"the young, the ignorant, the idle, to whom they serve as lectures of conduct and introductions into life"—they should set forth positive moral examples for the easily corrupted reader.[1] What remains relatively constant from Dr. Johnson to contemporary ideology critique is the belief that readers are easy prey for the snares of fiction, but where Dr. Johnson feared seduction, many contemporary analyses find domination. By assuming that the individual subject is easily subjected, deterministic accounts of novelistic discourse find individuals entering into a particular form of subjectivity not so much against their will as apart from any sense of violation, desire, or resistance. With the ideology proffered by novels understood as a powerful determinant of subjective states, every reader becomes Dr. Johnson's impressionable idler. History, it seems, is to blame.

If the subjected novel reader has been most prevalent in Victorian studies, where the action of what is taken to be the typical Victorian plot—the socialization of the protagonist—is said to be replicated in the normalization of the reader,[2] the modern novel has also been theorized as an agent of social discipline, even though the fragmentation of subjectivity in modernists such as Joyce or Woolf does not seem conducive to the contagious internalization of discipline often attributed to earlier fiction. In what is now a standard move in New Historicist readings, one critic has recently found in the discursive complexity of canonical high modernism "the machinery of an administered society that, in spite of its recurring protest, modernism could not help but serve."[3] Challenging the dystopian argument, theories of the novel as a form of subversion, typically relying on Bakhtinian heteroglossia or Kristevan semiotic disruptions of the Symbolic, invest novelistic discourse with the capacity to subvert the very operations of power described as hegemonic in dystopic readings. When applied to the modern novel, the subversion hypothesis can also invoke long-standing theories of modernism—from Oscar Wilde to Adorno—that ascribe liberating social effects to revolutions in formal conventions.

These polarized and polarizing arguments seem to me equally in danger of oversimplifying the relations between a particular literary text and its readership. As Dominick LaCapra has argued, relations between dominant powers and specific cultural practices are, at a given historical moment, both various and subject to historical variation,[4] and more work is necessary to theorize how, with a given text, one can reasonably gauge its relative complicity or resistance. Also needed, if "history" is to be invoked with such insistence and regularity, is more work that is genuinely historical. In the following pages I hope to contribute to this project by using some of the particulars of the British administration of Ireland to turn a dystopian reading of *Ulysses* inside out. The "Circe" episode, which registers various "oscillation[s] between events of imperial and of local interest" (*U* 17.428–29), is especially interesting in this context. Insinuating itself into the ongoing construction of the reader's subjectivity more extravagantly than the earlier episodes on which its effects depend, "Circe" reopens the possibility of resistance closed off by deterministic models of reading, and it does so without crediting the fiction of an autonomous will to subvert.

Subjects and Subjection: Disciplinary Power in Ireland

Given that Stephen's aphoristic attack on the English sovereign conjures, on the next page, Edward VII himself, dressed as a Freemason, wearing "an image of the Sacred Heart," and carrying "a bucket on which is printed *Défense d'uriner*" (*U* 15.4457), it is tempting to say that if king and priest cannot be killed, they can at least, in the manner of pantomime, be redressed. Carnivalized as

the goofy custodian of Leopold Bloom's emergency bladder movement, Edward steps into "Circe" only to have his sovereignty
derided as the war-mongering hypocrisy of an impostor. Yet the
idea of carnival has already been complicated in "Circe" by an
earlier appearance of Bloom, whose crowning is more dignified
than Stephen's: Leopold the First, ruler of the New Bloomusalem,
promises "General amnesty, weekly carnival with masked license,
bonuses for all" (*U* 15.1690). Administered by a king, Bloom's
carnival may simply operate as the "safety value" that elicits only
to recontain the desire for subversion. Does Joyce's Circean carnival, though administered to a king, have an equally regulatory
effect? Is every apparently subversive act in—and of—the novel
actually recontained within a more inclusive act of indoctrina-
tion?

The specifically Irish scene of social discipline provides entry
into the politics of *Ulysses*. Joyce's Dublin, it happens, was the
most heavily policed city in the United Kingdom, and both the
Dublin Metropolitan Police (DMP) and the Royal Irish Constabulary (RIC), which patrolled the rest of Ireland, were administered from the central site of Dublin Castle.[5] Lord Morely called
Dublin Castle "the best machine that has ever been invented for
governing a country against its will," and in 1937 Dorothy Macardle looked back on "the Dublin Castle system of espionage"
as "the most dangerous of all the instruments of England's policy
in Ireland":

> The enemy's resources in this respect were boundless. The
> R.I.C., with their intimate knowledge of the inhabitants, re-
> ported to the Castle from the most remote villages in the
> country; in Dublin a body of plainclothes detectives, the G
> Division of the Metropolitan Police, watched all places sup-
> posed to be visited by prominent Republicans, shadowed the
> leaders, identified political prisoners, and guided the military
> in searches, raids, and arrests. Into the Republican organisation
> were sent spies, paid informers, and *agents provocateurs*.[6]

It is easy to see Macardle's description of Dublin Castle, especially
the DMP's notorious G Division, as analogous to Foucault's ac-

count of Bentham's panopticon; each site of surveillance becomes a synecdoche for the way social and political institutions promote the internalization and dissemination of discipline.[7]

The influence of the Castle as the United Kingdom's most extensive antisubversion mechanism registers throughout Joyce's texts. Stephen must have the Castle in mind in *Portrait* when he bitterly tells Davin that he can easily find "the indispensable informer" for "the next rebellion" in Trinity College (*P* 169). Bloom, having watched a "squad of constables ... split up into groups" and scatter "towards their beats" (*U* 8.406–10), notes that Jack Power's father was a "G man," and the aptly named Power, the Good Samaritan of "Grace" who tries to recruit the Protestant Kernan to Catholicism, is employed in Dublin Castle's RIC office. Bloom's train of thought also returns to an earlier suspicion that Corny Kelleher is a police "tout," or informer: "Never know who you're talking to. Corny Kelleher he has the Harvey Duff in his eye. Like that Peter or Denis or James Carey that blew the gaff on the invincibles. Member of the corporation too. Egging raw youths on to get in the know all the time drawing secret service pay from the castle" (*U* 8.441–44). Bloom's suggestion that James Carey was from the start employed by the Castle is erroneous, but the tenor of his suspicion is, historically, fair enough. In "Ivy Day" Mr. Henchy may be guilty of little more than exaggeration when he claims to know for a fact that half the radical nationalists in Dublin are in "the pay of the Castle" (*D* 96). Bloom's suspicions that Kelleher is a police informer are confirmed later in "Wandering Rocks" by Kelleher's conversation with a passing constable, and Kelleher's cozy relations with the authorities in "Circe" will figure prominently in the aftermath of Stephen's confrontation with Privates Carr and Compton.

Advancing the argument for containment, one might take such details as well as the more general sense of watching and being watched in *Ulysses* as indicative of the way the British administration of Ireland circumscribes Joyce's characters: like the trams paralyzed at the foot of Nelson's pillar in "Aeolus" or like Gabriel Conroy enacting a horse's orbit around the statue of William III, Joyce's characters seem wholly subordinated to the circulation of imperial power. External evidence can also be assimilated into this logic: "To see Joyce at work on the Wandering Rocks," in Frank Budgen's words, "was to see an engineer at work with compass and slide-rule, a surveyor with theodolite and measuring chain. . . . [Joyce wrote the episode] with a map of Dublin before him on which were traced in red ink the paths of the Earl of Dudley and Father Conmee. He calculated to a minute the time necessary for his characters to cover a given distance of the city."[8] Consonant with this image of Joyce is Richard Ellmann's report that the sculptor August Sutler became "rather irritated to see how Joyce seemed to stage-manage conversations as if to use his friends as subjects for experiments."[9] If, as Budgen claims, "Dublin itself," not Stephen or Bloom, becomes "the principal personage" in "Wandering Rocks," that is because Joyce himself has become the arch-bureaucrat supervising the peregrinations of characters whose subjectivities—however minutely detailed by stream-of-consciousness techniques—are transformed into effects of structure within Dublin's urban labyrinth. In this reading *Ulysses* extends technologies of surveillance to an unprecedented extent by recording in the public space of the page what had previously been shielded in the domain of the private. The novelist who represents police touts himself becomes an informer: we read Bloom as Bloom, in the outhouse, reads *Titbits*. Many of Joyce's critics, turning to computer-generated word counts, maps and photographs of 1904 Dublin, and diagrams of Odysseus's supposed wanderings, may be equally disabled within a wholly administered society by becoming, in effect, census takers, surveyors, and assessors. Even bits of critical vocabulary specific to Joyce may register the paranoid implications of a fictional world behind which the author-god is not paring his fingernails but checking his stopwatch: David Hayman's concept of the Arranger, after all, is cited more frequently than Gérard Genette's more clinical "extradiegetic narrator."[10]

By this point several problems with this approach require attention. One wants to know, for starters, how the policing effect of a novel changes when the police form part of a colonial occupation whose individual members are recruited almost exclusively from the ranks of the occupied. When ordered, for instance, to take what amounted to military action against their fellow citizens, some members of the RIC refused to do so.[11] In such a case, the British subject within an individual policeman is at war with the Irish one. To elide such contradictions within the subject and the historical circumstances that produce them is to posit an abstract, unified subject, precisely the model of subjectivity that offers up readers as easy dupes. Although Foucault claims in "The Subject and Power" that power cannot be properly theorized apart from resistance, he never establishes how resistance could even exist within the "new economy of power relations" the essay envisions.[12] As Andreas Huyssen writes of Adorno and Horkheimer's culture industry, "emptied subject and totality immobilize each other. The world appears frozen into nightmare."[13]

In *Discerning the Subject* Paul Smith has argued that a more genuinely dialectical response to the nightmare of history can be derived from Louis Althusser's concept of interpellation, the process whereby an individual becomes a subject by recognizing and responding to the "call" of ideology.[14] Although the complaint subject theorized in Althusser's own exposition underlies many coercive models of cultural reading, the idea of interpellation remains important as a step toward theorizing how ideological messages do or do not become anchored in the individual. For in Althusser's seminal essay "Ideology and Ideological State Apparatuses," a narrative of subjectivity as process is acknowledged only to be suppressed, and from that suppressed narrativity the possibility of resistance can be recovered.

Althusser takes recourse to what he calls, somewhat apologetically, a "theoretical theatre" for the staging of face-to-face examples of interpellation.[15] A friend knocking at the door responds to the question, "Who's there?" with the response "It's me," and the opening of the door reveals that, sure enough, that's who it is. Or one friend calls to another on the street, and, having turned toward each other, they stop to shake hands and say hello. Althusser's "rituals of ideological recognition" hinge on the moments when individuals recognize themselves as "hailed" and turn to face whoever has done the "hailing." Recognition scenes of this kind exemplify the interpellation of bourgeois subjects, the process whereby people "discover" themselves to be "concrete, individual, distinguishable and (naturally) irreplaceable subjects." But how much can face-to-face examples contribute to an understanding of texts and readers? And if the response to or "turn" toward the hailer constitutes the moment of ideological "conversion," what if the individual responds inappropriately or turns only to turn away? His examples having opened up the possibility of nonresponse or misrecognition, Althusser tries to dispense with such questions by dismissing the examples themselves on the grounds that they project as narrative what is essentially "without succession"; individuals are always already interpellated as subjects by virtue of having responding to the call of ideology.

One need not posit a pure origin prior to the beginning of ideology—a kind of originary unlisted number, "Aleph, alpha: nought, nought, one" (*U* 3.39–40)—to see that the transformation of Althusser's call-and-response narrative into an inescapable mode of being elides the process whereby a concrete individual subject does or does not respond to a particular ideological hailing. Althusser prefers to focus on "ideology-in-general"—the formation of bourgeois subjectivity—rather than on specific ideological appeals operated by particular social institutions.

Yet failure to acknowledge the conceptual space between ideology in general and specific ideological appeals can lead to a conflation of Althusser's otherwise distinct categories of repressive state apparatuses, which operate through the threat of violence, and ideological state apparatuses, which depend on persuasion.[16] Althusser himself seems to want to finesse the problem with a strategic parenthesis when he refers in passing to "the most commonplace police (or other) hailing: 'Hey, you there!' "[17] But the difference between a police hailing and, say, a friend's is precisely the point. When a policeman calls out, "Hey, you there!" that utterance has a determinate performative effect in a way that a friend's does not. Whether or not you respond to the cop's call, you have, to some initially undefinable degree, become "wanted" and consequently are subject to legal regulations that allow the police to impose their authority. If the law occupies an ambiguous place in Althusser's model—Althusser lists it as both a repressive state apparatus and an ideological apparatus—where should the discourse of the novel be situated?

In D. A. Miller's brilliant readings of Victorian fiction the police function as an alibi for other controlling social institutions. Yet if the police in Ireland are brought forward not as the novel's most visible synecdoche for the circulation of disciplinary power but as indices of the historical particularities of the colonial situation, the political status of *Ulysses*—what might be called its ideological mode of existence in Irish culture—becomes more complex.

Consider again England's policing of Ireland. Although the DMP and the RIC were part of an imperial surveillance network, the divided loyalties of the RIC members who refused to fire on their fellow citizens complicate the relations among empire, its agents in Ireland, and its Irish subjects. Even the simplest police procedures were always more difficult in Ireland than in England, sometimes comically so and by 1901, when an inquiry was conducted into the DMP, Home Rule agitation had turned even "the more respectable element" against the police. In the plaintive words of one Inspector Hourahan:

> "[I]t is very hard to manage traffic in Dublin; the people here are not at all so pliable as those in London. . . . In London, as I have myself seen . . . a policeman has only to put up his hand, and it is sufficient. It is not so in Dublin." "The Irish carman rather likes driving on the wrong side?" inquired a member of the commission. "Yes sir," rejoined the Inspector, "he is inclined to be contrary. Even the upper classes frequently offend against regulations; and if you speak to a gentleman for doing it, many of them will tell you that you are a 'cad of a policeman' or use some other offensive expression."[18]

Bloom, we recall, having raised "a policeman's whitegloved hand" to stop an oncoming sandstrewer in "Circe," must leap to the curb to escape an abusive motorman. Police efforts were also hampered on the level of organization. Dublin Castle intelligence reports first published in 1966 reveal that even though the central offices of the RIC and the DMP were located in the Castle itself, the countrywide network of surveillance described by Macardle as "the most dangerous of all the instruments of England's policy in Ireland" was undermined by a failure to share information. Questions have also arisen about the very existence of the network. A 1911 article in the *Irish Freedom* entitled "The Police Game" claims that the " 'Dublin-Castle-knows-all-about-it' phrase" is part of a police strategy to promote the fear that anyone might be a traitor. Whatever the merits of this claim, in 1916 the Castle evidently had no informers among the small number of people who knew of the intention to rise on Easter.[19]

The generalized concept of policing thus founders on both theoretical and empirical grounds: Irish circumstances throw into relief the way in which the multiple subject-positions that constitute subjectivity may disrupt the internalization of discipline, and histories of the pertinent institutions reveal that discipline to have been poorly enforced.

This is not to say that radical nationalists did not have good reason to share Bloom's suspicion that you "Never know who you're talking to"; plenty of activists were sent to their deaths by, in Bloom's words, informers "drawing secret service pay from the castle" (*U* 8.441, 444). Nor is there reason to doubt that fear of betrayal from within was widespread; to this day the FBI (whose "G men" probably got their name from the DMP's G Division), acting in concert with the Royal Ulster Constabulary, is reputed to approach Irish immigrants and ask them to inform on members of the Irish community.[20] Rather, my point is that if we take seriously the importance of analyzing concrete individuals and specific institutions, it becomes clear that when a given call is directed toward individual subjects with divergent personal histories, that call will have a variable capacity to evoke recognition and elicit compliance. Continually bombarded with a variety of ideological messages, the individual subject may assume a subject position without "locking into" it, yet the trace of that subject position, even if discarded for another, persists. As Paul Smith puts it, "a singular history always mediates between the human agent and the interpellations directed [his or her way]."[21]

By preserving the narrative dimension that Althusser introduced only to elide, interpellation can be theorized as a process that involves moments of identification, partial identification, and the refusal of identification. In this way the "turn" toward the hailer that Althusser associates with the conversion to ideology can be "slowed down" to take into account the complicating mediations that enter into identification as process.

Bloom's installation as lord mayor of Dublin and Stephen's encounter with the military provide especially suggestive focuses in this context. With the imperial administration of Dublin Castle the true seat of political power, the municipal politics of Dublin were always ambiguously contingent, and Bloom's fantasy of political empowerment reflects that ambiguity by transforming the installation of Dublin's lord mayor into a ceremony modeled on the coronation of Edward VII.[22] Stephen's confrontation is staged in the international context of England's attempt to recruit Irish soldiers to the cause of empire. These attempts at ideological consolidation provide points of reference for gauging the place of the novel within discourses more pointedly devised to lock the individual agent into a particular form of subjectivity. Joyce does not suggest that the Irish individual is immune to the hailings of British ceremony, nor does he respond with idealized counter-images, like Synge's noble peasant or Yeats's Cathleen ni Houlihan, from Ireland's own storehouse of newly invented traditions. Rather, acknowledging the powerful influence of the Imperial Crown and the Roman Catholic church, Joyce shows how specific ideological appeals may inflect, though not necessarily determine, the operations of desire at their very inception.

Coronations and Conversions: Church, State, and Colonization

David Cannadine has shown that the purportedly timeless traditions of the British coronation were invented in the late nineteenth century as part of a large-scale strategy to identify an increasingly urban and centralized nation-state with the royal and imperial centrality of London. The ideology of the "British" nation-state, a reaction in part to the French Revolution, had been promulgated throughout the nineteenth century, but only at the time of Edward's coronation in 1902, when the nation-state had begun to compete in the international market of imperialism, did national allegiance actually begin to take precedence over local loyalties. In an era of "change, crisis and dislocation," Cannadine writes, "the deliberate, ceremonial presentation of an impotent but venerated monarch as a unifying symbol of permanence and national community became both possible and necessary."[23] If Victoria was named empress of India in 1877, it was of Edward's coronation that one appreciative observer wrote: "For the first time in the history of our land, did the Imperial idea blaze forth into prominence, as the sons and daughters of the Empire gathered together from the ends of the earth to take their part."[24] With colonial delegates from around the world ritually pledging their fealty alongside English peers, and the monarch increasingly identified with imperial ambition, Edward's 1902 ceremony reached beyond national subjects by means of a spectacle designed also for the colonized.[25] Popular royal biographies also date from this time, as does "the massive proliferation [of] popular works explaining, describing and commemorating great royal occasions."[26] The interspellative design of such texts is particularly well illustrated in Sir John Bodley's official account of Edward's coronation.

Well into Bodley's 1903 tome, the royal historian claims, "It has been shown in these pages that the conversation and consolidation of the British Empire has been chiefly due to the influence of the Crown on the imagination of the British race." The Crown itself, he asserts, is emblematic of "tradition," which has given the British Empire undisputed "supremacy in the world."[27] If royal ceremony solicits the imagination to participate in the construction and consolidation of imperial traditions, the insertion of Joyce's text into the contested terrain of ceremonial interpellation reveals those traditions to be vulnerable ideological inventions. Given the uncertain and disputed status of Irish national identity at this time, it is not surprising that the increasingly organized hailings of empire called into play with Edward's coronation elicited a complexly ambivalent response, and in *Ulysses* Joyce explores the confused response of a city that cheered Edward's visit in 1903 even as the Dublin Corporation refused to honor him with a municipal address.

Bloom's coronation articulates Dublin's ambivalent politics as a drama of confused desires. Having donned the purple dalmatic mantle of the English sovereign, Bloom is drenched in hair oil by the archbishop of Armagh, who, borrowing the formula used to announce the election of a new pope, proclaims: "Gaudium magnum annuntio vobis. Habemus carneficem" ("I have a great joy to announce to you. We have an executioner"; *U* 15.1487–88).[28] The intrusion of the formula announcing a new pope into Bloom's installation both associates Bloom with Pope Leopold XII, who happened to die the day after Edward's royal visit, and registers as parody the increasingly religious character of the king's coronation ceremony. Early in the previous century the Anglican church had not wanted to participate in the celebration of royal power, but by Edward's accession the church enthusiastically took up its role, and the ceremony's origins in the consecration of a bishop came lavishly to the foreground. Bodley, in a passage that could pass for a parody in "Cyclops," shamelessly invokes Catholic iconography, the *mater dolorosa*, in his description of king, queen, and prince during the ceremony:

> With a gesture of infinite tenderness, which needs the heart of a father to command, the royal sire drew to his arms his only remaining son and, in sight of his people, embraced him; while, in the majesty of motherhood, the Queen looked on with eyes which bore the divine trace of sorrows as well as of the joys of maternity and before which, perhaps, passed a vision, unperceived in the jubilant throng, save by the father upon the throne and the brother who knelt before him. The scene lasted only for an instant; yet in a certain sense it had a profound significance. The secret of England's imperial greatness was bound up in it.[29]

Anglicanism, here as a state religion, takes over Catholicism just as Catholicism had once absorbed paganism. Given that Edward's was the last English coronation to disparage Catholicism as a departure from the true faith (as Joyce bitterly points out in "Ireland at the Bar" [CW 198–99]), the image of the Holy Family as the linchpin of empire carries a nice irony here. In *Ulysses* Joyce subverts the appropriation of religious symbolism for political ends in his ironic invocation of Bloom, Molly, and Stephen as the Holy Family, a profanation that represents only one facet of his more general interest in the way ideological appeals issued by church and state may become mutually supportive. In "Circe," locating the complicity of secular and ecclesiastical authority in the installation/coronation of Dublin's chief administrative official, Joyce shows Bloom's fantasy of empowerment to be inflected by the hailing of an imperial message that has already appropriated the religious iconography of the colonized subject. Bloom's authority, like that of the Dublin Corporation itself, is marked by the institutional power of British Crown and the Catholic church.

The interwoven claims of church, state, and empire constituted part of the texture of everyday life in Dublin.[30] Although the Dublin Corporation narrowly voted against offering the king a municipal address, he was enthusiastically greeted by the young priests of Maynooth.[31] The readiness of the church to cozy up to the king was deplored by some but not all Dubliners, and a huge crowd warmly greeted Edward as he entered the city via Leeson Street, passing through a huge proscenium arch built, like a stage setting, solely for the occasion.[32] Edward's entry into "Circe," where he is greeted with "General applause" (*U* 15.4464), reflects this hospitality toward the stranger. Where in *Portrait* the antagonism between Irish nationalism and the church is represented in the Christmas dinner scene as divisive family conflict, in *Ulysses* contradictions between national church and quasi-imperial local government are revealed more generally as a constitutive feature of subjectivity in early twentieth-century Dublin.

These pressures receive further attention later in "Circe." The declaration of Bloom as executioner rather than as pope following his coronation oath echoes the extended execution scene in "Cyclops" and anticipates the horrific execution of the Croppy Boy dramatized in the midst of Stephen's encounter with Privates Carr and Compton. Throughout *Ulysses* the recurring ballad of the Croppy Boy, a young enthusiast on his way to fight in the Rebellion of '98, operates as an emblem of naive nationalism betrayed not simply by the church but by the implicit collusion between church and state, by the king disguised, like the ballad's British soldier, within the priest. The "Circe" execution, during which Edward contentedly sings a popular song celebrating his own coronation while Rumbold hangs and disembowels the Croppy Boy, reinterprets the identity of civic and religious duty encoded in the coronation ceremony by suggesting that to be a loyal Catholic and a committed nationalist in Ireland may constitute overlapping yet violently contradictory subject-positions. Presiding over this potentially disabling contradiction, as F. L. Radford has shown, is the true image of British authority: the executioner.[33]

The satiric superimposition of lord mayor, king, and pope in the narrative of Bloom's empowerment transforms him into a colonial incarnation of the English and Italian masters to whom Stephen feels subjected in "Telemachus." (If Stephen resents being solicited for the "odd jobs" of empire and church, it is Bloom in "Circe," it seems, who is obliged to perform them.) What is the reader to make of this curious transformation, and what does this transformation "make" of the reader?

Bloom's identification with the executioner—Stephen's *dio boia*, or hangman god—is amenable to a dystopic reading in which the very effort to resist dominant authorities is always already circumscribed by the mutually supportive powers momentarily located in Bloom; the Good Samaritan of "Circe," like Power in "Grace," can only abet institutional control. Not quite blaming history, Bloom himself has already indulged in a correlative moment of fleeting paranoia by viewing the global power of the church under the aspect of Dublin Castle's centralized administration of Ireland: "Squareheaded chaps those must be in Rome: they work the whole show. And don't they rake in the money too?" (*U* 5.434–45). If God as "playwright . . . wrote the folio of the world" (*U* 9.1047), the pope, in Bloom's view, acts as director of the global theater, insinuating the economic and social power of the church everywhere.

Yet in "Lotus Eaters" Bloom's suspicions about the centralized power of the church in Rome are qualified by a continual debunking of the particular mystifications being performed before him during the mass. Watching women take communion, Bloom acknowledges the unpredictable mobility of desire—his penpal Martha "might be here with a ribbon round her neck and do the other thing all the same on the sly"—before turning his thoughts to what seems a more puzzling constellation of beliefs: "That fellow that turned queen's evidence on the invincibles he used to receive the, Carey was his name, the communion every morning. This very church. . . . And just imagine that. Wife and children at home. And plotting the murder all the time" (*U* 5.376–77, 378–82). Bloom has difficulty holding Carey together as Catholic, husband, father, and political assassin, the last seeming to invalidate the authenticity of the first three. Deciding that there is always something "shiftylooking" about the ostentatiously devout, Bloom ultimately suppresses a confusing degree of "myriadmindedness" under the rubric of hypocrisy.

The curtailment of Bloom's insight notwithstanding, the very activity of mind catalyzed by the multiplicity of the individual subject permits Bloom a critical vantage on the Mass, Carey's political violence, and other interpellative messages. It is Bloom's personal history, mediating the ceremony, that permits him, in this instance and during the Catholic funeral services of "Hades," an inside/outside perspective. Born to a Catholic mother, later raised as a Jew by his father, then baptized as a Protestant before converting to Catholicism, Bloom the mature atheist bears traces of these subject positions without ever becoming bound to any in particular: "I remember slightly," he thinks while straining to hear the priest's words (*U* 5.422). The deeper connection between Bloom's reflections on the Phoenix Park murders and the activities of the church can only be formulated at a level of abstraction beyond his awareness: the turn of the century not only was the apogee of the age of empire, it was "the classic age of massive missionary endeavor."[34] Carey resisted British policy in his own way—with what anarchist discourse of the time called "propaganda by the deed"—and Bloom, listening to the mass, resists in another. Having spotted a notice for Father Conmee's sermon on the African Mission, Bloom ponders the idea of converting Africans to Catholicism, and his barely articulated awareness of the way the hailings of church and state may mirror each other as they are multiplied throughout society registers just enough to initiate a train of thought that must be completed by the reader: "Prayers for Gladstone they had too when he was almost unconscious. The protestants are the same. Convert Dr William J. Walsh D.D. to the true religion. Save China's millions" (*U* 5.323–24). The kingdoms of heaven and earth compete for subjects through a network of crisscrossing appeals, and to Bloom, for whom Gladstone, "almost unconscious," is commensurate with an "entranced" object of missionary zeal, that network becomes a more comic version of his earlier misreading of the Jewish Haggadah: instead of "everybody eating everyone else," however, here the world itself is consumed in efforts of mutual conversion—though Bloom's conversion, like Gladstone's, remains a matter of what Stephen would call "almosting it."

Reading "Circe": Inventing the Cosmopolitan Subject

If Bloom is represented as steeped in yet partially resistant to specific interpellative messages, what can be said of the reader? Colin MacCabe has argued that by destroying the idea of an authoritative perspective on the narrative, Joyce's text has a liberating effect on the reader, who, like Bloom, is forced to adopt multiple subject-positions. But for the reader, as for Bloom, interpellation is variable. Only by specifying both the nature of the appeals advanced and the kind of audience addressed can the ideological effects of a novel be gauged. Which readers are at issue: Irish, English, European? Male or female, Protestant or Catholic?

Though identifying the audience for *Ulysses* is problematic, side-stepping questions of readership altogether effaces the particular social and political contexts that influence the act of reading in a given historical moment. MacCabe raises the issue of readership only to privilege Joyce himself as the solitary individual to whom *Ulysses* is addressed,[35] but depoliticizing *Ulysses* in this way vitiates what I take to be a major aim of Joyce's project: the invention of a cosmopolitan subject that incorporates without fully assimilating the colligated subject-positions of the Irish colonial subject. The strategies of that project, at work throughout *Ulysses*, can be found in their most extravagant form in "Circe."

"Circe" has been called "a nightmare sent by God-Joyce to the reader,"[36] and the nightmarish effect depends on readers having already been deeply absorbed in the materials of the previous fourteen episodes. *Ulysses* "transposed and rearranged,"[37] the episode transforms into nightmare historical features of Dublin life that for contemporary Dubliners were not necessarily nightmarish in the least. Cheryl Herr has pointed out that many Dublin theatergoers seem to have sat through, unconcerned, as Irish performers sang music-hall songs that assumed "a total identification of the Irish actors, singers, and audience with their English government," even songs celebrating Britain's colonial prowess.[38] Edward himself, I have already noted, was welcomed into the city by the majority of its citizens. At the same time, given the vitality of various nationalist activities—the Gaelic League, the Gaelic Athletic Association, the Land League—the Irish as a whole cannot be considered gratefully oppressed. In "Circe" such contradictions do not remain latent for long, and the political work performed by the episode derives from the way phantasmagoric drama catalyzes a heightened experience of the confused loyalties that characterize the Irish colonial subject.

Joyce wrote to Valery Larbaud that Stephen's "mind is full like everyone else's of borrowed words,"[39] and in "Circe" those borrowed words become the fleetingly embodied voices of contradictory ideological appeals. In Joyce's treatment, the drunken confrontation between citizen and soldier—no doubt a common occurrence in 1904 Dublin—is almost overwhelmed by the babble of voices and stage directions that compete for the reader's attention: Edward quoting "The Ballad of Joking Jesus," Kevin Egan quoting a French journalist mocking Queen Victoria, Old Gummy Granny plumping for Stephen's martyrdom. Consider again, in this context, Joyce's use of Edward's coronation.

By the time Edward sings his coronation ditty at the Croppy Boy's execution, the song has already been sung in "Telemachus" by Buck Mulligan, who plays on "coronation day" as slang for payday in anticipation of sharing in the "crowns" or "sovereigns" Stephen will receive from the Anglo-Irish Deasy. The repetition suggests that Edward, like Mulligan, is a pretender or usurper, and each, Stephen knows, wants his money, either to underwrite "some brutish empire" or to buy drinks for Haines (U 15.4569–70). It is fitting that Stephen finds no money in his pockets to hand over to Carr: the "noose"—Stephen's word for Deasy's payment in "Nestor"—has just been used for the hanging of the Croppy Boy. The linking of Mulligan, Edward, and Deasy in this way effectively relocates the politics and violence of empire in the transactions of everyday social existence.

The presence of the church is also registered in the execution of the Croppy Boy, a young man who forgot to pray for his mother's rest (U 15.4547). The Fenian ballad recited by the Citizen just before the Croppy Boy's execution—"May the God above / Send down a dove / With teeth as sharp as razors / To slit the throats / Of the English dogs / That hanged our Irish leaders" (U 15.4525–30)—invokes memories of the church's role in cutting the throats of Irish leaders like Parnell, and the handkerchief-bearing society women who sop up the dying ejaculation of the Croppy Boy travesty Mary Magdalene's ministrations to Jesus at the Crucifixion. As these women quickly coalesce into Joyce's version of Cathleen ni Houlihan—Old Gummy Granny—the collusion of religious and political narratives is seen to converge in the meaningless sacrifice of a "hero martyr" (U 12.609). Having witnessed the execution of the Croppy Boy, the old woman of Ireland tempts Stephen with martyrdom—"At 8:30 A.M. you will be in heaven and Ireland will be free" (U 15.4737–38)—and so represents Joyce's grim counterpart to Bodley's *mater dolorosa*.

The effect of this confusing chorus of jostling appeals is to instill in the reader a sense of the international and factional pressures that animate what otherwise might seem to be a local dispute. Compton accuses Stephen of being pro-Boer, as many Dubliners were, and Bloom, attempting to placate the soldiers, declares: "We fought for you in South Africa. . . . Isn't that history? Royal Dublin Fusiliers. Honored by our monarch" (U 15.4606–7). Indeed it is history, as is the fact that, recruiting drives notwithstanding, Irish troops also sided with the Boers against the British; Bloom himself recalls having been caught up in a pro-Boer demonstration during Chamberlain's 1899 visit to Dublin. Bloom's allusion to the Royal Dublin Fusiliers immediately conjures his father-in-law, Major Tweedy, who emanates, as does Edward's Masonic apron, from the trace left in Bloom's mind by the recruiting poster he examined in "Lotus Eaters." (Tweedy is dressed as the grenadier Bloom first mistook for a fusilier on the poster; the Royal Dublin Fusiliers and their band often played a prominent role in recruitment drives from 1900 on.)[40] The divided loyalties peculiar to Ireland's colonial history, and in particular, the clash between recruiting forces, is played out in "Circe" in the confrontation between Major Tweedy, sprung from a poster, and the Citizen, whose pro-Irish battle cries join with Tweedy's anti-Boer slogans in the cacophony surrounding Stephen's confrontation with Carr.

With tensions rising, Bloom, reinvoking Bodley's queen, hopes that "woman, sacred lifegiver," can avert the violence, but Cissy Caffrey, unable to pull Carr away, can only call for the police, a call that quickly becomes a general alarm. Given Carr's increasingly violent if self-defeating desire to protect the name of his "bleeding fucking king," and given the imperial status of the DMP, it is only fitting that following the alarm the violence impending against Stephen is displaced onto the city itself in the ensuing stage directions, an apocalyptic paragraph that mixes bits of Revelation and a black mass with details from the Rebellion of '98 and the British shelling of Dublin in 1916. Though the DMP themselves were unarmed (and thus conspicuously absent during the Easter Rising), the police, as tall reminders that Dublin was a garrison town occupied by a foreign power, conjure a vision of the urban destruction that was very much on Joyce's mind as he wrote *Ulysses*.[41] Despite having momentarily become a policeman himself in the first of his Circean costume changes, Bloom is able to rescue Stephen only with the aid of someone closer to Castle authority than are the police, Corny Kelleher. Having to depend on the "indispensable informer," Bloom and Stephen are able to enjoy whatever limited communion they later achieve, it seems, only by sufferance, once again, of the centralized authority established by England to regulate its Irish subjects.

Yet it is crucial to recognize that Bloom's rescue of Stephen also constitutes a triumphant *exploitation* of Kelleher's role as a cog in Ireland's antisubversion system. If "in Ireland, just at the right moment," as Joyce wrote in 1907, "an informer always appears" ("Fenianism," in *CW* 190), *Ulysses* transforms that dystopic observation. Long recognized as an Odyssean strategist, Bloom, to use Michel de Certeau's distinction, is both a strategist and a tactician.[42] Always on the watch to "work . . . a pass" or some favor from the powers that be (*U* 4.453), Bloom in his exchanges with Kelleher and the police demonstrates that even powerful systems may be worked from the inside out. Playing one system against another can offer a respite from the totalizing power of a single system, and Bloom, "his fingers at his lips in the attitude of secret master" (*U* 15.4956–57), apparently owes his success to one gap in particular: the policeman's oath, according to Dublin's 1908 *Policeman's Manual*, ends with a promise not to join any secret society—except the Society of Freemasons.[43]

What we see with particular vividness in these scenes are moments in which Joyce fashions a political theater more attuned than is Althusser's to the ways in which individual subjects, ideological appeals, and the interactions between them are constituted only as contested terrain. It is only partly true to say that the unconscious of particular characters or "the collective unconscious" of the city is represented in "Circe." If the possibility of individual agency exists within and between the potential contradictions of multiple subject-positions, then "Circe," insofar as it projects as dramatic spectacle the partially introjected appeals that converge in the individual subject, may work to heighten the enabling conditions of resistance. In Althusser's political theater the individual invariably turns toward the hailer. In Joyce's theater, efforts to interpellate the individual as a subject—the coronation ceremony, the Mass, recruiting posters—are staged in the liminal space where an individual's experience of the world confronts institutional attempts to shape that experience. Before being rescued by Bloom, Stephen, however oppressed, is permitted to ask, "Will someone tell me where I am least likely to meet these necessary evils?" (*U* 15.4575–76). The reader, like Stephen, meets them in the pages of "Circe," where Joyce, registering the degrees of likelihood that govern collisions between individuals and the forces that would subject them, makes that subjection less likely.

Notes

Portions of this essay were originally published as "Bloom's Coronation and the Subjection of the Subject," *James Joyce Quarterly* 28, no. 4 (1991) and are reprinted courtesy of the editor. I thank Ian Duncan and Victor Luftig for their astute comments on earlier drafts of this essay.

1. Johnson, "The Rambler," no. 4, reprinted in *Samuel Johnson: Selected Poetry and Prose,* ed. Frank Brady and W. K. Wimsatt (Berkeley and Los Angeles: University of California Press, 1977), 156.

2. See D. A. Miller, *The Novel and the Police* (Berkeley and Los Angeles: University of California Press, 1988). Conduct books are invested with a similarly coercive and insidious power in some studies of the eighteenth-century novel. See, for instance, Nancy Armstrong, *Desire and Domestic Fiction: A Political History of the Novel* (New York: Oxford University Press, 1987).

3. Vincent Pecora, *Self and Form in Modern Narrative* (Baltimore, Md.: Johns Hopkins University Press, 1989), 6.

4. Dominick LaCapra, *History, Politics, and the Novel* (Ithaca, N.Y.: Cornell University Press, 1987). For a debate between LaCapra and D. A. Miller on the viability of the potentially transformative powers of the

novel, see "Ideology and Critique in Dickens's *Bleak House,"* *Representations* 6 (Spring 1984): 116–29.

5. See Joseph V. O'Brien, *"Dear, Dirty Dublin": A City in Distress, 1899–1916* (Berkeley and Los Angeles: University of California Press, 1982), 180.

6. Lord Morely is quoted in Dorothy Macardle, *The Irish Republic: A Documented Chronicle of the Anglo-Irish Conflict and the Partitioning of Ireland, with a Detailed Account of the Period 1916–1923* (London: Victor [Gollancz], 1937), 53. Macardle's own description is on p. 319.

7. For Foucault, see *Discipline and Punish: The Birth of the Prison,* trans. Alan Sheridan (New York: Vintage, 1979), 195–228.

8. Frank Budgen, *James Joyce and the Making of "Ulysses"* (Oxford: Oxford University Press, 1989), 123.

9. See Richard Ellmann, *James Joyce,* rev. ed. (Oxford: Oxford University Press, 1982), 438. Ellmann notes that Joyce often liked to orchestrate his conversations by floating a topic in order to garner responses.

10. For the Arranger, adopted by Hugh Kenner and others, see David Hayman, *"Ulysses" and the Mechanics of Meaning,* rev. ed. (Madison: University of Wisconsin Press, 1982), 88–104. For Gérard Genette, see *Narrative Discourse: An Essay in Method,* trans. Jane E. Lewin (Ithaca, N.Y.: Cornell University Press, 1980), 228.

11. See Macardle, *Irish Republic,* 376.

12. See Foucault, "The Subject and Power," in *Art after Modernism: Rethinking Representation,* ed. Brian Wallis (New York: New Museum of Contemporary Art, 1984).

13. Andreas Huyssen, *After the Great Divide: Modernism, Mass Culture, Postmodernism* (Bloomington: Indiana University Press, 1986), 23.

14. See Paul Smith, *Discerning the Subject* (Minneapolis: University of Minnesota Press, 1988). The development of my argument is at several points indebted to Smith's excellent critique of models of subjectivity that have dominated poststructuralist literary theory.

15. Althusser, "Ideology and Ideological State Apparatuses," in *Lenin and Philosophy and Other Essays,* trans. Ben Brewster (New York: Monthly Review Press, 1971), 172. The following discussion draws quotations from pp. 172–75.

16. See Smith, *Discerning the Subject,* 16–17.

17. Althusser, "Ideological State Apparatuses," 174.

18. Earnan P. Blythe, "The D.M.P." *Dublin Historical Record* 20, nos. 3–4 (June–September 1965): 122–23. Though Blythe always invents excuses for hostility to the police, he acknowledges a political motivation for

that friction only when observing that the nationalism of the Dublin Corporation denied municipal employment to police pensioners. Between attempts to downplay the problem, Blythe notes, "Some landlords were prepared to reduce rent for constables, but others would not let houses to constables at all"; he also admits that "the public at large wouldn't cooperate with the police" (122, 123).

19. See Breandàn MacGiolla Choille, ed., *Intelligence Notes, 1913–16* (Dublin: Government Publication Sale Office, 1966), xvii–xix, and León Ó Broin, *Dublin Castle and the 1916 Rising* (London: Sidgwick and Jackson, 1970), 141.

20. See Patrick Farrelly, " 'Come Forward' Appeal to Blackmail Victims," *Irish Times*, September 8, 1990.

21. Smith, *Discerning the Subject*, 37.

22. See Don Gifford, *"Ulysses" Annotated* (Berkeley and Los Angeles: University of California Press, 1988), 472–74.

23. David Cannadine, "The Context, Performance, and Meaning of Ritual: The British Monarchy and the 'Invention of Tradition,' c. 1820–1977," in *The Invention of Tradition,* ed. Eric J. Hobsbawm and Terence Ranger (Cambridge: Cambridge University Press, 1983), 122. It was the rise of national daily newspapers and the yellow press late in the century, Cannadine points out, that delivered the imperial spectacle of Edward's coronation "with unprecedented immediacy and vividness" to "a broader cross section of the public than ever before" (123). See also Eric J. Hobsbawm, *The Age of Empire, 1875–1914* (New York: Pantheon, 1987), chap. 3.

24. Quoted in Cannadine, "Context, Performance, and Meaning," 125.

25. The postponing of Edward's coronation owing to the king's poor health heightened the imperial aspect of the event insofar as only the delegates who had traveled farthest remained in England to await the indefinitely delayed ceremony.

26. Cannadine, "Context, Performance, and Meaning," 123.

27. Sir John Bodley, *The Coronation of Edward the Seventh* (London: Methuen, 1903), 307, 322.

28. See Gifford, *"Ulysses" Annotated,* 474; his translation.

29. Bodley, *Coronation,* 306–7.

30. For an informal account of city life at this time, see P. L. Dickinson, *The Dublin of Yesterday* (London: Methuen, 1929), who comments on the effects of the military on Dublin's social life.

31. Sir Sidney Lee, *King Edward VII* (London: Macmillan, 1927), 2:167–68.

32. In extant photographs the arch looks to be built of solid stone, but according to Phil McCann of the Irish National Library the monument was taken down soon after Edward's visit and was, suggestively enough, probably a hollow structure designed to look permanent.

33. See F. L. Radford, "King, Pope, and Hero-Martyr: *Ulysses* and the Nightmare of Irish History," *James Joyce Quarterly* 15 (1978): 310.

34. Hobsbawm, *Age of Empire*, 71.

35. Colin MacCabe, *James Joyce and the Revolution of the Word* (London: Macmillan, 1978), 156–57. MacCabe does not address the fact that a great deal of what now appears willfully difficult in *Ulysses,* such as allusions to the minutiae of Irish history or everyday life, was immediately accessible to a contemporary Dubliner.

36. Marilyn French, *The Book as World: James Joyce's "Ulysses"* (Cambridge, Mass.: Harvard University Press, 1976), 187.

37. Hugh Kenner, "Circe," in *James Joyce's "Ulysses": Critical Essays,* ed. Clive Hart and David Hayman (Berkeley and Los Angeles: University of California Press, 1974), 356.

38. Cheryl Herr, *Joyce's Anatomy of Culture* (Urbana: University of Illinois Press, 1986), 112–14.

39. To Larbaud, June 4, 1928. Quoted in MacCabe, *James Joyce,* 117.

40. Pro-German and anti-British posters and publications, as well as a huge public funeral procession for the Fenian O'Donovan Rossa, countered the messages sent out by recruiters and managed to hold down enlistment. The threat of conscription later turned even more citizens away from the British army and instead swelled enlistment in the military organization that later staged the Easter Rebellion, the Irish Volunteers. See O'Brien, *"Dear, Dirty Dublin,"* 251–57. For a sustained investigation of the conjunction of *Ulysses* and recruiting posters, see Mark A. Wollaeger, "Posters, Modernism, Cosmopolitanism: *Ulysses* and World War One Recruiting Posters in Ireland," *Yale Journal of Criticism* 6, no. 2 (1993): 87–131.

41. Budgen records Joyce's famous remark that if Dublin were destroyed, it could be rebuilt from the pages of his novel. See Budgen, *James Joyce,* 69. As for the "giant" policemen reported by visitors to Dublin, the minimum height for the DMP was five feet, nine inches, for the RIC five feet, eight inches.

42. A "strategy" operates within existing structures of power by util-

izing the circuitry already laid out; a "tactic" functions oppositionally within the interstices of existing systems by productively exploiting the potential for contingency within otherwise hegemonic structures of determination. See Michel de Certeau, *The Practice of Everyday Life*, trans. Steven Rendall (Berkeley and Los Angeles: University of California Press, 1984), xviii–xx.

43. Hume R. Jones, *The Policeman's Manual*, 7th ed. (Dublin: Alexander Thom, 1908), 2.

Ulysses, Narrative, and History

EMER NOLAN

◆   ◆   ◆

> The naive or mythical view of Irish history is
> important for readers of Joyce, since he uses it
> throughout *Ulysses* and *Finnegans Wake*. The
> fact that it is endlessly interesting to most Irish-
> men and infinitely tedious to most Englishmen
> can be a serious obstacle to the understanding of
> Joyce's major works.
>
> —Matthew Hodgart, *James Joyce:*
> *A Student's Guide*

Preface: Stories and Styles

Toward the end of chapter 15 of *Ulysses* ("Circle") Major Tweedy,
father of Molly Bloom, and member of the Royal Dublin Fusiliers,
who "rose from the ranks" (*U* 4.63–64) of the British army, confronts the Citizen, a dropsical Irish nationalist: "(*Major Tweedy and
the Citizen exhibit to each other medals, decorations, trophies of war, wounds.
Both salute with fierce hostility*)" (*U* 16.4622–24). "*Massed bands,*" further
stage directions tell us, "*blare* Garryowen *and* God Save the King."
Garryowen is the name of the Citizen's dog in chapter 12 ("Cyclops") and of a place in Limerick. It is also the title of an Irish
drinking song. Don Gifford and Robert J. Seidman gloss this reference with a quotation from its refrain:

> Instead of Spa we'll drink brown ale,
> And pay the reckoning on the nail,

155

No man for debt shall go to gaol,
From Garryowen in glory.[1]

"God Save the King" is the title of the national anthem of Great Britain. Verse and chorus (although annotation may be judged unnecessary) are:

> God save our gracious king,
> Long live our noble king,
> God save the king.
> Send him victorious,
> Happy and glorious,
> Long to reign over us,
> God save the king.

This short exchange illustrates certain features of narrative and style typical of *Ulysses* as a whole. Perhaps the first thing to note of the confrontation between the Major and the Citizen is that it comes to nothing. The fight which Cissy Caffrey, Cunty Kate, and Biddy the Clap eagerly anticipate does not materialize. In their disappointment, the prostitutes stand for any reader of *Ulysses* who has not yet abandoned his or her expectation of narrative progression. Second, the two songs are evidently to be understood as playing simultaneously, the one utterance melting indifferently into the other. The styles of language associated with them are here merely suggested by the citation of their titles. The songs are not quoted, nor subjected to the comic exaggeration or distortion which might amount to parody. But in their literal indistinguishability they serve to demonstrate what is implicit elsewhere: in *Ulysses* it is usually impossible to say whether parody elevates or ridicules any particular style, as each blends with the next in the frenzy of textual play.

In this small way, therefore, the absence of evident plots and any ethical notion of style in *Ulysses* is already obvious. However, this passage has not been chosen at random, but because of its specific content. The lines which describe the Major and the Citizen indicate antagonism but suggest symmetry. Their salutes are signs of recognition as well as of respect to mutually exclusive and supposedly opposing loyalties. They are both ridiculous; however, if either of them looks funnier it must be the Citizen, for at least Tweedy really is a military man. The Irish nationalist merely mirrors the uniform and gestures of the soldier although he is hardly able to stagger from his bar stool to the door of the pub, as we have already seen in chapter 12. The encounter here stages and defuses a scene of possible aggression. And if the passage reveals the secret equivalence of British soldier and Irish nationalist, such a process of leveling might also be understood as being at work in the juxtaposition of the British national anthem and the Irish drinking song. The confrontation between the two figures can thus serve to illustrate the critical case that this practice of writing erodes the grounds on which we could evaluate or seek to choose between the ideologies for which the pair stand, British imperialism and Irish nationalism, respectively. My reading of the text, however, is devoted to challenging this conclusion. I will examine how such a view of *Ulysses'* "antinationalism" is associated with a certain interpretation of Joyce's abandonment of narrative or plot in the text.

Simply by dint of its realism—the material the text supplies for a diagnosis of the economic and political malaise of the group of lower-middle-class men who constitute its primary focus, its descriptions of their proneness to alcoholism, violence, and debt (as indeed the words of "Garryowen" suggest) and of the bleak lives of their dependents, especially the Dedalus family—*Ulysses* powerfully suggests Joyce's hostility to British colonial rule in Ireland. But for many commentators, this does not amount to nationalism: indeed, according to some of Joyce's more recent critics—hostile alike to what Tweedy and the Citizen stand for—it in fact adds up to something a great deal more radical and valuable, exposing the contradictions and weaknesses inherent in the nationalist project from the start. Colin MacCabe, for example, remarks that Joyce's life before 1914 lent the writer the opportunity to observe the three great movements of twentieth-century history (anticolonialism, communism, and fascism) constitute themselves around the three great themes of nineteenth-century history (democracy, socialism, and nationalism).[2] This formulation admits of *no* alliance between nationalism and anticolonialism: it is not surprising, then, that in its opposition to nationalism, MacCabe reads *Ulysses* as adumbrating an alternative form of anticolonial politics. Seamus Deane argues that the modernist Joyce, in severing the traditional affiliations between narrative and history, opens up a vision of apparently endless possibility at the level of language while incorporating into his writing the terrible burden of Irish historical experience by displaying the failures of nationalist imaginings at the level of content.[3] Joyce's departure from novelistic convention attests to his historical consciousness, exposing the collusion between literary form and a drastically impoverished version of history. Resistance to narrative continuity is thus itself an oblique political act. Similarly, for Colin MacCabe, Joyce's liberation of narrative fiction from the categories of character and plot signals his "more and more desperate attempt to deconstruct those forms of identification which had allowed the national revolution to mean the very opposite of a liberation for Ireland. . . . such a nationalism confers identity and belief where we would find desire and knowledge."[4] It is as though, from this critical viewpoint, Joyce is wise before the revolutionary event precisely because he is writing after it, prefiguring in (say) the sterile mirror image of soldier and citizen what he takes to be the deadlocked outcome of the free state itself.

Because the topic of narrative in *Ulysses* is inevitably linked with oral performance and storytelling, it is closely associated with the question of style. In the next chapter [of *James Joyce and Nationalism*], therefore, my emphasis will be on the way in which such questions of narrative and style converge around the problem of Joyce's aesthetic exploitation of what he calls in *A Portrait of the Artist* "the sacred eloquence of Dublin" (P 164). This in turn raises the specter of "Irish style," and the cliché of the quaint but hopelessly impractical Irish talker, in the light of what Declan Kiberd describes as modern Irish writers' "dignified assertions of a people's right to be colourless."[5] But the relationship between style and parody is also complex. In general, parody involves a deliberate disjunction of style and content to comic effect: high style to low content, or an elevated content to low style, or both, as in the case of "Garryowen" and "God Save the King." I want to examine the consequences of the adaptation of a low style to a low content, particularly through themes and languages of violence. Joyce significantly emphasizes the violence of his stylistic parodies in a 1919 letter to Harriet Shaw Weaver:

> The word *scorching* . . . has a peculiar significance for my superstitious mind not so much because of any quality or merit in the writing itself as for the fact that the progress of the book is in fact like the progress of some sandblast. As soon as I mention or include any person in it I hear of his or her death or departure or misfortune: and each successive episode, dealing with some province of artistic culture (rhetoric or music or dialectic) leaves behind it a burnt up field. (*SL* 241)

But Joyce's hatred of violence is consistently read by, for example, Hugh Kenner, Richard Ellmann, and Dominic Manganiello as the very cornerstone of his politics: these accounts of his pacifism, at least as it is articulated by *Ulysses*, need qualification. To this end, we should consider the linguistic styles linked to Irish nationalism—in both its elevated versions which predominate in chapter 7 ("Aeolus") and in the demotic rhetoric which characterizes chapter 12—in order to suggest how the language of, say, "Garryowen" differs in both the way it is deployed and in its political significance from the kind of language associated with "God Save the King."

I am concerned first, however, to examine the category of narrative as it is deployed by Joyce's poststructuralist commentators. In particular, I will pay attention to the ways in which such a sense of narrative intersects with a certain sense of history—a history which is insistently foregrounded in those early episodes which best exemplify the "stream of consciousness" of Stephen Dedalus and Leopold Bloom, respectively. In these early chapters of *Ulysses*, complex and contradictory associations between "history" and "narrative" emerge. Recent celebrations of the novel's apparent deconstruction of plot would seem implicitly to characterize narrative in highly traditional ways: the point of my own reading, however, is to extend the category of narrative to include just the kind of very short story that the confrontation of Tweedy and the Citizen typifies. *Ulysses* is not, to be sure, a continuous linear story; it is composed of a multiplicity of such stories, a knot of superimposed, complementary narratives in which the individual actors often appear to be dispensable while the underlying narrative paradigms persist. These microevents, by force of their repetition and variation, can indeed be read as constituting a set of ironically and conflictively interrelating narratives, such that no one of these textual events can be taken in isolation. To view the confrontation between citizen and soldier as complete in itself is likely to involve a somewhat different judgment on political nationalism from a reading which reinserts that encounter into the narrational complex of the text as a whole. Similarly the apparently private consciousness of the three central characters, Dedalus, Leopold, and Molly Bloom look different when seen as implicated in the collective stories of the community.

Let us consider these questions in the light of parts of chapter 15 ("Circe"), and Joyce's introduction to the novel, chapter 1 ("Telemachus"). Here, certain strategies employed by Stephen Dedalus at the level of literary content in his negotiations with Dublin on "Bloomsday" can be read as corresponding to major formal strategies of Joyce's in *Ulysses*. In his encounter with the British soldier Private Carr, Stephen behaves "antinarrationally," refusing to play the role allotted to him by the colonial power, but in doing so simply succeeds in becoming the victim of its violence. A modernist refusal of narrative and emancipation from colonial power may not, in short, be as unproblematically conjoined as some contemporary critics assume.

Like the prostitutes, Private Carr is a notably vulgar reader of Joycean narrative, struggling to interpret Stephen's enigmatic utterances. Stephen knows that he is being understood as anti-British—"Green rag to a bull" (*U* 15.4497) as he confides to Bloom—but makes no attempt either to placate or confront the soldier. Carr threatens violence: "I'll wring the neck of any fucker says a word against my bleeding fucking king" (U 15.4643–44). Stephen evidently wants to continue the argument with the soldier because "He provokes my intelligence" (U 15.4513), even though the intellectual potential of this dialogue seems from the outset to be pretty limited. Ultimately, in his attempt to meet violence with brilliance, Stephen is knocked to the ground, to be hauled away by a few cronies of his father, kowtowing to the civil authorities at the same time as they try to extract him from their clutches. Stephen disdains the simple narrative of aggression proposed by the soldier, and suffers for it: modernist fiction may refuse plot in order to deny the reader's "pleasure" but open up "desire" (MacCabe, *James Joyce and the Revolution of the Word*, 156), but here, at least, pain is the result.

But if Dedalus eschews the vulgarity of plot, he is elsewhere politically constrained to resist that freewheeling modernistic parody which might appear to be its alternative. That parody, as practiced by Buck Mulligan, represents for Stephen a fundamental indifference to (and hence complicity with) colonial domination, for all its superficial subversiveness. Just as Stephen deliberately talks over the head of the soldier, so Mulligan chats patronizingly to Haines about the milkwoman in chapter 1. Mulligan glosses for Haines the woman's pious exclamation: "The islanders . . . speak frequently of the collector of prepuces" (U 1.393–94). This might be read as a parody of Haines, as Mulligan exploits the comically technical language of anthropological research. He makes fun of Haines, as much as or indeed perhaps more than of the woman, but of course Haines is not mocked in the same way because he can understand the joke. The woman, who unlike the soldier is powerless, makes no response. Mulligan treats Haines, who is the local representative of imperial England—"His old fellow made his tin selling jalap to Zulus or some bloody swindle or other" (U 1.156–57)—in the same indifferent comic manner as he treats everything else. Stephen, in his insistence to Mulligan on the moral seriousness of his behavior toward his dying mother, and in his refusal to banter with Haines, appears to believe that certain issues should be protected from Mulligan's rationalist demystifications and vacuous parodies. Mulligan, according to Stephen, plays the role of "A jester at the court of his master, indulged and disesteemed, winning a clement master's praise. Why had they chosen all that part?" (*U* 2.43–45). He has become another gifted Irishman who plays to the British audience. His mockery of the Irish is entirely consistent with the fact that he himself embodies a certain stereotype of the linguistically gifted Irishman. Stephen's ultimate charge against Mulligan, however, is not that of "mocker" but "Usurper" (*U* 1.744). I would suggest that what Mulligan, Ireland's "gay betrayer," has *usurped* is precisely Dedalus's self-appointed role as Ireland's very serious betrayer. It is Stephen's reluctance to scoff at what he opposes that leads Mulligan, in turn, to accuse him of simply inverting, rather than dismantling, traditional pieties: "Because you have the cursed jesuit strain in you, only it's injected the wrong way" (*U* 1.208–9).

It is often noted that *Ulysses'* parodic strategies are paralleled by Mulligan's, though as Colin MacCabe argues, with perhaps suspicious vehemence, we must "ruthlessly distinguish" between these two modes of parody, the one radically challenging the positions of author and reader, unsettling and unlimited in its effects, the other straightforward, comic, and didactic.[6] This emphatic distinction—odd for a poststructuralist to enforce—can be questioned: character and novel do indeed share certain strategies, one of which is simple repetition. This is evinced by their attitude, for example, toward sacred ritual. Mulligan claims that he can joke about death because he sees so much of it, and the majesty of the single death is consequently eroded: "You saw only your mother die. I see them pop off every day in the Mater and Richmond and cut up into tripes in the dissectingroom" (*U* 1.204–6). This prefigures Bloom's demystifying reflections at Paddy Dignam's funeral:

> He must be fed up with that job, shaking that thing over all the corpses they trot up here. Every mortal day a fresh batch: middleaged men, old women, children, women dead in childbirth, men with beards, baldheaded business men, consumptive

girls with little sparrows' breasts. . . . Says that over everybody. Tiresome kind of a job. But he has to say something. (U 6.621–30)

Mulligan's spoof, electric-powered transubstantiation, also parallels Bloom's scandalously irreverent musing on the eucharist:

> For this, O dearly beloved, is the genuine christine: body and soul and blood and ouns. Slow music, please. Shut your eyes, gents. One moment. A little trouble about those white corpuscles. . . . That will do nicely. Switch off the current, will you? (U 1.21–29)

> Shut your eyes and open your mouth. What? *Corpus*: body. Corpse. . . . Rum idea: eating bits of a corpse. (U 5.349–52)

The former, of course, proceeds from the blasphemous delight of the lapsed Catholic, the latter from the observations of the non-Catholic. However, this registers a distinction between insider and outsider which *Ulysses* as a whole, as "the type of all anti-auratic texts, a mechanical recycling of a sacred document,"[7] is unable to preserve, as it passes all that was holy through the processes of modern, mechanical reproduction and repetition, leveling the distinction between sacred and profane, high and low. Through Stephen, the novel recognizes the political limitations of parodic practice, while engaging in precisely such practices on its own part. Indeed as such parody becomes less constrained and more general, it can be seen as becoming less dangerous and less critical, rather than (as MacCabe claims) more so. In the complete absence of a possibly "normative" speaking voice, the practice of modernist parody gives way to one of postmodern pastiche. As Jameson comments:

> Pastiche is, like parody, the imitation of a speaker or unique style, the wearing of a stylistic mask, speech in a dead language: but it is a neutral practice of such mimicry, without the satiric impulse, without laughter, without the still latent feeling that

there exists something *normal* compared to which what is being imitated is rather comic.[8]

The scene with Mulligan, Haines, and Stephen, then, dramatizes a Joycean dilemma: how to process the styles of Irishness, the verbal habits of the "islanders," from the point of view not only of a "sympathetic alien" (as Stephen describes himself in *Stephen Hero* and as Haines represents here), nor simply from the standpoint of a disdainful native (Mulligan), but from the position of an engaged but critical insider. But it is a question of who will receive this discourse as well as produce it: the milkwoman, the "Poor old Woman," stands as the representative of an uncomprehending Irish audience and Haines for a readily available metropolitan readership. This dilemma is understood as colonial from the outset.

The Living Dead

Many critics have remarked that in *Ulysses* Joyce presents us with an image of a city in which not much happens or is likely to happen, apparently oblivious to the fact that "these same streets were to become the scene of fierce revolution within little more than a decade."[9] Such judgments as Franco Moretti's that "the status of history in *Ulysses* is intrinsically rather low"[10] are more usually founded on those episodes which centrally feature Leopold Bloom, rather than on the speculations of Stephen Dedalus. In particular, such readings tend to focus on chapter 8 ("Lestrygonians") and on the image there of Bloom as a version of the modernist *flâneur*, an advertising agent moving through the streets of Dublin, a desacralized and endlessly distracting urban space. Stephen, even if only as intellectual, remains in contact with different and historically prior conceptions of space. This divergence is dramatized by their contrasting meditations on repetition and simultaneity. For Stephen, repetition can still evoke communion and sacredness. In chapter 3, for example, he reflects on the fact that at any given time several celebrations of the Mass are likely to be proceeding in churches very close to each other:

> And at the same instant perhaps a priest round the corner is elevating it. Dringdring! And two streets off another locking it into a pyx. Dringadring! And in a ladychapel another taking housel all to his own cheek. Dringdring! Down, up, forward, back. Dan Occam thought of that, invincible doctor. . . . Bringing his host down and kneeling he heard twine with his second bell the first bell in the transept (he is lifting his) and, rising, heard (now I am lifting) their two bells (he is kneeling) twang in diphthong. (*U* 3.120–27)

What Stephen apprehends as ritual, Bloom wearily perceives as meaningless proliferation: "Funerals all over the world everywhere every minute. Shovelling them under by the cartload doublequick. Thousands every hour. Too many in the world" (*U* 6.514–16).

In chapter 7 ("Aeolus") repetition and apparently infinite production come dramatically to the fore at the level of content. The processes of modern industry and printing, which constantly threaten the observer with the possibility of endless repetition— "Now if he got paralysed there and no-one knew how to stop them they'd clank on and on the same, print it over and over and up and back" (*U* 7.102–3)—are depicted through the medium of a language which also displays the first spectacular evidence of the syntactical and typographical experiments which eventually come to predominate in *Ulysses* as a whole: "Grossbooted draymen rolled barrels dullthudding out of Prince's stores and bumped them up on the brewery float. On the brewery float bumped dullthudding barrels rolled by grossbooted draymen out of Prince's stores" (*U* 7.21–24). It is significant to note that mechanical reproduction enters the text simultaneously at the levels of content and language. However, either mechanical or organic images can be employed to describe the perpetual circulation of the various elements of urban life—trams, sacks of letters, barrels of Guinness, people—and Bloom uses both during his reflections in chapter 8: "And we stuffing food in one hole and out behind: food, chyle, blood, dung, earth, food: have to feed it like stoking an engine" (*U* 8.929–30). Bloom's vision of repetition within a closed system, in which nothing can substantially change, achieves its most pessimistic formulation in his conclusive summary of life in the city:

> Things go on same, day after day: squads of police marching out, back: trams in, out. Those two loonies mooching about. Dignam carted off. Mina Purefoy swollen belly on a bed groaning to have a child tugged out of her. One born every second somewhere. Other dying every second.... Cityful passing away, other cityful coming, passing away too: other coming on, passing on. (*U* 8.477–85)

Bloom's remarks can persuasively be read as also offering themselves as a resumé of *Ulysses* as a whole. As Daniel Moshenberg comments: "Thus, though much happens, not much changes or is changed. Even the few changes of the human population that do occur have a kind of equalising content: one birth, one death, the accounts of humankind remain balanced."[11] It is, however, this conclusion which I seek here to challenge. Although Joyce's text does significantly register the advent of mechanical reproduction in the modern city, this is largely mediated through the consciousness of a figure (Bloom) who compulsively generalizes his own specific condition to a pervasive mechanization of social experience as such.

Homer's Lestrygonians are cannibals, but they are represented here for Bloom simply by carnivores, and indeed eaters of all kind. He observes a great deal of food and consumption in this episode simply because he is so hungry: "The heavy noonreek tickled the top of Mr Bloom's gullet" (*U* 8.233–34), "Pungent mockturtle oxtail mulligatawny. I'm hungry too" (*U* 8.271), "Hope they have liver and bacon today" (*U* 8.498). It is his own appetite, then, which inspires this appalling vision of endless glut-

tony and savagery. Bloom, however, decides not to gratify his
carnivorous desires at lunchtime. He is so sickened by the sight
of the lunchtime diners in Burton's restaurant that he retires to
the pub for a quiet sandwich instead:

> Smells of men. Spat on sawdust, sweetish warmish cigarette
> smoke, reek of plug, spilt beer, men's beery piss, the stale of
> ferment.
>   His gorge rose.
> Couldn't eat a morsel here. Fellow sharpening knife and fork
> to eat all before him, old chap picking his tootles. Slight spasm,
> full, chewing the cud. . . . Scoffing up stewgravy with sopping
> sippets of bread. Lick it off the plate, man! Get out of this. (*U*
> 8.670–77)

"Eat or be eaten. Kill! Kill!": this is Bloom's judgment on the
spectacle of this greed. Earlier in the day, during the "Hades"
episode, Bloom announced his philosophy of "Let the dead bury
the dead" and affirmed vitality in the midst of morbid depression:
"In the midst of death we are in life. Both ends meet. Tantalising
for the poor dead. Smell of grilled beefsteaks to the starving" (*U*
6.759–61). The earlier episode appeared to conclude with Bloom's
embrace of human fellowship and closeness: "Plenty to see and
hear and feel yet. Feel live warm beings near you. Let them sleep
in their maggoty beds. They are not going to get me this innings.
Warm beds: warm, fullblooded life" (*U* 6.1003–5). However, in the
face of actually existing human community and warm human
bodies, this robust common man proves unable to imagine, for
example, communal eating outside an economy of greed and
selfishness:

> Suppose that communal kitchen years to come perhaps. . . .
> Devour contents in the street. . . . All for number one. Chil-
> dren fighting for the scrapings of the pot. Want a souppot big
> as the Phoenix Park. Harpooning flitches and hindquarters out
> of it. Hate people all around you. (*U* 8.704–16)[12]

He represents the citizens of Dublin both as savagely appetitive and, because of the circularity and ultimate futility of the "peristaltic" processes in which they are engaged, materially insubstantial and ghostly. In short, whereas in "Hades" he speculated that the dead are jealous of and taunted by the living, he here presents the living as ghosts, and charges the hungry with gluttony: "Hot fresh blood they prescribe for decline. Blood always needed. Lick it up smoking hot, thick sugary. Famished ghosts" (*U* 8.729–30).

Significant dissonances begin to emerge in the representation of Bloom. He appears in *Ulysses* both as life-affirming *homme moyen sensuel*, contentedly fleshy and lustful, and as extraordinarily squeamish and reserved in his negotiations with actual human bodies. This contradiction enables us to call into question the picture he paints of the citizens of Dublin, in which they appear as versions of Pound's "impotent, impetuous dead," perpetually demanding their libation of blood, but never managing to escape from the monotonous, infernal round of life in death. In "Lestrygonians" Bloom views the human body as a consumption machine. At an earlier point in the text this carries comic and demystifying implications in its refusal of somber religiosity, but seems here increasingly the mark of an alienated vision. Society presents itself to him merely as a panorama of blood lust and natural appetite: the modern world is grasped as a post-historical era, inhabited only by living dead, whose very possession of human instincts is horrifying.

This ghostliness is symbolized and given a precise political context by Bloom's sighting of John Howard Parnell, the great man's brother, a less vivid version of the lost leader: "Image of him. Haunting face. . . . Look at the woebegone walk of him. Eaten a bad egg. Poached eyes on ghost" (*U* 8.502–8). Parnell, as we have seen in "Hades," had quickly become the focus of the messianic hopes of his disappointed supporters. As the mourners pay their respects at the grave of "The Chief" in Glasnevin, Mr. Power reports: "—Some say he is not in that grave at all. That the coffin was filled with stones. That one day he will come again" (*U* 6.923–24). In Bloom's remembered or quoted version of Simon

Dedalus's Parnellism, it appears as an even more futile utopianism—a hope not just that Parnell never really died, but that he might be resurrected: "Simon Dedalus said when they put him [David Sheehy] in parliament that Parnell would come back from the grave and lead him out of the House of Commons by the hand" (*U* 8.517–19). So these ghostly citizens await a suitably phantasmal deliverance. The episode is scattered with promises of "great times coming" (*U* 8.454), although these are merely quotations. The prospect of better times is degraded to the level of an advertising jingle: "Elijah is coming. Dr John Alexander Dowie restorer of the church in Zion is coming. Is coming! Is coming!! Is coming!!!" (*U* 8.13–15). Even when such expressions of utopian longing do not reach Bloom in this degraded form, it is consistently the medium into which he translates them. In the newspaper office, for example, Bloom notes the resemblance between the backwards letters manipulated by the typesetter and the Hebrew script he remembers his father reading at Passover. At first glance, this might seem an act of discerning a meaningful history within the alienated modern language of the machine. He recalls the chant:

> All that long business about that brought us out of the land of Egypt and into the house of bondage *alleluia*.... And the angel of death kills the butcher and he kills the ox and the dog kills the cat. Sounds a bit silly until you come to look into it well. Justice it means but it's everyone killing everyone else. That's what life is after all. (*U* 7.208–14)

Gifford and Seidman gloss this as a rendition of the cumulative chants of the *Chad Gadya*, which includes the lines:

> And the Holy One, blessed is He, came and killed the Angel of Death that slew the slaughterer and slaughtered the ox that drank the water that quenched the fire that burned the stick that beat the dog that bit the cat that ate the kid that father bought for two zizium. One kid, one kid.[13]

They also refer to one account of the traditional interpretation of this chant:

> The history of successive empires that devastate and swallow one another (Egypt, Assyria, Babylon, Persia, etc.). The kid, bottom-most and most injured of all is, of course, the people of Israel. The killing of the Angel of Death marks the day when the kingdom of the Almighty will be established on earth; then, too, Israel will live in perfect redemption in the promised land.[14]

Everything preys on and devours that which is smaller than itself, the prayer declares, but the most vulnerable and long-suffering of all will finally be elevated and redeemed. Bloom, however, interprets this merely as a description of the *lex talonis*, the law of "an eye for an eye" or, as he puts it, "everyone killing everyone else." He negates the promise of liberation by his significant verbal slip, his repetition of "bondage."

To the extent, then, that Bloom's flawed and homogenizing historical memory eradicates from the history of the Jewish people the promise of a better future, it also proves insensitive to the similar messianic hopes of the Irish in the aftermath of Parnell. In this, Joyce is attentive to the loss of aura or charisma in the modern world in general and early twentieth-century Ireland in particular; but the fact that this secularization is largely registered through Bloom highlights its source in a particular history, and dramatizes its links with that uncritical acceptance of the discourse of modernity which he represents.

Notes

1. Don Gifford and Robert J. Seidman, *Notes for Joyce: An Annotation of James Joyce's "Ulysses"* (New York: Dutton, 1974), p. 262.

2. Colin MacCabe, *James Joyce and the Revolution of the Word* (London: Macmillan, 1978), p. 159.

3. See Seamus Deane, "Joyce and Nationalism," in *Celtic Revivals: Essays in Modern Irish Literature* (London: Faber & Faber, 1985).

4. MacCabe, *James Joyce and the Revolution of the Word*, pp. 167–70.

5. Declan Kiberd, "Anglo-Irish Attitudes," in *Ireland's Field Day* (London: Hutchinson, 1985), p. 98.

6. Colin MacCabe, "The Voice of Esau: Stephen in the Library," in *James Joyce: New Perspectives*, ed. Colin MacCabe (Brighton; England: Harvester, 1982), p. 118.

7. Terry Eagleton, *The Ideology of the Aesthetic* (Oxford: Blackwell, 1990), p. 375.

8. Fredric Jameson, "Postmodernism and Consumer Society," in *The Anti-Aesthetic: Essays on Postmodern Culture*, ed. Hal Foster (Port Townsend, Wash.: Bay Press, 1983), p. 114.

9. J. C. C. Mays, "Some Comments on the Dublin of *Ulysses*," in *Ulysses: Cinquante ans après*, ed. Louis Bonnerot et al. (Paris: Didier, 1974), p. 86.

10. Franco Moretti, "The Spell of Indecision," in *Signs Taken for Wonders*, rev. ed. (London: Verso, 1983), p. 247.

11. Daniel Moshenberg, "The Capital Couple: Speculating on *Ulysses*," *James Joyce Quarterly* 25, no. 3 (1988), p. 333.

12. As Mary Lowe-Evans remarks, this is a reference to Soyer's Dublin soup kitchen which operated during the Famine of the 1840s. As she describes: "At the sound of a bell, one hundred of the destitute entered and, using chained soupspoons, consumed what was euphemistically called The Poor Man's Regenerator. As soon as the bowls and spoons had been swabbed and the bowls refilled, another hundred starving Irish men, women and children were ushered in. . . . After making a chemical analysis of the soup, the English medical journal the *Lancet* pronounced it worthless: 'This soup quackery (for it is no less) seems to be taken by the rich as a salve for their consciences'." M. Lowe-Evans, *Crimes against Fecundity: Joyce and Population Control* (Syracuse, N.Y.: University of Syracuse Press, 1989), p. 19. Here, as so often with Bloom's historical references, it is difficult to say whether one should congratulate him on his historical memory, or remark on its neutral vagueness.

13. Don Gifford, *Ulysses Annotated: Notes for James Joyce's "Ulysses,"* 2d ed. (Berkeley: University of California Press, 1988), p. 132.

14. Ibid., p. 133.

The Decomposing Form of Joyce's *Ulysses*

HENRY STATEN

◆ ◆ ◆

A T T H E E N D of "Calypso," Bloom defecates while reading
a story, a "prize titbit" in an old number of a journal called
Titbits (*U* 4.502); when he finishes his business, he tears away "half
the prize story" and wipes himself with it (*U* 4.537). I read this
moment as a witty and profound allegory of literature touching
reality. One might be tempted to think that the incident is merely
Joyce's little joke, a comment on the subliterary character of the
titbit in question, yet *Ulysses* is a text that freely allows the subliterary to circulate within it. And Bloom's reading of the story,
embedded in a scene of perhaps unprecedented novelistic realism,
touches off a reflection on mimetic truthfulness: "Life might be
so," Bloom thinks (*U* 4.511). In Bloom's toilet, both literary mimesis, in the form known as realism, and *Ulysses* itself are *mises en
abyme* in more ways than one.[1]

Yet realism is *abimé* only through a process that simultaneously
reconstitutes it in a way inconceivable by the laws of classical
representation.[2] In *Ulysses* realist mimesis is reconceived as the
isomorphism of two decompositional series, one involving lan-

guage and the other the body: the smearing of the logos with shit emblematizes the correspondence between these two series. It might be argued that this correspondence is illusory, since everything takes place in language—toilet, bowel movement, and all. But this objection would be as out of date as the metaphysics to which it replies, a substantialist metaphysics that asserts a simple correspondence between words and things. What is in question here is, rather, the movement of form making and of the dissolution of form that is the common matrix of text and body. In "Scylla and Charybdis" Stephen Dedalus declares the identity of this double movement in body and in text: "As we, or mother Dana, weave and unweave our bodies . . . from day to day, . . . so does the artist weave and unweave his image" (*U* 9.376–78). The analogy of the living body indicates that the artist's weaving and unweaving, unlike Penelope's, is not an alternation. What Stephen names is, rather, the simultaneity, if not the unity, of composition and decomposition; and *Ulysses* acts out this simultaneity.

At a certain point, however, the individual life ceases, and yet this process of "(de)composition" goes on (this is Bloom's vision in "Hades" [chap. 6]). The decomposition of the individual body and its incorporation into the transindividual organic cycle mark the limit of what the Western philosophical tradition can understand and assimilate and thus set off its most profound anxiety or hysteria, the anxiety of individualization. *This hysteria should not be repressed*—as it is, for instance, in the Heideggerian "confrontation" with death, which makes scorn for mere biology a fundamental principle of authenticity (Heidegger 290–93; Staten, *Eros*, 59). There is value in the hysterical insight that no ultimate distinction can be drawn between formlessness as degradation of the logos—even to the point of absolute loss of sense—and formlessness as the becoming-feces of the human body. *Ulysses* secures the isomorphism of these decompositional series at the level of this indistinction, as the ground of a profligate generation of new forms.

Is it still mimesis when what is enacted is the becoming-formless of form? What seems clear is that *Ulysses* achieves some of its most characteristic effects by pressing the internal logic of mimesis to the limit, above all through onomatopoeia, which manifests in a peculiarly condensed way the self-contradictory character of the realist project. Ideally, onomatopoeia should be the unmediated presentation of the form of the represented, but such a presentation would transcend the medium of language, without which onomatopoeia is impossible (see Attridge 156). Onomatopoeia is thus a figure for the abyss into which mimesis falls. Form in the sense of the repeatable identity of the thing—the Aristotelian definition that grounds classical mimesis—comes unglued from itself in the onomatopoeic project. And this ruin of form reverberates at every level of *Ulysses* as the undoing of all ontological security and the unleashing of the anxiety of individuation. How this anxiety, linked at one pole to onomatopoeia and the ruin of mimetic form, is linked at the other pole to the fear of infidelity is the substance of my argument.

I

Onomatopoeia occurs frequently in the text, especially in "Sirens" (chap. 11), which ends with the sound of Bloom farting, and it is given a metaphysical grounding in Bloom's and Stephen's animistic reflections on the speech of inanimate things: "Listen: a fourworded wavespeech: seesoo, hrss, rsseeiss, ooos," Stephen thinks as he watches the incoming tide (*U* 3.456–57). Similarly, Bloom, hearing the sound of machinery in the newspaper office, muses, "Sllt. Almost human the way it sllt to call attention. . . . Everything speaks in its own way. Sllt" (*U* 7.175–77).

Stephen and Bloom conceive their onomatopoeias as the pure self-expression or self-annunciation of reality. This notion of self-annunciation is suggested as well by Stephen's remark that he is here to "read" the "[s]ignatures of all things" (*U* 3.2), a signature being (at least notionally) the singular mark of a unique individual. The metaphor of reading evokes a more mediated relation to the thing than does that of hearing things speak, yet Stephen is reading the "signature" of the waves when he onomatopoeically represents "wavespeech." He thus conflates reading and hearing:

the signature of a thing, unlike that of a human being, would be, if it existed, not a conventional notation but the radiance or resonance of the thing's quiddity.

Even a human signature, however, though a form of writing operating within linguistic convention, lies at the boundary of the linguistic. Even the most legible human signature remains the token of a proper name, the name of a finite, contingent individual, who is not iterable as individual; thus even if the name or the signature is itself essentially iterable, it implies or evokes the presence, as its cause or origin, of an absolute singularity.

The illusion of this presence is created in large part by the isolation of the signature or onomatopoeia from the web of syntax and of the linguistic system of differences. Because this isolation corresponds to the singularity of the entity, the function of signature and onomatopoeia is analogous to that of the demonstrative adjective in Bertrand Russell's logical atomism. Russell in his atomist phase argued that words like *this* and *that*, uttered in the presence of the isolated particulars to which they refer at the moment of utterance, are the only true names "in the logical sense" (62–63). The encounter with the real here becomes the kind of madness satirized by Wittgenstein in his portrait of a philosopher who stares at an object and keeps repeating, "This! This!" (19).

The isolated signature, onomatopoeia, name, or demonstrative adjective suggests the encounter with the real by denying the mediating medium that nevertheless, as Derek Attridge shows (136–57), hovers in the background and makes the suggestion possible. From Plato on, philosophy and often literature have aimed to secure the direct impression of the entity on perception or cognition and to do so at least in part by suppressing the role of language. Jacques Derrida has argued that the Platonic *eidos*, "idea," is in its essence a *tupos*, "type," a model that can be impressed directly on the substance of the soul ("Plato's Pharmacy" 108–13). Aristotle, the philosopher who is repeatedly evoked in *Ulysses*, holds a doctrine of perception that is even more clearly a doctrine of the direct imprint.[3] Wherever there is knowledge of a thing, according to Aristotle, what is known is the *eidos*, "form," of the thing, which is detachable from the matter in which it is embodied. Perception and knowledge are not mediated relations to a thing that remains in itself inaccessible; they constitute the actual reception into the *psukhe*, "soul," of the thing's *eidos*. The conclusion Aristotle reaches in *On the Soul* concerning this analysis of knowledge, the statement that sums up his whole system, is a remark Stephen quotes several times: "the soul is the form of forms" (Aristotle 3.8).[4] In describing the process by which the soul is to be understood as the "form of forms," Aristotle deploys the "typographical" image used by Plato: "sense perception is that which is receptive of the forms of things without their matter, just in the same way as wax receives the impress of the seal without the iron or the gold of which it is composed" (Aristotle 2.12).

Onomatopoeia as Stephen and Bloom imagine it carries to the limit the ancient fantasy of the direct impress of the real on the psyche. Yet as *Ulysses* proceeds—notably, as Karen Lawrence has shown (*Odyssey* 61–62), from "Aeolus" (chap. 7) on—it undermines the illusory transparency of language, extravagantly calling attention to the textuality of its text. The onomatopoeic fantasy may thus appear to be presented merely as a sign of the nostalgia for presence that the work as a whole deconstructs. But mimesis in *Ulysses* is entangled with its deconstruction in complex ways. In "Aeolus" itself, the irruption of autonomous textuality goes hand in glove with the most striking mimetic effects; the chapter is, in Lawrence's words, a "whimsical pun of form and content" (*Odyssey* 58). Set in a newspaper office, the scene resounds with the movement of typographical machinery, and the section headings, suggestive of headlines, manifest the direct impress of "newspaperness" on the face of the literary text.

Both onomatopoeia and the "pun of form and content" of "Aeolus" are kinds of "imitative form."[5] Whereas literary mimesis predominantly exploits the semantic and referential functions of language, which call into play the arbitrary relations among signifier, signified, and referent, imitative form attempts to embody or mime what is represented—to carry something of the phenomenal form of the referent directly into the sensual substance of the linguistic medium, as onomatopoeia does at the level of sound or as the headlines of "Aeolus" do at the level of typography. What *Ulysses* as a whole imitates, however, is not any phenomenal form but rather its making and unmaking at the limit where imitative form becomes indiscernible from deconstruction.

In moving beyond the referential function of language to the level of imitative form, Joyce raises the philosophical as well as the literary stakes of his deconstruction. The pages of "Aeolus" are directly imprinted by the trope of the direct imprint, a philosophical trope fundamental to the concept of perception that underwrites the possibility of realist mimesis. The narration becomes the receptive substance or support of inscription, but it receives the form of the modern media, of advertising, sensationalism, rumor, misrepresentation—as in Bloom's request that the reporter add a name to the list of Dignam's mourners (*U* 6.882). Thus this scene at once mimes and satirizes the classical model of the soul as a medium for the direct inscription of reality, as the "form of forms."

Deeper than the possibility of misrepresentation, however, lies a principle of death belonging to the essence of the trope of the truthful imprint. The soul is in its inmost nature that which lives, pure spontaneity, a principle of vitality that must infuse itself into the mere materiality of the sense impression in general and of the letter in particular. But the impression of a type onto the vital substance is a mechanical action: at the moment of transmission, the soul must, if only for the most fleeting instant, abandon its spontaneity in submission to the rectitude of the impression. The typographical machinery of "Aeolus" functions as a hyperbolic image of this action of death, and thus figures a textual and linguistic machinery in which death, infidelity, and mechanical reproduction are inextricably linked.[6]

II

This linguistic machinery, which involves various reversals or "mirror transformations," is evoked most vividly in Bloom's reflections on the typesetter's skill: "Reads it backwards first. Quickly he does it . . . mangiD kcirtaP" (*U* 7. 205–6). The typographical imprint is here a proper name, but the antitype of a signature: the name is that of a dead man, and it has been reproduced mechanically, defaced by the application of a mechanical principle of reversal—a mirror transformation that enacts death as the operation of linguistic and technological mechanisms indifferent to the presence of a living consciousness that could sign its own name.

The principles of reversal and reversibility condense the signification of death in *Ulysses*. For instance, the series of associations set off in Bloom's mind by "mangiD kcirtaP" lead to his father's "backwards" reading of the Haggadah, which leads to the comment that "the angel of death kills the butcher and he kills the ox and the dog kills the cat. . . . Justice it means but it's everybody eating everyone else. That's what life is after all" (*U* 7.205, 212–14). Bloom understands the passage as signifying the pure transitivity of the eater-eaten relation, a phenomenon that would manifest itself at the grammatical level as the reversibility of subject and object. In this reciprocal devouring, everyone is both eater and eaten.

This reversibility of activity and passivity is in *Ulysses* not one grammatical transformation among others but the formal matrix of its mimesis. The transformation is introduced as formal play in "Aeolus" when for no apparent reason a sentence is repeated in its passive form: "Grossbooted draymen rolled barrels dullthudding . . . dullthudding barrels rolled by grossbooted draymen" (*U* 7.21–23). The mechanical indifference of this object-subject switch in surface grammar manifests the deep effacement in *Ulysses* of the action-suffering binary. This effacement comes to bear with a special force on certain determinate facts of human existence, on eating and death, as I have noted, and also on sex: "She kissed me. I was kissed" (*U* 8.915). "[Shakespeare] is bawd and cuckold. He acts and is acted on" (*U* 9.1021–22). And Bloom, who like Shakespeare is bawd and cuckold, is described as having a "firm full masculine feminine passive active hand" (*U* 17.289–90).

A "passive active hand," like a hand that writes, composing

and decomposing. In *Ulysses* the linguistic form of (de) composition continually entrains the biological, as in Cunningham's
"spellingbee conundrum," of which Bloom thinks: "It is amusing
to view the unpar one ar alleled embarra two ars is it? double ess
ment of a harassed pedlar while gauging au the symmetry with
a y of a peeled pear under a cemetery wall. Silly, isn't it? Cemetery
put in of course on account of the symmetry" (*U* 7.166–70). This
conundrum is generated by the quasi-phonemic character of English spelling, which only partly corresponds to the sound of the
spoken word. As in "mangiD kcirtaP," the alphabetic character of
the written language is in this passage foregrounded; words begin
to decompose into their consitutive units as individual letters
emerge into quasi autonomy. Yet this decompositional play is
contained within a compositional frame dominated by the action
of symmetry effects. The last sentence in the passage suggests that
cemetery is "put in . . . on account of" its symmetry with *symmetry*;
but *embarrassment* and *harassed* are also there "on account of the
symmetry" at the level of sound and alphabet. Such symmetry
is a major principle of the wordplay in *Ulysses*—for instance, Stephen's "Oomb, allwombing tomb" (*U* 3.402), where once again
word symmetry evokes a cemetery. The principle of wordplay, of
linguistic symmetry, magnetically draws *cemetery* into the text, and
once the word is in play, it becomes a nodal point that produces
textual effects.

The passage also has a sexual resonance, for the "under a wall"
motif, without the "cemetery," turns up in "Nausikaa," when
Bloom thinks, "Molly, lieutenant Mulvey that kissed her under
the Moorish wall beside the gardens" (*U* 13.889–90). In "Sirens,"
while Bloom is in the Ormond Bar, he thinks of "[s]ymmetry
under a cemetery wall" (*U* 11.833). And the association between
the cemetery and kissing is developed at length in "Hades":
"They'd kiss all right . . . love among the tombstones" (*U* 6.756–
59). Eating is suggested in the conundrum too, since the pear is
"peeled," ready to eat in the shadow of the cemetery wall; it is
this pear to which symmetry is attributed (though the symmetry
of the letter *y* intervenes in the conundrum).

The essential connection between the autonomization of the

alphabet and the fundamental reversal of eating / being eaten is illustrated in "Lestrygonians" in capital letters. The letters are *H,E,L,Y,* and *S,* which wander about Dublin like animated figures on the hats of the five "sandwichmen" (*U* 8.123). Once again it is a matter of a proper name (a family name, actually, which is "proper" in a sense that already involves the fraying of singularity) and of the defacing—in this case, by partial decomposition—of the name: Y (why *Y* again?) leaves his proper place because he happens to be hungry. "Y lagging behind drew a chunk of bread from under his foreboard, crammed it into his mouth and munched as he walked" (*U* 8.126–28). There is no explicit reference to the cemetery, but in *Ulysses* every time food or eating is mentioned, the cemetery is also there, because of "everybody eating everyone else." This phrase entails not only human beings eating one another, as in the cannibalism of the eucharist (*U* 5.352), but also the circulation of living beings in general through one another's digestive systems—for instance, that of the "obese grey rat" Bloom sees at the graveyard, for whom a dead human being is just "ordinary meat" (*U* 6.973, 981).

Y, who eats the bread, is himself a sandwich man, and Bloom leaves the butcher's shop lusting for the "[p]rime sausage" of the woman whose "hams" move in front of him (*U* 4.172, 179). Everyone in *Ulysses* is a sandwich man or woman, a sandwich person or wafer person, like Jesus, whose sacrament is ubiquitous in the novel. "This is my body," Jesus says in the Gospel of Luke when he declares himself food for the disciples, meat in the form of bread (22.19). Bloom uses the same words when he imagines the "flower" of his phallus floating in his bathwater (*U* 5.566, 572). In "Proteus," Stephen thinks of the drowned man's phallus as a "spongy titbit" to be eaten by the minnows flashing through the slits of the man's fly (*U* 3.477): this phallophagia prefigures the fellatio Molly imagines (*U* 18.1351–57). There is nothing phallocentric about this invocation of the phallus, for this phallus is ordinary meat, this letter utterly incapable of resisting division (Joyce's prescient reply to Lacan). The "spongy titbit" of the drowned man's penis echoes the "prize titbit" of the logos with which Bloom wipes himself. Flaccid or erect, passive or active, the phallus succumbs to the universal reversibility of the cycle of (de)composition that encompasses the text, a principle that I call "general gastronomics." Stephen's thoughts shift from the minnows nibbling the dead man's penis to this gastronomics: "God becomes man becomes fish becomes barnacle goose becomes featherbed mountain. Dead breaths I living breathe, tread dead dust, devour a urinous offal from all dead" (*U* 3.477–80).

III

Every aspect of organic life—especially sexuality—is comprehended in *Ulysses* as a moment or aspect of a general circulation whose primary figure is eating and the digestive process, "we stuffing food in one hole and out behind" (*U* 8.929), as Bloom says. The whole of *Ulysses* is the epiphany of general gastronomics, the sacramentalization of shit. Molly's imagined "lick my shit" (*U* 18.1531–32) to Bloom is the corollary or ring closure of the same circulation or gastrosexual communion involved in Bloom's taking the already partially digested seedcake from her mouth ("Softly she gave me in my mouth the seedcake warm and chewed. . . . Joy: I ate it: joy" [*U* 8.907–8]).[7] "Both ends meet," Bloom thinks in "Hades" (*U* 6.760). Yet if in these cases Molly is the priestly dispenser of communion food, she also imagines drinking something "like *gruel*" from Stephen's penis (*U* 18.1355, emphasis added). The female is neither more nor less bodily or "foodly" than the male in this general gastronomics: "I am the sacrificial butter," Stephen thinks in "Scylla and Charybdis" (*U* 9.64). Nevertheless, the Molly function must be situated in the general gastronomics of *Ulysses* so that its dialectical or deconstructive force may be felt in contrast to the idealizing tradition that still has a powerful grip on Stephen. Molly's gastrosexuality is abstractly the answer to his desire ("And my turn? When?" [*U* 9.261]), but concretely it may be his nightmare, since he is still mired in an ideology that confuses the corruptibility of the body with a moral and metaphysical taint linked to sexuality. In response to his ambivalent sexual need ("in my mind's darkness a sloth of the underworld"), Stephen's thoughts turn to Aristotle and to the "tranquil brightness" of the master formula "the soul is the form of forms," as though it could offer him shelter from "the sin of Paris" (*U* 2.72–73, 74, 75).

In a gesture that is culturally unimaginable in the West, *Ulysses* posits a beautiful heroine who is self-pleasuring, promiscuous, and full of corpse gas.[8] Stephen calls the drowned man a "[b]ag of corpse-gas sopping in foul brine" (*U* 3.476), and Molly's menstruating, urinating, farting body corresponds not to the motherly or fatherly archetypal sea in which the drowned man floats but to the drowned man's bloated, decomposing body. In the graveyard Bloom explicitly associates corpse gas with Molly's flatulence: "Molly gets swelled after cabbage. . . . [T]hey have to bore a hole in the coffins sometimes to let out the bad gas and burn it" (*U* 6.606–11). The "allwombing tomb" is thus also an anus, or has an anus, a hole through which noxious gases escape, and this equation or analogical relation is a reminder that digestion is a form of decomposition, the switch point through which *Ulysses* juggles its many figures. The stomach is a tomb in which dead beings decompose. These figures are all aspects of "that same multiplicit concordance" involving the "retrogressive metamorphosis" of "growth from birth" that Stephen contemplates in "Oxen of the Sun," a process by which the "ends and ultimates of all things accord . . . with their inceptions and originals" (*U* 14.389, 390, 387–89). In the context of a discussion of conception, gestation, and birth, Stephen's thought blends the "retrogressive" movement toward "minishing and ablation" (*U* 14.391) with the drive toward an Aristotelian end (*telos* or *entelecheia*).[9]

In the design of *Ulysses*, "Oxen of the Sun" is the antiphonal response or chiastic inversion of "Hades," where the predominant theme is death and decomposition. Gestation is invoked in "Oxen" as the composition of which putrefaction is the decomposition. Just as in "Hades" Mr. Power and Simon Dedalus, not knowing about Bloom's father, attack suicides as cowards, in "Oxen" Stephen, who does not know about Rudy, makes in Bloom's presence a ghoulish and immensely droll reference to newborns as "staggering bob," which, the narration informs us, "in the vile parlance of our lowerclass licensed victuallers signifies the cookable and eatable flesh of a calf newly dropped from its mother" (*U* 14.1292, 1298–99). As the narration reports, Stephen states

> that an omnivorous being which can masticate, deglute, digest and apparently pass through the ordinary channel with pluterperfect imperturbability such multifarious aliments as cancrenous females emaciated by parturition, corpulent professional gentlemen, not to speak of jaundiced politicians and chlorotic nuns might possibly find gastric relief in an innocent collation of staggering bob. (*U* 14.1286–92)

The identity of the "omnivorous being" is not clear; the most obvious candidate is the maggot ("your worm is your only emperor for diet," Hamlet says [4.3.21]), but there is also the obese grey rat in the graveyard; and of course human beings are omnivorous too, and some even like the taste of incipient decomposition ("there are people like things high," Bloom thinks in "Lestrygonians" [*U* 8.868]). Insofar as it evokes the progress of humanity through the guts of a maggot, the passage describes the microprocess of the digestive cycle, the moment of the most extreme inversion or introversion in the eater-eaten cycle. (Is there not, however, a profound pathos and even a sacramental resonance in the invocation of the innocence of the "innocent collation," a subtle echo of the baby Jesus and the eucharist as well as of Rudy Bloom?)

IV

In the gastronomics of *Ulysses* biological decomposition is formally enacted as textuality, and onomatopoeia, the figure of representational fullness, provides the opening for the movement of textual decomposition. In Stephen's and Bloom's thoughts, "slit" and "seesoo . . . ooos" appear as sounds, but in the text they appear, like "mangiD kcirtaP," as unconventional groupings of letters.

And as the English language resolves into unfamiliar and sometimes unpronounceable groups of letters (as in the "Mrkrgnao" of Bloom's cat [*U* 4.32]), the quasi-phonemic character of its alphabet is once again foregrounded.

In this way the entire problematic of mimesis is reconstituted at its most elemental level, for the alphabet is a conventional notation that attempts to represent the constitutive sounds of the language and is thus the proto-onomatopoeia. The ABC is the "typing" of the elements of sound out of which sense is constituted. And like ordinary onomatopoeia the alphabet is constituted, though more radically, through the decomposition of sense, for the significant sounds represented by letters exist "naturally" only as constituents of words and utterances, which represent higher levels of integration. When these higher levels of integration are analyzed into their irreducible constituents, what remains (in the form of letters) is the residue of meaningfulness, itself meaningless or the vanishing point of meaning.

Even though letters, being only markers of the linguistic system of differences, do not "naturally" function as isolated entities, they become available as individually manipulable units once the alphabetical analysis has been performed. And once letters are available, language can operate as a "combinatorium," producing the unities of word, utterance, and discourse simply by generating combinations of letters. Such a process is at work in the section of "Ithaca" (chap. 17) that records the anagrams Bloom once made with his name:

> Ellpodbomool
> Molldopeloob
> Bollopedoom
> Old Ollebo, M.P.
> (*U* 17.406–9)

Unlike "Mrkrgnao," these anagrams abide by the rules of syllable formation in English. Although mostly nonsensical, at times they point to an aleatory generation of meaning, as in "Moll dope." "Old Ollebo, M.P." suggests a possible alternative life for Bloom, one that would have involved a career in politics and a different name as well—but "Bloom" is not his "real" name anyway. "Old Ollebo, M.P." could be the germ of a narrative, since the next section of "Ithaca" might easily have developed the biography of this alternative Bloom ("What future careers had been possible for Bloom in the past . . . ?" the narration asks a little later [*U* 17.787]). Narrative, too, is a product of the generative formalism of language, of the principles of the alphabetic combinatorium.

The autonomization of the various machines of language is most clearly indicated by an analogy with mathematics. When Stephen and Bloom write out for each other some characters of the Irish and Hebrew alphabets, Bloom explains the "arithmetical values" of each of the Hebrew letters (*U* 17.739). Then mathematics is applied to speculative biography when Bloom is reduced by "cross multiplication of reverses of fortune" and "by elimination of all positive values" to a "negligible negative irrational unreal quality" in the "[n]adir of misery," a "moribund lunatic pauper" (*U* 17.1933, 1934, 1935, 1946, 1947). This is not real math, yet there is a structural analogy between the discursive and the mathematical mechanisms that, once set in motion, generate their consequences in a rigorous, inexorable, and arbitrary fashion— arbitrary in the sense that these consequences are not dictated by a preexisting reality. "Do anything you like with figures juggling," Bloom thinks in "Sirens" (*U* 11.832). The combination of mathematical inexorability with arbitrariness is visible in what is perhaps the most lunatic passage of "Ithaca," in which Stephen's and Bloom's future ages are calculated using the ratio between their ages in 1883: "when Stephen was 22 Bloom would be 374 and in 1920 when Stephen would be 38, as Bloom was then, Bloom would be 646," and so on (*U* 17.453–55).

If, however, mathematics exemplifies the autonomy of pure formalism, it is also, as philosophers since Pythagoras and Plato have stressed, the most reliable signification of the real, and Joyce in this chapter bombards the reader with numbers that measure, refer, and name. The purest formalism may be the most indifferent to the particularity of the real, but it captures the real in the net of an abstract universality.[10] As Hegel remarks, universality is the element even of "this!": "What we say is 'This,' i.e., the *universal* This. . . . Of course, we do not *envisage* the universal this . . . but we *utter* the universal" (60). The universal or form (*eidos*), which alone makes reference possible, is also the solvent of particularity. The automatisms of mathematics and language manifest the inhumanity of the ineluctable movement of universality, which at once makes and unmakes the form of the individual. The infinite expansiveness of the macrocosm and the infinite divisibility of the microcosm on which Bloom meditates (*U* 17. 1040–69) have as their corollary the infinitely recursive mechanisms of mathematical writing. Bloom knows of a number that would fill thirty-three thousand-page volumes, "the nucleus of the nebula of every digit of every series containing succinctly the potentiality of being raised to the utmost kinetic elaboration of any power of any of its powers" (*U* 17.1079–82). This infinite expansiveness poses a threat to the existence of the self-identical individual, even the whole set of such individuals. Thus immediately after the expansion beyond human limits of Bloom's and Stephen's future ages, the text evokes "the inauguration of a new era or calendar, the annihilation of the world and consequent extermination of the human species, inevitable but impredictable" (*U* 17.463–65).

Earlier I focused on the madness of particularity; "Ithaca" evokes the madness of universality as the vastness of the cosmos or the infinite expansibility of a recursive series. If the mechanisms of linguistic generativity are isomorphic with those of nature, this fact provides cold comfort. When Stephen leaves, Bloom feels "[t]he cold of interstellar space, thousands of degrees below freezing point or the absolute zero of Fahrenheit, Centigrade or Réaumur" (*U* 17.1246–47) and flees to the "human" warmth of Molly's body, with its "superior quality" of "(mature female) . . . calefaction" (*U* 17.2032, 2037–38). This desire for the warmth of a shared bed echoes a moment in "Hades": "Feel live warm beings near you. Let them sleep in their maggoty beds. They are not going to get me this innings. Warm beds: warm fullblooded life" (*U* 6.1003–5). In both passages a bed warmed by a human body is imagined as the antidote to an inhuman coldness: the coldness of space, of an infinite recursive series, or of the grave. In the end, however, the encounter with Molly's bed does not sustain this antithesis.

V

It should by now have been evident for some time why, when Bloom wipes his posterior with a page of fiction, it is no mere joke to suggest that what is staged is the meeting of language and reality. At the confluence of the two decompositional series designated by these terms, an effect is created that is not the reality effect but the reality *affect*. The reality affect is anxiety, the pervasive, overwhelming, boundless anxiety of individuation, of being a contingent particular. To be a contingent particular means that one might not have existed and will certainly cease to exist (a cessation that entails the decomposition of the body); it also means that one is a member of a species, therefore a term subject to a recursive operation that generates an indefinitely extensible series of terms. Because being the object of infidelity makes one feel so eminently contingent and replaceable, this circumstance sets off an anxiety of nonbeing that resonates with the pain of death.

Nevertheless, the real joke is on Blazes, not Bloom, because infidelity is a transcendental structure, belonging to the very nature of individuation as membership in a species. It is Blazes who is the unwitting dupe of Eros; Bloom, "[i]f he had smiled," would have smiled at the thought that "each one who enters imagines himself to be the first to enter whereas he is always the last term of a preceding series even if the first term of a succeeding one, ... neither first nor last nor only nor alone in a series originating in and repeated to infinity" (*U* 17.2126–31). The list of Molly's lovers, no longer taken literally by critics, makes a transcendental point. The joke of the infinite series, which also imports the most extreme anxiety as its obverse, does not concern how many men Molly has fucked, or even (such is its rigorous logic) Molly herself. The crux is the nonuniqueness of the individual, the force of the universal, of eros, the species drive as the annihilation of the contingent individual. The infidelity principle belongs to the essence of sexed being (whether hetero- or homosexual): it always already inhabits not only the sexual act but love itself, above all in its most rapturous or self-abandoned forms.

Bloom's potential smile is poised between comedy and tragedy, between two perspectives on the same phenomenon: the (comic) triumph of the species that is one with the (tragic) foundering of the individual. In Shakespeare the exemplary perspective on this phenomenon belongs to a cuckold; in Joyce this cuckold is the conscious agent of his own cuckolding, "bawd and cuckold," actor and acted upon. He might be a tragic actor-patient: "horn-mad Iago ceaselessly willing that the moor in him shall suffer" (*U*9.1024–25). Or he might take part in a manic sort of comedy:

BLOOM

(*his eyes wildly dilated, clasps himself*) Show! Hide! Show! Plough her! More! Shoot!

BELLA, ZOE, FLORRY, KITTY

Ho ho! Ha ha! Hee hee! (*U* 15.3814–18)

In either case, the cuckold represents the individual as the dispensable refuse of the species drive; but since everyone shares this fate, bawd-cuckoldry can be read as a representative and ultimately sacramental stance. Sacramentalization is the making manifest in an individual body of the action of "lifedeath" or universality, the action I call (de)composition, and the discovery in this action of the communion of all those beings that circulate through the intestines of universality. But just short of the erotic epiphany of general gastronomics, out of which being can both blaze and bloom, there is anxiety without limit.

Stephen's concern with Aristotle's doctrine of possibility manifests this anxiety. Stephen, whose ambivalence toward sex I have noted, is gripped by the fear, no doubt triggered by his mother's death, that he might have died in infancy, that he might have been aborted or even lost through contraception or masturbation before being conceived—"impossibilized," like all those other "Godpossibled souls that we nightly impossibilise," as he says in "Oxen" (*U* 14.225–26). The theme of "impossibilization" is first introduced in "Nestor" (chap. 2), when Stephen ponders the deaths of Pyrrhus and Caesar, meditating that these events have "ousted" all the "infinite possibilities" whose place they have taken. Then he wonders whether those other, unactualized possibilities were really possible, "seeing that they never were"—or whether that was "only possible which came to pass" (*U* 2.51, 50–51, 51–52, 52). Identifying with the feeble Sargent, Stephen then thinks of his own dead mother as having "saved him from being trampled underfoot" (*U* 2.46–47). At the beginning of "Proteus," he shuts his eyes to the "[i]neluctable modality of the visible," wondering if he can make it disappear, but concludes that his existence is not essential, for the world is "[t]here all the time without [him]: and ever shall be, world without end" (*U* 3.1, 27–28). Immediately after seeing the midwife Florence McCabe, he remembers that it was a midwife who "lugged" him "squealing into life" and speculates that it must be a "misbirth" that she carries in her bag (*U* 3.36, 37).

Stephen tries to reassure himself that his life was never subject to contingency: "From before the ages He willed me and now may not will me away or ever" (*U* 3.47–48). In "Scylla," where Stephen grapples with the question of his own existence and identity, he cites Aristotle's formula that "[n]ecessity is that in virtue of which it is impossible that one can be otherwise" (*U* 9.297–98). The phrase "form of forms" turns up once again to secure Stephen's self-identity: "Molecules all change. I am other I now. . . . But, I entelechy, form of forms, am I by memory because under ever-changing forms" (*U* 9.205–9). Yet he slides through the agency of the first-person pronoun back into the soup of alphabeticity:

> I that sinned and prayed and fasted.
> A child Conmee saved from pandies.
> I, I and I. I.

A. E. I. O. U.

(*U* 9.210–13)

The problem of the flux of matter in Stephen's body recurs in
a complex passage that ties the theme of the two
(de)compositional series to one of the preponderant concerns of
"Scylla"—the father-son relation:

> As we, or mother Dana, weave and unweave our bodies, Ste-
> phen said, from day to day, their molecules shuttled to and
> fro, so does the artist weave and unweave his image. And as
> the mole on my right breast is where it was when I was born,
> though all my body has been woven of new stuff time after
> time, so through the ghost of the unquiet father the image of
> the unliving son looks forth. (*U* 9.376–81)

Stephen draws an analogy between this mole and the introjected
or incorporated image of the "unliving son." The signifier *mole* is
a nodal point for a dense associative cluster in *Hamlet* (Lukacher
212–19). In Shakespeare's play Hamlet refers to his father as "old
mole" and in reference to himself speaks of "some vicious mole
of nature" (1.5.162, 1.4.24). Although Stephen invokes it as a principle of permanence across change, *mole* suggests a web of identifications (involving at least the pairs Shakespeare and Hamlet,
Hamlet and his father, Leopold and Rudy, Hamlet and Gertrude,
Stephen and Mrs. Dedalus) that carries along with it a tangle of
ambivalent feelings: mourning, guilt, and sexual anxiety.

Since Stephen identifies, in his anxiety over his own possible
impossibilization, with a dead son ("I am in his son" [*U* 9.390])
and Bloom is an "unquiet father" still mourning his own dead
son, one might suspect that Stephen and Bloom communicate
at the level of a common anxiety, anxiety over the fragility of
the son's existence—the impossibilization that has already overtaken one son (Rudy) and might as easily have overtaken another
(Stephen).[11] Bloom's grief for Rudy merges with his anxiety over
death and putrefaction, which drives him, lover of entrails, to

consider the attractions of vegetarianism (*U* 8.720–21), apparently
in the aftershock of his graveyard reflections on decomposition.
Stephen for his part is suffering from vitiation of his being as a
consequence of his mother's death, his penury, his humiliation
by Mulligan, and his sense of failed or at least unproven vocation.
He identifies with his shadow ("form of my form") but just as *I*
dissolves into the alphabet, this form dissolves into the cosmic
infinite, thus overflowing the boundaries of his individuated
("ended") being: "Why not endless till the furthest star?... I
throw this ended shadow from me, manshape ineluctable, call it
back. Endless, would it be mine form of my form?" (*U* 3.414, 412,
408–14).

An anxiety and a grief are inextricably bound together for both
Bloom and Stephen. For Bloom, unterminated mourning for the
child who never was, or never quite was, who existed just long
enough to acquire a proper name and to warrant a funeral, appears to dictate his interrupted coition with Molly.[12] Why not try
again when Molly thinks she might want to bear another child?
Perhaps Bloom is afraid of undergoing the same grief again, or
perhaps he is in the throes of some phobic reaction against the
emission of his substance into a woman's vagina.[13] In either case,
what he experiences is the great anxiety of individuation.

VI

Molly may be unfaithful (as, at least in spirit, is Bloom), but she
does not deceive. There is a tacit understanding between them.
That the thing is nevertheless massively traumatic for Bloom is
evidenced by his physical avoidance all day of Blazes and his mental recoil from the thought to which he keeps returning. The
psychopathia sexualis of "Circe" (chap. 15) makes explicit the massive
libidinal charge Molly's infidelity carries for Bloom, a charge that
shoots like electricity into the most tangled roots of his sexuality
and phantasmatically lights up its most "perverted" potentialities.
(I use "perverted" as shorthand even though *Ulysses* teaches that
what is today called perversion is merely the repressed portion of

sexuality.) At the deepest level sexual economy involves a series of (grammatical) reversals and active-passive transformations: male/female, sadism/masochism, pleasure/pain. In "Circe," Bloom has a vagina, wants to be punished, masturbates while he watches Molly coupling with Blazes.

The fantasia of Bloom's voyeurism and masturbation places onstage the event around which the entire novel is constructed. His physical and mental wanderings constitute an endless allusion to this event, which is not represented in its real, fictional presence. And from four o'clock on, the moment approaches of actual physical encounter with the scene and signs of the event's perpetration, as well as with the body of the (female) perpetrator. As the moment draws near, Bloom appears to think of the act in a direct way, applying to it the most uncompromisingly candid verb available. In a passage notable even in *Ulysses* for the circumspection of its periphrasis, Bloom reflects on

> the natural grammatical transition by inversion involving no alteration of sense of an aorist preterite proposition (parsed as masculine subject, monosyllabic onomatopoeic transitive verb with direct feminine object) from the active voice into its correlative aorist preterite proposition (parsed as feminine subject, auxiliary verb and quasimonosyllabic onomatopoeic past participle with complementary male agent) in the passive voice. (*U* 17.2217–23)

The proposition in question is evidently "He fucked her," with its passive "correlative": "She was fucked by him."[14] The unconfrontable fact is suggested in the most linguistically mediated way, and yet the verb *fuck* is evoked as onomatopoeic, thus as immediate linguistic representation of the unrepresented and unrepresentable. The event of infidelity is so vivid that it exceeds the grasp of cognition and escapes the realm of "this." Hence Bloom's inability, despite his use of the most explicit phrasing, to think about the fact head-on. He thinks instead about "the natural grammatical transition by inversion" of the "active" into the "passive" proposition.

Yet the extreme circumspection with which the crucial propositions are narrated blends the automatism of language (specifically of the active-passive transformation) with that of the body. If Bloom's abstractions indicate a continued evasion, this strategy fails, because the indifferent transformations of grammar portend the same fate for the individual as does the sexual-gastronomic cycle's transcendental law of infidelity. The mixture of grammatical form and imitative form is so tangled that one might be forgiven for coming away from this amazing passage with the confused impression that inversion naturally makes a fucking sound or even, thinking ahead to the position Bloom habitually occupies in Molly's bed, that grammatical inversion is symmetrical with the "perverted" positioning of sexual bodies.

VII

When Bloom arrives at his final resting place, his planetary motion at last arrested, he encounters a remarkable manifestation of imitative form: beside Molly is "the imprint of a human form, male, not his" (*U* 17.2124). Because no actual bed would register the readable imprint of a body identifiable by gender and distinguishable from that of its habitual occupant, this imprint must take shape in Bloom's soul. There is a deep philosophical satire here: the words "imprint of a form" cannot be merely casual coming from Joyce's pen, especially not in this book. Furthermore, in "Scylla," in the discussion of infidelity in Shakespeare, it is said that Shakespeare "makes Ulysses quote Aristotle" (*U* 9. 996)—a remark requiring only that one word be italicized to mean that the formulas of the Aristotelian ontology cited in *Ulysses* are motivated at a level of being other than that which Aristotle addresses. Shakespeare makes *Ulysses* quote Aristotle: the Shakespeare who is obsessed with his wife's infidelity. The imprint of a male form, not Bloom's, in Molly's bed signifies the intangible *not thing* itself, the thing called infidelity, improper essence, or essence of impropriety for the ethical-ontological schema *Ulysses* cites. But that schema is placed in a textual circulation it cannot dominate or even comprehend.

Everything that the metaphysics of form and of the proper cannot comprehend is summed up in the apparent affirmation with which the book ends, Molly's yes to Bloom when he proposed marriage.[15] In this remembered scene, Bloom's heart beats madly as Molly draws him into the erotic abyss of her breasts. Yet this scene of sexual rapture or erotic folly, *foudatz* in the troubadour sense,[16] rewrites another famous Joycean passage in which erotic rapture founders. When Bloom first pops the question, Molly does not answer, because she "was thinking of so many things he didn't know of" (*U* 18.582). At the conclusion of "The Dead," another husband, Gabriel Conroy, has his erotic excitement dashed by his wife's preoccupation with a past unknown to him; the revelation of Gretta's youthful, ill-starred romance hurls him into an agonized awareness of his nonuniqueness, his contingent place in a series (*D* 175–76). In *Ulysses*, Molly does not disillusion her lover by revealing her thoughts to him, but the reader knows what Bloom at that moment does not. Thinking of her first lover, Mulvey, the first man who kissed her "under the Moorish wall," Molly decides to say yes to Bloom because she thinks "well as well him as another" (*U* 18.1604–5). The ground of her affirmation is thus that very nonuniqueness or substitutability that constitutes the abyss of erotic anxiety. Not, of course, that just anybody will do but that there is always a set of possible erotic partners (for either the male or the female), that one is always subject to, and subject of, an eeny meeny miney moe among the members of a set. Erotic rapture is a fall into this same abyss of the decompositional combinatorium, only with a yes and a madly beating heart.

Molly's final lines bring together textual forces from elsewhere in *Ulysses*:

[Y]es and how he kissed me under the Moorish wall and I thought well as well him as another and then I asked him with my eyes to ask again . . . and yes I said yes I will Yes. (*U* 18.1603–9)

The *a, e, i* of the progression "wall . . . well . . . well . . . will" in these lines evoke Stephen's "A. E. I. O. U." in "Scylla." The Moorish wall under which Molly was kissed echoes the graveyard wall of Cunningham's conundrum and recalls the cemetery symmetry of poor, bare, forked Y, which becomes the *y* of Molly's reiterated yes. And "will," the key word of "Scylla" as Shakespeare's first name, suggests Mulligan's question, "Which will?" parsed by John Eglinton into the distinction between the will to live, ascribed to Shakespeare, and the will to die, ascribed to "poor Ann, Will's widow" (*U* 9.794, 795–96). At the end of "Penelope" this distinction no longer holds sway; Molly's yes entails both the will to die and the structural law of infidelity and in this is all the more affirmative of life.

Leopold, however, seems more ambivalent than Molly about the will to live-die. Yet when he sleeps with her, he instinctively draws near to her all-tombing, "allwombing" anus, traditionally the most privatized of the organs, though by nature (if "nature" means that which is most indigestible or nauseating to the logos) it is the Grand Central Station of life, the point at which decomposed life redisseminates itself, smears itself once more across the page.[17] Poldy doesn't say yes, but he doesn't say no. At the end of this epochal day, he continues to linger on the verge.

Notes

1. On anality and fecality in *Ulysses*, and in Joyce in general, see Anderson, Hart, and especially Anspaugh. Anspaugh's essay is an essential companion piece to mine; it treats a number of issues I do not have the space to address: feces as the abject in Kristeva's sense, the relation between feces and writing in the Shem portion of *Finnegans Wake*, and the relation of Joyce's "excremental vision" to Rabelais's and to Bakhtin's reading of Rabelais.

2. See the deconstructive problematization of mimesis laid out by van Boheemen (132–69). As she says, *Ulysses* "tries to rewrite the logos and to open it to what it must necessarily exclude" (163). However, I disagree with her judgment that in the end Joyce opts for a "wholeness" based on "an oral incorporative strategy" (184). For a more open-ended deconstructive approach to *Ulysses*, see McGee.

3. In Plato's *Theaetetus*, Socrates images the mind as a "block of wax"

on which it is possible to "imprint" (Plato uses the word *apotupousthai,* which can be translated as "transfer the type") perceptions or ideas "as [one] night stamp the impression of a seal ring" (191d). In the ensuing discussion, however, Socrates declares this model inadequate.

4. In this passage Aristotle distinguishes the rational faculty (glossed as "form of forms"), as the higher part of the soul, from sensation (glossed as "form of sensible objects"), as the lower part; but then Aristotle states that "the forms of the rational faculty are contained in the forms of sensible objects" ("en tois eidesi tois aisthetois ta noeta esti"). On Joyce's intense interest in—and study of—Aristotle's writings on mind and mimesis, see Aubert 83–99, 131–37.

5. Attridge speaks of "iconic" and "directly imitative devices" (136). "Iconic," however, seems inapt to describe an imitation of the process of decomposition, and "device" loses contact with the notion of form on which I focus; the old term *imitative form* thus seems best for my purpose.

6. See Ziarek's discussion of "the interrelation between mechanical reproduction and female sexuality" (269). Unlike Ziarek, I do not see infidelity in *Ulysses* as tied only to the female.

7. See Lawrence, "Legal Fiction," for a discussion of the sacramental character of the seedcake chewing.

8. On Molly's relation to her social-cultural context, see Pearce, *Molly Blooms.*

9. See the account of this discussion in Brown 63–78.

10. On form and the universal as a classical problem in philosophy, see Staten, *Wittgenstein,* 5–8.

11. Compare Rabaté's discussion of Bloom as Lacanian symbolic father.

12. My thoughts on Molly and Leopold's relationship owe much to McMichaels (172–94).

13. On this well-attested fear, widespread both in the history of Western culture and in anthropological accounts of non-Western cultures, see Herdt and Stoller 145, 81–83, 188–89.

14. Joyce calls the verb involved "quasimonosyllabic" because the "t" sound at the end extends the "fuck" monosyllable in a way that does not quite count as a second syllable.

15. See Derrida (*"Ulysses"*), who calls the yes in *Ulysses* "the transcendental condition of all performative dimensions" (62). See also Pearce's analysis of Fionnula Flanagan's dramatic reading of "Penelope." According to Pearce, Flanagan emphasizes the less enraptured dimensions of

Molly's use of the word: "Flanagan's Molly . . . ends in tears as she faces
the fact, yes, that she locked herself in 7 Eccles Street when she got
Bloom to say yes" ("Molly Bloom" 57).

16. On the troubadour *foudatz* see Staten, *Eros*, 77–91.

17. On the notion of the privatization of the anus, see Hocquenhem,
esp. 93–112. Hocquenhem remarks, with an intention different from but
not, I believe, unrelated to mine, that "the anus's group mode is an
annular one, a circle which is open to an infinity of directions and
possibilities for plugging in, with no set places" (111).

Works Cited

Anderson, Chester G. "On the Sublime and Its Anal-Urethral Sources
in Pope, Eliot, and Joyce." In *Essays in Honor of William York Tindall*.
Ed. Raymond J. Porter and James D. Brophy. New York: Iona College Press, 1972. 235–49.

Anspaugh, Kelly. "Powers of Ordure: James Joyce and the Excremental
Vision(s)." *Mosaic* 27, no. 1 (1994): 73–100.

Aristotle. *On the Soul*. Ed. and trans. W. S. Hett. Cambridge, Mass.: Harvard
University Press, 1964.

Attridge, Derek, *Peculiar Language: Literature as Difference from the Renaissance to
James Joyce*. Ithaca, N.Y.: Cornell University Press, 1988.

Aubert, Jacques. *The Aesthetics of James Joyce*. Baltimore, Md.: Johns Hopkins University Press, 1992.

Brown, Richard. *James Joyce and Sexuality*. Cambridge: Cambridge University
Press, 1985.

Derrida, Jacques, "Plato's Pharmacy." In *Dissemination*. Trans. Barbara Johnson. Chicago: University of Chicago Press, 1981. 61–171.

———. "*Ulysses* Gramophone." Amended trans. by Shari Benstock. In
Acts of Literature Ed. Derek Attridge. New York: Routledge, 1992. 253–
309.

Hart, Clive. "The Sexual Perversions of Leopold Bloom." In *"Ulysses":
Cinquante ans après*. Ed. Louis Bonnerot, with J. Aubert and C. Jaquet.
Paris: Didier, 1974. 131–36.

Hegel, G. W. F. *Phenomenology of Spirit*. Trans. A. V. Miller. Oxford: Oxford
University Press, 1979.

Heidegger, Martin. *Being and Time*. Trans. John Macquarrie and Edward
Robinson. Oxford: Blackwell, 1980.

Herdt, Gilbert, and Robert J. Stoller. *Intimate Communications*. New York:
Columbia University Press, 1990.

Hocquenhem. Guy. *Homosexual Desire.* Trans. Daniella Danghoor. Durham, N.C.: Duke University Press, 1993.

Lacan, Jacques. "Seminar on 'The Purloined Letter.' " Trans. Jeffrey Mehlman. *Yale French Studies* 48 (1972): 38–72.

Lawrence Karen. "Legal Fiction or Pulp Fiction in 'Lestrygonians.' " In *"Ulysses": En-gendered Perspectives* Ed. Kimberly J. Devlin and Marilyn Reizbaum. Columbia, S.C.: University of South Carolina Press, 1999.

———. *The Odyssey of Style in Joyce's "Ulysses."* Princeton, N.J.: Princeton University Press, 1981.

Lukacher, Ned. *Primal Scenes: Literature, Philosophy, Psychoanalysis.* Ithaca, N.Y.: Cornell University Press, 1986.

McGee, Patrick. *Paperspace: Style as Ideology in "Ulysses."* Lincoln: University of Nebraska Press, 1988.

McMichaels, James. *"Ulysses" and Justice.* Princeton, N.J.: Princeton University Press, 1991.

Pearce, Richard. "How Does Molly Bloom Look through the Male Gaze?" In Pearce, *Molly Blooms,* 40–60.

———, ed. *Molly Blooms: A Polylogue on "Penelope" and Cultural Studies.* Madison: University of Wisconsin Press, 1994.

Plato. *The Theaetetus.* Ed. Lewis Campbell. New York: Arno, 1973.

———. *Theaetetus.* Trans. F. M. Cornford. In *The Collected Dialogues of Plato.* Ed. Edith Hamilton and Huntington Cairns. New York: Pantheon, 1961. 845–919.

Rabaté, Jean-Michel. "Fathers, Dead or Alive, in *Ulysses.*" In *James Joyce's "Ulysses."* Ed. Harold Bloom. New York: Chelsea, 1987. 81–98.

Russell, Bertrand. *The Philosophy of Logical Atomism.* Ed. David Pears. La Salle, Ill.: Open Court, 1985.

Shakespeare, William. *Hamlet.* In *The Riverside Shakespear.* Ed. G. Blakemore Evans. Boston: Houghton, 1974. 1141–86.

Staten, Henry. *Eros in Mourning: Homer to Lacan.* Baltimore, Md.: Johns Hopkins University Press, 1994.

———. *Wittgenstein and Derrida.* Lincoln: University of Nebraska Press, 1984.

van Boheemen, Christine. *The Novel as Family Romance: Language Gender, and Authority from Fielding to Joyce.* Ithaca, N.Y.: Cornell University Press, 1987.

Wittgenstein, Ludwig. *Philosophical Investigations.* Trans. G. E. M. Anscombe, New York: Macmillan, 1958.

Ziarek, Ewa. "The Female Body, Technology, and Memory in 'Penelope.' " In Pearce, *Molly Blooms,* 264–84. [And above, 103–28.]

Against *Ulysses*

LEO BERSANI

❖ ❖ ❖

L ET US APPROACH *Ulysses* as naively as possible, while ad-
mitting that in the case of *Ulysses* this decision can hardly be
anything but a ruse. The ruseful naiveté I have in mind will
consist in our pretending not to have any extratextual information about the novel—in particular, information about Joyce's
elaborate scheme of Holmeric correspondences and about the geography and history of Ireland's capital city. In saying this, I of
course expose our naiveté as, precisely, a decision: it is only because we know how important Homer and Dublin are in *Ulysses*
that we can refer to a reading ignorant of that importance as
naive. I do not mean that it is natural to read any novel in a
state of cultural ignorance. I do, however, want to suggest that
it would not be naive to set about reading *La chartreuse de parme,*
War and Peace, and *Moby Dick* without, in the cases of Stendhal and
Tolstoy, more than a fairly general, nonspecialist's knowledge of
Napoleon's campaigns in Belgium and Russia, and, for Melville's
work, cetological expertise. This also means that the difficulties
of these novels cannot in any way be resolved by consulting

sources external to them. Our ideally uninformed reader of *Ulysses*, on the other hand, may very well be overcome with embarrassment to discover, when he opens his first work of criticism on the novel, that what he had been thinking of quite simply as chapters 8 and 10 are universally referred to as "Lestrygonians" and "Wandering Rocks," or that wholly impenetrable passages have in fact the most satisfying transparence to cognoscenti, say, of nineteenth-century records of Gaelic legends or of theater programs and journalistic *faits divers* in turn-of-the-century Dublin.

Naiveté, then—when it is not the sophisticated and artificial luxury which I propose we briefly enjoy—perhaps inevitably becomes a retroactive judgment: how could I have read *Ulysses* without at least trying strenuously to exploit the cue provided by the novel's title, and—what is even more humiliating—how could I have mistaken cryptic or truncated allusions to the minutiae of Dublin life around 1900 for passages of textual ambiguity or complexity? The title itself, in addition to furnishing an important clue, was after all also a clear warning against the perils of innocence: the Latinized version of Odysseus obliquely alludes to one of literature's most resourceful and wily heroes, and—as if that were not enough—Buck Mulligan draws our attention on the novel's very first page to Stephen Dedalus's "absurd name, an ancient Greek" (*U* 1.34), the name, that is, of the cunning artificer who both constructed and escaped from Minos's labyrinth.

In short, we have only to glance at the title and read page one of *Ulysses* to be forewarned: trickery, cunning, and ruse are the novel's first connotations, and the possibility is thus raised from the very start that those qualities not only belong to certain characters within the novel but, much more significantly, that they define an authorial strategy. And in that case naiveté is tantamount to walking into a trap. We would therefore do well to take trickery, cunning, and ruse as hortative and not merely psychologically predictive connotations: they propose the ideal reader response for *Ulysses* as one of extreme—of extremely nervous, perhaps even somewhat paranoid—vigilance.

The tensest vigilance will, however, allow us safely to approach *Ulysses* with what may at first have seemed like a dangerous naiveté. For we may now go on to suspect that the connotative cluster of trickery may itself be part of a superior trickery. Might it after all be possible that Joyce wastes no time in encouraging us to find the novel more complicated, more devious, than it actually is, and that a comparatively simple and uninformed reading may not be that inappropriate after all? An intentionally *or* unintentionally naive reading of *Ulysses* can perhaps reveal things about the novel which our inevitable loss of readerly innocence will obscure. Since my emphasis will be mainly on the nature and consequences of the ideally informed reading of *Ulysses*, we should begin by doing justice to the insights of ignorance, the interpretive gains to be had from the naive assumption that *Ulysses* can be read as if it were a nineteenth-century realistic novel.

In fact, those gains are far from negligible. If we were unaware of the avant-gardist claims made for Joyce's novel, we would, I think, have little hesitation in speaking of it as a psychological work, as a novel of character. We might of course be bothered by what old-fashioned critical discourse would call—indeed, has called—a disproportion between the technical machinery and the psychological or "human" content, machinery which frequently obscures our view of what is happening. For it is undeniable that a certain type of story—or rather, a story *tout court*—has awakened in us certain desires by which the second half of the novel seems embarrassed and to which the most chic contemporary critics of Joyce implicitly claim to be immune. *Ulysses* is an exceptionally detailed study of character—especially of the character of Leopold Bloom, but also of Stephen Dedalus, Molly Bloom, and even of Gerty MacDowell, who appears in only one episode. We know these characters inside out, and both from the inside and from the outside. There is plenty of evidence of how they look to others, and long sections of internal monologue and free indirect style make us more than familiar with their most intimate habits of mind. There is even an entire episode—"Eumaeus"—written in the manner of Bloom, that is, in the style he would presumably use were he to try his hand at writing (a possibility he himself raises to himself in this very chapter). Since the style of "Eumaeus" also suggests—not unpainfully—why Bloom will always prefer talking to writing, the episode can be considered as still another and quite novel characterizing technique: this very late section (it is episode 16) lets the reader know the character even more intimately than before by temporarily turning the narrator into the dummy-double of a ventriloquistic Bloom.

Has any fictional character ever been so completely known? Warm-hearted, commonsensical, and appealingly unfanatic in politics and religion; a loving son, father, and even husband, full of enterprising (if unrealized and impractical) commercial schemes; slightly but not unappealingly pretentious intellectually; horny and a bit guilty sexually; garrulous but a stylistic outsider in a city of besotted skilled rhetoricians; perhaps a bit tight by Dublin pub standards (where the one unpardonable sin is failing to pay one's round); something of a loner (but by no means a rebel or an outcast) with his daydreams of travel in exotic Eastern lands—Bloom is eminently appealing and eminently ordinary. In one of the exchanges which constitute the impersonal catechism of "Ithaca," Bloom is called "Everyman or Noman." Perhaps. In any case he is a sweet man, and if Joyce has inspired a kind of attachment and anecdotal curiosity (about him, about the streets of Dublin) curiously evocative of that affection for Jane Austen which was for so long an obstacle to her being thought of as a serious and important writer, it is largely due to his success in creating Bloom. The Joyceans are quite a bit raunchier than the "Janeites," but the extraordinarily prosperous Joyce industry (with organized visits to the holy spots in Dublin and Zurich) depends in large part, as in the case of Austen, on the by no means unfounded or inconsiderable pleasure of recognition. The Blooms are an identifiable couple, and it is an extraordinary tribute to Joyce's power of realistic evocation that all the fancy narrative techniques of *Ulysses* are unable to smother or even dim the vivid presence of Poldy and Molly. For hordes of aficionados, June sixteen will always be celebrated as Bloomsday, and it would be not only snobbish but critically wrong to suggest that the innovative power of Joyce's novel lies in a questioning or breakdown of traditional novelistic assumptions about personality.

THERE ARE, HOWEVER, from the very beginning, certain knots, or certain gnats, in the narrative which disturb our relaxed reading and easy appreciation of *Ulysses'* fairly rounded characters. Much of the novel's difficulty, especially in the early sections, is the result not of our having to learn to think about novelistic names (such as Stephen Dedalus and Leopold Bloom) in nonpsychological terms, but rather of the uncompromising nature of the mimetic techniques. An "accurate" rendering of a character's consciousness presumably requires that the narrator do nothing to help us understand or follow the moves of that consciousness. Confronted with characters at once vivid and obscure, the reader may be inspired to take on the exegetical task of reducing the obscurity, of getting to know Bloom, Molly, or Stephen even better by completing their sentences and explaining their allusions. Far from destroying a mimetic effect which may seem to depend on a certain degree of maintained obscurity in the recorded consciousness, exegesis in this case is itself a secondary mimetic technique: a certain type of textual research is experienced as an investigation into real lives. Thus we are required to complete the portraits of Bloom and of Stephen, an activity which includes but which is very little threatened by the perception of their absorption into a variety of alien styles and nonrepresentational techniques. Indeed, in Joycean criticism the most sophisticated technical analysis comfortably cohabits with the most naive reading. John Paul Riquelme's intelligent and thorough study of mimetically disruptive techniques in *Ulysses* apparently intensified his affection for Bloom. In the midst of the most trenchant, no-nonsense type of point-of-view analyses, Riquelme frequently praises Bloom as a man who avoids extremes, one who "perceives what Boylan is blind to: a basis for human action in concern for others rather than primarily in self-interest."[1] Is there no relation between elaborate analyses of *Ulysses* as pure linguistic effects and a type of psychological and moral appreciation already made obsolete by the New Criticism of half a century ago? My point is, of course, that the relation is only too clear, and that Joyce's avant-gardism largely consists in his forcing his readers to complete the rearguard action which the novel itself simultaneously performs and elaborately disguises.

Filling in the blanks of consciousness is, however, only part of the game, although none of the more sophisticated moves into which Joyce maneuvers us will seriously undermine the traditional view of human identity which *Ulysses* implicitly defends. The novel is full of what has rather curiously been called stylistic intrusions, as if literature were ever anything but just that. Most frequently, these "intrusions" take the form of discontinuities or inconsistencies in point of view. I have in mind passages in which Bloom abruptly begins to think with stylistic resources obviously not his, as well as those other moments when, as Hugh Kenner puts it, "The normally neutral narrative vocabulary [is pervaded by] a little cloud of idioms which a character might use if he were managing the narrative,"[2] or, finally, when different characters' points of view are briefly merged. The celebrated perspectival jolts and mergers of *Ulysses* include the paragraph in "Nausikaa" that abandons Bloom's limited angle of vision and takes us on a panoramic tour of the entire Howth neighborhood, the name distortions in "Scylla and Charybdis" (which may be Stephen's mental horseplay with his companions' names or the fooling around of a lexically ebullient narrator), and, in "Sirens," the subtle invasion of Bloom's consciousness by the "musicalizing" tics of the dominant narrative style (alliterations, verbal echoes, staccato rhythms).

All of this has quite appropriately made of Joyce one of the darlings of that branch of narratology obsessed with narrative origins, with determining where narrators are located, over whose shoulder they may be speaking, from what temporal perspective and in whose voice they address us. In its more ambitious manifestations, this school of literary analysis moves from particular literary works to the drawing up of a master plan of possible narrative points of view—a model which can of course then serve in future readings. With a writer as perspectivally shifty as Joyce, we can easily imagine how handy, and how comforting, such pocket codes of narrative perspective can be. Now he's there and now he's not; point-of-view analysis is the literary-criticism version of hide-and-seek. It is the paranoid response to what might be called the ontological irreducibility of voice in literature to locations and identities.

Joyce both provokes and soothes our critical paranoia (he provides it with exorcising exercises); the difficulty, or even impossibility, of attribution in *Ulysses* is almost always a local affair, one which takes place against a background of firmly identified and differentiated personalities. Since, for example, we could no more confuse Bloom's voice with Stephen's than we could mistake Gibbon's style for Malory's in the pastiches of "Oxen of the Sun," the intrusions, confusions, and discontinuities of point of view in *Ulysses* must, I think, be read as an important element in the strategic centering of the narrator's authority. That is, they should be read as part of his aggressively demonstrated superiority to the patterns and models of representation which he insists that we recognize and analytically elaborate while he himself partially neglects them.

I do not mean by this that the perspectival agitations of *Ulysses* are insignificant. The question of point of view is essentially a question of citation: whose voice is the narrative quoting? And citation is crucial to the intra- and intertextual authority of Joyce's novel as a masterwork. Indeed, Joyce's occasionally grand indifference to consistency of point of view should perhaps be read as a way to redirect our attention from the comparatively trivial quotations of consciousness to what I will call the quotation of essential being. And in this he brings to the mimetic tradition in literature what may be its most refined technique. Consider the first sentence of *Ulysses*: "Stately, plump Buck Mulligan came from the stairhead, bearing a bowl of lather on which a mirror and a razor lay crossed" (*U* 1.1–2). "Bearing" instead of "carrying" is part of the "novelese" characteristic, as Kenner reminds us, of the first episode;[3] both it and the two adjectives used to describe Buck also reflect his particular rhetorical pomposity. But it is not exactly as if Buck had written that sentence; nor do we have an otherwise "neutral" narrative vocabulary pervaded by "a little cloud of idioms which a character might use if he were managing the narrative."[4] Rather, Buck's verbal mannerisms are a necessary part of a *wholly objective* presentation of him. "Plump" somewhat deflates "stately"; it helps us to visualize the character in a way which does not exactly support the vaguer connotations of "stately." The sentence is at once seduced by Mulligan's rhetoric and coolly observant of his person. I do not mean that Buck would have been incapable of writing that sentence (which is a rather silly issue for criticism to address at any rate), but in writing it he would already, so to speak, have stepped out of himself; he would have performed himself with irony. And we could say that a complete or objective view of Buck can be given neither by a direct quote nor by an analytical description, but only by a self-performance at a certain distance from the performing self. In other terms, the sentence objectifies the point of view which it takes.

It is, so to speak, this nonperspectival point of view which explains the peculiar and disturbing power of *Dubliners*, where Joyce characterizes not only individuals but also a kind of collective consciousness through such objectified subjectivity. This impressive achievement should, I think, be considered in the light of Stephen's definition of beauty in *A Portrait of the Artist as a Young Man*, as well as his references, in *Ulysses*, to Aristotle's notion of entelechy and the "form of forms." In trying to understand what St. Thomas means by "radiance" (or *claritas*) in his enumeration of the "three things needed for beauty" (*integritas, consonantia, claritas*), Stephen comes to the following solution: "The radiance of which he speaks is the scholastic *quidditas*, the whatness of a thing" (*P* 79). It is as if literature could quote being independently of any particular being's point of view. We would, that is, have the point of view of neither a narrator nor a character; rather, we would have the *quidditas* of Buck Mulligan, and even of Dublin. The individual's or the city's point of view has been purified or raised to their essence, to a "whatness" ontologically distinct from the phenomenality of having a point of view.

The somewhat comical side of this "realization" of Aquinas in some narrative techniques of realist fiction are evident in the following sentence from "The Boarding House," which describes Protestant Dubliners going to church on "a bright Sunday morn-

ing of early summer": "The belfry of George's church sent out
constant peals and worshippers, singly or in groups, traversed the
little circus before the church, revealing their purpose by their
self-contained demeanour no less than by the little volumes in
their gloved hands" (*D* 47–48). An essence of Dublin churchgoing
receives expression here not as a result of either a dramatic or
an analytic approach; instead, the most scrupulously impersonal
description manages to raise the object of description to a kind
of objectifyingly ironic self-description. The very neatness of that
sentence, with its elegantly controlled but somewhat fancified
syntax and its concluding succession of nouns each with a single
modifier ("self-contained demeanor," "little volumes," "gloved
hands") actually speaks the activity itself as a somewhat trivial
manifestation of the human taste for ritualized order. But the
language also demystifies the very idea of an essentialized self-
expression by allowing us to *locate* its transcendental, its nonperspectival point of view. If Dublin speaks itself in *Dubliners*, the
essentializing voice itself cannot escape having a social and psychological identity. The pitiless *quidditas* of realist fiction allows for
the dephenomenalizing of character only as a phenomenon of
point of view. Who can "repeat" Dublin with particular "radiance"
without, however, being able to take *another* point of view (and
another point of view would, precisely, however superior it might
be, destroy the essentializing repetitions)—who, if not an educated Dubliner, or Dublin schoolteacher, for example, one who,
like Stephen in the "Nestor" episode of *Ulysses*, fully assumes the
continuity between his dull-witted student and himself, thereby
perhaps plotting his escape from Dublin through his articulated
recognition of his own Dublin-ness in art? The schoolteacher can
speak only Dublinese (unless—and this is of course the difference
between *Dubliners* and *Ulysses*—he borrows voices from other
places): we can hear, in the second half of our sentence from
"The Boarding House," those adeptly poised rhythmical designs,
so receptive to hyperbole ("revealing their purpose by . . . no less
than by") which, in *Ulysses*, animate the endless recitation of local
news in public meeting places. The *quidditas* of a Dublin church
group is, then, itself a kind of secondary or occasional form within

the superior, more general form of Dublin-ness. *Quidditas* here is manifested most profoundly as a kind of respiratory pattern in language, a pattern which then has the potential, associated by Aristotle with entelechy, to engender actualities (fictional characters and events) of the same kind, which repeat it. In Joyce, the Schoolman is reformulated as the schoolteacher; an educated but inescapable provincialism is the social precondition of an art content to give *claritas* to the artist's inherited consciousness.

CLARITAS IS AN EFFECT OF quotation, although, as I have been suggesting, the quote is at the ontological level of essence and not of existence. Of course in *Ulysses* Joyce does not merely cite Dublin; the novel is an encyclopedia of citational references. And this means that in *Ulysses* voices are always on loan. Several critics have noted the absence of what we would call a personal style in Joyce. Stephen Heath, writing—for the most part brilliantly— as a representative of poststructuralist (and mainly French) readings of Joyce, notes: "In place of style we have plagiarism," and then goes on, as might be expected in a critical essay printed in *Tel Quel* in 1972, to speak of Joyce's writing as "ceaselessly pushing the *signified* back into the *signifier* in order to refind at every moment the drama of language, its production."[5] I will not linger over the always satisfying spectacle of a professor praising plagiarism (high-class plagiarism, it is true); the notion of a plagiaristic wandering among signifiers—of the writer as a kind of open switchboard picking up voices from all over—does, however, deserve more attention. For it raises a question of major interest to us: that of the authority, possibly even mastery, of literature over the materials which it incorporates. The incorporating process is perhaps most visible in the encyclopedic novel, which tends toward a massive, ideally total, absorption of the real into a novelistic structure. And yet among encyclopedic novels there are significant differences in the ways in which this general project is carried out. At one extreme the citation can be presented as a redemptive substitute for its source; at the other the mode of encyclopedic quotation can suggest the irrelevance of literature to what might be called the work of civilization, to its technological, scientific, even philosophical development. These alternatives, and their importance for *Ulysses*, will be clearer if we put Joyce's novel alongside Flaubert's *Bouvard et Pécuchet*, another encyclopedic novel which also appears to indulge in massive quotation. . . .

In *Bouvard et Pécuchet* Flaubert makes a perhaps unexpectedly modest claim for the authority of art. *Bouvard et Pécuchet* does not imply—as *Ulysses* does—that its own performance can redemptively replace all the culture which it seeks to incorporate. At the price of a certain indifference to the beneficial effects of thought's mastery over nature (as well as over its own nature), art cultivates a deliberately fragmentary, unusable, even ignorant relational play with the entries of its culture's encyclopedia. . . . In *Bouvard et Pécuchet*, style caresses an encyclopedic culture out of its projects of mastery, into a liberalizing impotence.

In *Ulysses*, Joyce implicitly makes very different claims for art, claims mediated through the novel's encyclopedic intertextuality. The intertextuality of *Bouvard et Pécuchet* is highly deceptive: the textual act of quotation is, as I have suggested, simultaneously a disqualification of the citational process. Flaubert erases our cultural memory at the very moment he awakens it. The mutations of epistemological discourses in *Bouvard et Pécuchet* plunge the novel into a kind of ontological isolation, removing it from the cultural history which it nonconnectedly absorbs. Nor does the work's intratextuality create connective designs or structures; each section repeats a process of solipsistic play which cuts it off from the other sections echoed in that repetition. Finally, not only does the work of art *know nothing*, but in its incommensurability with all cultural discourses of knowledge, it can only exist in a state of continuous anxiety about its capacity to sustain itself, perhaps even to begin itself.

For Joyce, on the other hand, art is by definition the transcendence of any such anxiety. *Ulysses* is often hard to read, but, more than any other work of literature, it is also a guidebook to how it should be read. Actually, a guidebook was issued before the novel was published. Partly for reasons beyond Joyce's control (the delay of more than ten years between the publication of

Ulysses in Paris and its appearance in England and America) and partly because Joyce wanted it that way (he sent the first known schema for *Ulysses* to Carlo Linati in September 1920, more than a year before Shakespeare and Co. published the book, and a second schema to Valéry Larbaud in late 1921), *Ulysses* was an object not only of discussion but also of interpretation long before its major audiences had access to the complete text. Thousands of readers thus had lessons in reading before they had anything to read. In itself, this is sufficient evidence of this great modernist text's need for the reader, of its dependence on a community of comprehension. If the modernist artist refuses to make his work accessible to a mass audience, he is nevertheless, as Richard Poirier has argued, far from indifferent to being read and understood.[6] Joyce, like Eliot in his notes for *The Waste Land*, helps us on the road to all those recognitions and identifications necessary for the "right" reading of *Ulysses:* recognitions of the elaborate network of repetitions within the novel, identifications of all the other cultural styles and artifacts alluded to or imitated.

There is in *Ulysses* an intratextuality meant to guide us in our intertextual investigations, to teach us how to leave the novel and, above all, how to return to it in our exegeses. This training is given in a series of graduated lessons, ranging from single-word repetitions to structural analogies between entire episodes. As we read, and reread, more and more circuits are lighted up; the movement forward, from episode to episode, is simultaneously a spatialization of the text, which is transformed into a kind of electrical board with innumerable points of light connected to one another and having elaborate, crisscrossing patterns. "Circe" condenses the activity of textual remembrance ceaselessly taking place throughout the novel. *Ulysses* is itself the hallucinating subject of "Circe"; the episode is the book dreaming itself even before it is finished, with anticipatory echoes of things yet to come. To a certain extent, it is even Joyce's oeuvre both calling up moments from its past and, in certain wordplays, announcing the verbal textures of *Finnegans Wake*. Reading "Circe" also allows us to check our textual memory, to be tested on how well we have read, to find out to what extent *Ulysses* has occupied our mind. Even more: it is a model dream for the ideally occupied, or possessed, reader of *Ulysses*. "Circe" implicitly defines an absolute limit of readerly absorption. Not only would Joyce's work provide all the terms of our critical activity, but it would also be the inexhaustible material of our dreams, in Freudian terms both the daytime residue and the unconscious drives. Before *Finnegans Wake*, Joyce already projects in *Ulysses* the literary textualization of the entire mind, of our day consciousness and our night consciousness. In so doing, he unwittingly exposes what may be the secret project behind all talk of the mind or of the world as text: the successful positing of the Book—or, more accurately, of books, that is, of a certain type of *professional* activity—as the ontological ground of history and of desire.

The "drives" of the Book are, however, drives without affects. "Circe" hallucinates the unconscious as wordplay. The unconscious, it is true, never is anything but wordplay in literature, and while this should probably be taken as the sign of an incommensurability between mental life and the instruments of literary expression, it has recently authorized interpretations of the unconscious as a structure "in some way" analogous to that of language. Thus a sublimating bookishness domesticates the unconscious, enacting the very repudiations which it purports to analyze as linguistic effects. The violations of logic and linearity, the displacements and the condensations of discourse in which we are inclined to read the operations of unconscious processes are themselves constitutive of the vast sublimating structure of human language. That structure—perhaps thought itself, as Freud suggested—may have evolved as the result of a primary displacement of a wish—a displacement from the untranslatable terms of a drive to so-called linguistic metaphors of desire, metaphors which "express" drives only on the ground of their self-constitutive negation of drives.

"Circe" is Joyce's most explicit and, we might say, most Flaubertian insistence on the nonreferential finality of the signifier in literature. To a certain extent it counters the mimetic effects which I began by emphasizing. It is the episode which most openly invites a psychoanalytic interpretation, at the same time that it compels us to acknowledge impenetrable resistance to any such interpretation. As part of a book's hallucinatory play with its own elements, Bloom's presumed masochism, for example, can only be a joke. Bloom's psychology is elaborated in "Circe"— given the dimension of unconscious drives—as it is nowhere else in *Ulysses*, but the elaboration is a farce, and the suggestion is that in writing, psychology can never be anything but farce. A desire with nothing more than a textual past has the lightness and the unconstrained mobility of farce. In "Circe," Joyce exuberantly stages masochism with wild inventiveness, as if to insist on the profound difference between two kinds of masochism: the mysterious and monotonous repetition of a painful pleasure, which Freud obscurely posits as the essence of human sexuality in *Three Essays on the Theory of Sexuality*, and masochism as an occasion for extravagantly varied scenic effects. In "Circe" the book "dreams" masochism without pain (or with an inconsequential pain, one that can be erased from one page to the next), and in so doing it appears to leave behind it not only the "burnt up field" of *Ulysses'* own mimetic seriousness, but also the devastated terrain of a more general cultural discourse. (In a letter to Harriet Shaw Weaver, Joyce spoke of the *scorching* effect of his writing: "each specific episode, dealing with some province of artistic culture . . . , leaves behind it a burnt up field" [*LI*, 129].) Toward the other texts which it quotes in various ways—especially Sacher-Masoch's *Venus in Furs*, Krafft-Ebing's *Psychopathia Sexualis*, and Flaubert's *Tentation de St. Antoine*, all textual elaborations of the "perverse" in human conduct—"Circe" engages in an extremely intricate operation of what we might call a resublimating desublimation. In his farcical treatment of other cultural discourses, Joyce could be understood as proposing, first of all, that the claim to truth of any cultural artifact is its primary mystification. The farcical here operates as the sign of a desublimated discourse—although it is not the sexual in this case which is revealed as the referent of an allegedly higher discourse. On the contrary: the works which "Circe" quotes claim in different ways to analyze or to represent sexual drives, but, Joyce suggests, the reality which those claims disguise is nothing more than the arbitrary play and productiveness of the signifier. The virtuosity of desire *as* linguistic effects is, I think, meant to lead us to conclude that language cannot represent desire.

This, however, does not necessarily diminish the authority of literary language. We will have to look more closely at the re-sublimating aspect of the operation I have just referred to. Let's begin by noting that the frequently marvelous comedy of "Circe" is much more ambiguous—I might even say suspect—than I have suggested so far. First of all, there is in Joyce, from *Stephen Hero* to *Ulysses*, a scrupulously serious use of techniques obviously meant to represent characters realistically, as well as the culti-vation of a remarkable perspectival strategy which suggests, as we have seen, that we have the essence of a character independently of his or her point of view. Not only does Joyce work within formal conventions which we inescapably associate with a refer-ential bias in fiction; his departure from more or less familiar techniques of novelistic "reporting" actually reinforces the illu-sion of referentiality. The quotation of characters in their essential being, while it violates a certain literalism in realistic point of view, actually suggests that characters exist outside their novelistic appearances. The narrator quotes them at a level of reality which they are themselves incapable of representing, and this means that the narrative frequently refers to, say, a Bloom or a Mulligan more real than the Bloom or the Mulligan whom it allows us to see and to hear. Thus the reduction of Bloom's depths to verbal farce in "Circe" is countered by the very passages to which "Circe" refers us. The novel has already committed itself to illusions of truth, that is, to a belief in novelistic language as epistemologically trustworthy, as almost nonproblematically capable of recreating the density of human experience, of referring to or carrying more than its own relational play.

Furthermore, if Joyce somewhat fitfully and ambivalently makes the points I have associated principally with "Circe," they are not exactly new points. In different ways, the works of Flau-bert and of Henry James already make the case for knowledge as a matter of style, and for the self as a play of the signifier. What is original in Joyce is the use to which he puts this awareness.

James's *The Europeans*—and I realize the bizarreness of the comparison—could be read in terms not too different from those I have used for "Circe." The farce of "Circe" is a function of the melodramatic associations it evokes. Just at the point when Bloom is to be characterized in depth, he disappears as a self, and a cultural discourse on the perverse in human nature is comically replayed devoid of a referent, as part of the more general comedy of entertaining but epistemologically insignificant mutations in, precisely, the history of cultural discourse. And, at least in the immediate context in which this demonstration is made in *Ulysses*, there is, so to speak, no one around whom it might affect. What interests James, on the other hand, is the effect of something like the disappearance of a self on human relations. Rather than propose an extreme (and extremely theoretical) skepticism about our ability to report on anything at all, James in *The Europeans* stages a confrontation between characters who expect their inherited moral and psychological vocabulary to correspond to something real in human nature, and a woman (Eugenia) who may be nothing but a play of styles. James suggests, with great originality, that Eugenia's lack of a self may be the most morally interesting thing about her, while the Wentworths' need to know others severely limits them (they are finally compelled to label Eugenia as a liar).

I will make an even more incongruous juxtaposition by suggesting that Beckett is closer to James in this respect than to his friend and compatriot. From *Waiting for Godot* to *Company*, Beckett suggests that while there can no longer be "characters" in literature, that very deprivation throws into sharper relief than ever before the infinite geometry of relational play among human subjects. *Godot* demonstrates the inevitability of conversation at a cultural juncture when there may be nothing left to talk about; furthermore, the strategies for continuing talk survive the absence of psychological subjects. And *Company*, even after the elimination of a human other, performs a solipsistic sociability inherent in the grammar of language itself. (Sociability in Joyce is a function of realistically portrayed characters and not, as in Beckett, the fascinatingly anachronistic remnant of the disappearance of such

characters.) Beckett's authentic avant-gardism consists in a break
not only with the myths fostered by cultural discourse, but more
radically, with cultural discourse itself. The mystery of his work
is how it is not only sustained but even begun, for intertextuality
in Beckett (the echoes of Descartes and of Malebranche in the
early works, for example) is not a principle of cultural continuity
(as it is in Joyce, in spite of the parodic nature of the repetitions),
but the occasion for a kind of psychotic raving. Cultural memories exist in the minds of Beckett's characters like fossils which
belong to another age, like instruments which no one knows how
to use any more. Beckett's work remembers culture as Lucky
remembers the structure of a logical argument in *Godot*: they are
played like the broken records of language and consciousness.

Joyce, for all his parodic intentions, modernizes and to a certain extent rejuvenates the Homeric myths which, somewhat
above the characters' heads, give an epic dimension to a prosaic
day in Dublin life. Thus *Ulysses*, however crookedly and mockingly, resuscitates and assimilates Odysseus, and Joyce's ambivalent
argument against the mimetic seriousness of literature, unlike
Beckett's or Flaubert's, actually works to increase literature's authority, to realize a dream of cultural artifacts as both unconstrained by and superior to life, superior by virtue of the intertextual designs which they silently invite us to disengage. The
resublimation of cultural discourse in "Circe" is a function of the
episode's intertextuality. Joyce ultimately "saves" the other texts
which "Circe" parodistically quotes, and he does this simply by
putting them into relation with "Circe." Joycean parody simultaneously "scorches" the other texts to which it refers and reconstitutes them as cultural artifacts within the intertextual designs woven by *Ulysses*. Intertextuality is, of course, not a
phenomenon peculiar to *Ulysses;* what *is* peculiar to *Ulysses* is the
novel's use of the intertext as a redemptive strategy. The Joycean
intertext rescues Western literature from the deconstructive effects of the intertext itself. The parodistic replays of Homer,
Shakespeare, and Flaubert—not to speak of all the authors
"quoted" in "Oxen of the Sun"—are neither subversive of nor

indifferent to the fact of cultural inheritance; rather, Joyce relocates the items of that inheritance with *Ulysses* as both their center and belated origin.

This is very different from Flaubert's insistent demonstration, in *Bouvard et Pécuchet*, of art's indifference to its sources. There is no pastiche in *Bouvard et Pécuchet*, which means that Flaubert never advertises his authority over other cultural texts. Flaubert's novel is deliberately monotonous and narrow, as if it could not do anything with the mass of human knowledge which it incorporates except to submit all of it to the same, tirelessly repeated stylistic operation. The originality of *Bouvard et Pécuchet* is identical to its epistemological and cultural incompetence. In a sense, the artist is even revealed (and this remark might not have displeased Flaubert) as somewhat stupid: no matter what is presented to him, he reacts with the same stylistic reflex, with, we might almost say, a cliché. And, as I argued earlier, the writer's limited authority, even his political effectiveness, depends on this stripping away of all authority, on the recognition of the work of art as an impotent discourse. The work's solipsistic existence in the margins of history undermines, or at least helps to delay, the eventual, inevitable complicity of all art with a civilization's discourse of power.

Beckett, and not Joyce, would be the most attentive reader of the Flaubert I have been discussing. The very variety of stylistic designs in *Ulysses* reveals Joyce's designs on culture. Far from transmuting all his cultural referents into a single, recognizably Joycean discourse, Joyce scrupulously maintains the distinctness of innumerable other styles in order to legitimize misquoting them. The accuracy is not merely a referential scruple, just as the inaccuracies are far from being mere sloppiness. We have to recognize the sources of *Ulysses* if we are to acknowledge its superiority to them. *Ulysses* indulges massively in quotation—quotation of individual characters, of social groups, of myths, of other writers—but quoting in Joyce is the opposite of self-effacement. It is an act of appropriation, one which can be performed without Joyce's voice even being heard. It is as if Joyce were quoting Western culture itself in its *quidditas*—except that the "whatness" of all those cultural referents is implicitly designated not as the most essential property of the referents themselves, but rather as a consequence of their being (mis)quoted. Joyce miraculously reconciles uncompromising mimesis with a solipsistic structure. Western culture is saved, indeed glorified, through literary metempsychosis: it "dies" in the Joycean parody and pastiche, but, once removed from historical time, it is resurrected as a timeless design. Far from contesting the authority of culture, *Ulysses* reinvents and reanimates our relation to Western culture in terms of an exegetical devotion, that is, as the exegesis of *Ulysses* itself.

Beckett, on the other hand, babbles culture, as if its cultural memories *afflicted* the work of art—afflicted it not because they stifle its originality, but because they infect it like foreign or prehistoric organisms. The difficulty of art in Beckett is in no way connected to the encyclopedic nature of the work's intertextual range; rather, it is the function of an art alienated from culture, the consequence of Beckett's extraordinary effort to stop remembering, to begin again, to protect writing from cultural inheritance. As his latest work suggests, the most refined stage of Beckett's artistic consciousness is identical to a moving back, to a return to that stage of difficulty which, he may feel, he left too early: the stage at which the writer is paralyzed by the inherently insurmountable problem of description, of saying what he sees. It is perhaps only at that stage that the writer discovers the nature of writing; "ill seen, ill said" defines nothing less than the essence of literature.

U*LYSSES* IS A NOVEL CURIOUSLY unaffected by its most radical propositions. Perhaps because the realistic psychology of its characters is barely affected by, to quote Heath again, Joyce's "ceaselessly pushing the signified back into the signifier in order to refind at every moment the drama of language, its productions," this "pushing" never engenders any oppositional pressures. To put this schematically, the finality of the signifier is at once posited and ignored. We have, however, learned from other writers that literature's greatest ruse may be to insist that language perform the function of knowledge which the writer's special intimacy with language has taught him radically to doubt. This is the ruse of a reflexive "I" conscious of its aberrant consciousness of both its inner and outer worlds, and yet skeptical of that very consciousness of error. For the epistemological nihilism which may be the consequence of our sense of the human mind as a language-producing mechanism (linguistic signifiers can proliferate independently of what they signify and what they refer to) is of course itself the event of a linguistic consciousness, and the most daring move of all in this "prison house of language" may be to insist that language give us the truth which it falsely claims to be able to contain.

I will name three writers who make this insistence: Proust, D. H. Lawrence, and Georges Bataille. One could hardly imagine more different artists, and yet all three share a sense of the implausibility *and* the necessity of forging a correspondence between language and being. In his foreword to *Women in Love*, Lawrence writes that the "struggle for verbal consciousness should not be left out in art. It is a very great part of life. It is not superimposition of a theory. *It is the passionate struggle into conscious being*"—the sign, in art, of the writer's struggling "with his unborn needs and fulfilment," with the "new unfoldings" struggling up "in torment in him, as buds struggle forth from the midst of a plant."[7] The Lawrentian struggle—the word is repeated five times in the short paragraph from I have been quoting—is perhaps not too far from what Bataille calls, in his foreword to *Le bleu du ciel*, that "intolerable, impossible ordeal [which alone] can give an author the means of achieving that wide-ranging vision that readers weary of the narrow limitations imposed by convention are waiting for." "An anguish to which I was prey" was, Bataille remembers, at the origin of the "freakish anomalies" of *Le bleu du ciel*.[8] Thus Bataille obliquely announces his complicity with his frenetically restless narrator Troppmann, and in so doing he argues, from the very start, for an abdication of the novelist's mastery over his material. *Le bleu du ciel*—like *Women in Love* and, to a certain extent, *A la recherche du temps perdu*—has trouble settling on its own sense, and this is, in large part, how these works revolutionize the practice of writing novels. They have to be performed before any technique for dominating their sense has been worked out. Most important, the struggles and ordeals of which Lawrence and Bataille speak are incorporated into, made visible in, the very work of their writing, with the result that their fiction is perhaps ultimately compelled to abdicate any authority for resolving the dilemmas it poses, any superior point of view that could justify a broader cultural claim for art as a vehicle of truth.

The "freakish anomalies" of *Ulysses*, far from threatening the author's control over his material, are the signs of that control. Consider "Oxen of the Sun," which may be the most difficult and the most accessible episode of the novel. Once we have identified all the referents in this virtuoso pastiche of prose styles from Sallust to modern slang, what else does the episode give us? How does its language enact—or refer to—its sense? While the narrator is engaging in this stylistic tour de force, several of the characters, including Bloom and Stephen, are sitting around drinking and talking in a maternity hospital, where Mrs. Purefoy is going through the final moments of a long and difficult labor. With some help from a letter Joyce wrote to Frank Budgen while he was working on "Oxen of the Sun" (*LI*, 139–40) critics have proposed a series of parallels between the evolution of English prose and (1) biological gestation and birth, (2) the development of the embryonic artist's prose style, (3) faunal evolution, and (4) Stephen's rebirth, or his birth as an artist. The episode is perhaps the most extraordinary example in the history of literature of meaning unrelated to the experience of reading and to the work of writing. What Joyce obviously worked on was a series of brief pastiches which he aligned in chronological order. The characters and plot of *Ulysses* provide the material for the pastiche, although Joyce wants to think of the relation between the stylistic exercise and its anecdotal context in more organic terms. And so we have a series of imitative fallacies. In what way is the historical transformation (which is of course *not* a "development" or the maturation of an organism) of English prose styles "parallel" or "analogous" to (and what do those words mean here?) the real biological development of an embryo in a womb? Also, the beginnings of a twentieth-century writer's work obviously in no way resemble Anglo-Saxon; the transformation of an individual prose style reflects an experience of language wholly unrelated to the reasons for the difference between Dickens's style and that of Malory's *Morte d'Arthur*. Finally, the idea of some significant connection between Mrs. Purefoy's gestation *or* the history of English prose styles to Stephen's development or emergence as an artist is so absurd that it is difficult even to find the terms in which to object to it.

Now I may of course be taking all these analogies too seriously, and Joyce's letter to Budgen, characteristically, manages both to sound quite earnest and to strike a note which it is hard not to find comic: "Bloom is the spermatozoon, the hospital, the womb, the nurse, the ovum, Stephen the embryo." (Joyce even adds: "How's that for high?" [*LI*, 140] Joyce's shifty tone suggests a wager: let us see how much I can be credited for, and, in the worst of cases (if my critics are uncomfortable with these analogies), it can always be argued that I proposed them with tongue in cheek. It is true that the "Oxen of the Sun" analogies are not the sort of thing looked at too closely by the most sophisticated of Joyce's admirers, but they have, for example, led Richard Ellmann to suggest that "Mrs. Purefoy has laboured and brought forth a Purefoykin, English has laboured [?] and brought forth Stephen," and even to speak of "Mrs. Purefoy's oncoming baby" as "paralleled by the outgoing Stephen" (he leaves the hospital before Bloom, who entered it first and who "is hospitably received by the nurse"—remember that the nurses are, according to Joyce, the "ovum"), Stephen who, with his friends, can also be thought of, as they rush from the hospital to a pub, as "the placental outpouring . . . (it is the afterbirth as well as an ejaculative spray)."[9]

Such criticism is of course itself a joke, but my point is that it is not unauthorized by the novel (not to speak of Joyce's suggestions for reading the novel), and that authorization is itself a moment of great significance in the story of how literature has been thought about. If the history of philosophy can no longer measure approximations to truth but must rather be satisfied with chronicling the mutations of fictions, and if hermeneutics can no longer provide a "science" of interpretation but rather becomes

itself a stage in the history of the forms of intelligibility, "Oxen
of the Sun" might be thought of as one of the contributions to
the literature section of such a history. Joyce initiates us to a
radical separation of interpretation from the phenomenology of
reading. The announced correspondences and meanings of *Ulysses'*
episodes could be thought of as a way not of elucidating the
novel's sense, but of forcing us to see that *sense is a series of ingenious
jokes on the signifier.* It is the prose styles themselves of "Oxen of the
Sun" which are parodied by their repetition in Mrs. Purefoy's
womb. And the idea of Stephen's literary or spiritual birth in this
chapter is a magnificently irresponsible way of "understanding"
the insignificant role he plays in the episode, as well as of "interpreting" the possibility (suggested by Kenner)[10] of his having
slugged Mulligan (and thus repudiated the sterile past connected
with Mulligan) in the interval between episodes 9 and 14.

The Lawrentian (and, as I have shown elsewhere, the Mallar-
méan)[11] attempts to coerce language into an espousal of the
moves of an individual consciousness—moves which an impersonal linguistic coherence necessarily "skips," to which that coherence is even ontologically alien—is implicitly rejected in
"Oxen of the Sun" as an insidious fallacy. And yet a whole set of
conventional psychological and moral significances coexist quite
comfortably in Joyce with a radical skepticism concerning the
validity of any move whatsoever beyond or behind the line of the
signifier. (This cohabitation is of course familiar to us today. For
example, the Lacanians' ritualistic repetition of the word *signifiant*
as the key to the Master's radical rethinking of the Freudian unconscious has in no way affected the normative status, in their
thought, of the psychologically and morally specific referent of a
phallocentric heterosexuality.) The perception of human reality
as a language-effect has generally had the curious consequence
of forestalling, of leaving no terms available for, the criticism of
psychological, moral, and social orders elaborated by the quite
different view—now seen as epistemologically naive—of language
as essentially descriptive of a preexistent real. The rhetorical criticism associated with Derrida and, more properly, de Man has,
for example, much to say about the deconstructive effects of the

figural on politically or morally assertive statements, and very
little to say about the strategic nature of its own analytic enterprise. The decision to treat history as rhetoric must itself be
deconstructed—which is of course to say *re*constructed—as a
profoundly reactionary move: it deliberately ignores how independent networks of power can be of the subversive effect presumably inherent in their own discursive practices. The internal
resistance of language to its own performance provides insufficient friction to curtail the operational efficiency of even the most
"mystified" (but powerful) linguistic performances. Foucault, it
seems to me, had the great merit of seeing that effects of power
are indifferent to their rhetorical legitimacy, and that a predominantly rhetorical analysis of a society's discursive practices
therefore runs the risk of collaborating with precisely those coercive intentions which it protects even while ceaselessly demonstrating their (inescapably but on the whole ineffectually) self-
menacing nature.

   Ulysses substitutes for the interpretive ordeals through which
such writers as Lawrence, Mallarmé, and Bataille would put us a
kind of affectless busyness, the comfortable if heavy work of finding all the connections in the light of which the novel can be
made intelligible but cannot be interpreted. The experimentalism
of *Ulysses* is far from the genuine avant-gardism of *Women in Love,
Le bleu du ciel,* or almost any of Beckett's fictions. The intertextual
criticism invited by *Ulysses* is the domestication of literature, a
technique for *making familiar* the potentially traumatic seductions
of reading. Even more: *Ulysses* eliminates reading as the ground
of interpretation, or, to put this in other terms, it invites intertextual elucidations as a strategy to prohibit textual interpretations. In much contemporary criticism reading no longer provides
a hermeneutical ground of interpretive constraint—by which I
naturally do not mean that there should be or ever was one
legitimate interpretation of each text. Rather, in what we might
call the critical progeny of *Ulysses*, texts are made intelligible by
the intra- and intertextual cues which they drop rather than by
the work of reading. *Ulysses* is a text to be deciphered but not
read. Joyce's schemas already provide a model of interpretive ni-

hilism. They propose, with a kind of wild structural neatness, meanings so remote from our textual experience as to suggest that there is no other basis for sense than the "line" that can be drawn between two intratextual and intertextual points. The exegetical work to be done is enormous, but in a sense it has already been done by the author, and we simply have to catch up with him. *Ulysses* promises a critical utopia: the final elucidation of its sense, the day when all the connections will have been discovered and collected in a critical Book which would objectively repeat *Ulysses*, which, in being the exegetical double of its source, would express the *quidditas* of Joyce's novel, would be, finally, *Ulysses* replayed as the whole truth of *Ulysses*.

FINALLY—AND PERHAPS NOT SO strangely—the very nihilism I have referred to goes along with a promise of salvation. Not only does *Ulysses* keep its conservative ideology of the self distinct from its increasing emphasis on the finality of language's productiveness; not only does it display a perspectival technique which brings to psychological realism the prestige of a Thomistic confidence in art's ability to radiate with the essence of things; Joyce's novel also refers us to a mind purified of "impossible ordeals" or "struggles" and reduced—or elevated—to the serene and perhaps redemptive management of its cultural acquisitions. Where *Ulysses* really leads us is to Joyce's mind; it illuminates his cultural consciousness. At the end of the reader's exegetical travails lies the promise of an Assumption, of being raised up and identified with the idea of *culture* made *man*. Joyce incarnates the enormous authority of sublimation in our culture—of sublimation viewed not as a nonspecific eroticizing of cultural interests but as the appeasement and even transcendence of anxiety.

   Ulysses is modernism's monument to that authority, although— in what I take to be the most authentic risk Joyce takes in producing this monument—it also includes, or at least alludes to, the anxiety from which we escape in our exegetical relocation of the work itself within the masterful authorial consciousness at its origin. I am referring to certain moments in the representation of Bloom's solitude—not to his social solitude as a Jew in Ireland, or even to his estrangement from Molly, but rather to a kind of cosmic lack of linkage, a singleness that can be rendered only by images of his floating in interplanetary space. In one of the moral clichés to which this presumably revolutionary novel has given rise, Stephen's coldness and inability to love is often opposed to Bloom's warmth and frequent expressions of concern for others. But Stephen's solitude is psychological (it includes his estrangement from his father, and his unshakable sense of a crime against his mother); Bloom's aloneness is, we might say, metaphysical. Furthermore, Stephen is as sociable and loquacious a boozer as all the other characters we meet in the editorial offices of the *Freeman* or in Barney Kiernan's pub; like them, he spends his day in talk and even plots his oratorical effects (in "Scylla and Charybdis") and blushes with pleasure (in "Aeolus") as he listens to the rhetorical flourishes in J. J. O'Molloy's recitation of the lawyer Seymour Bushe's "polished period" describing "the Moses of Michelangelo in the Vatican." If, in "Ithaca," both Bloom and Stephen are said to be comforted by the spectacle of "the heaventree of stars hung with humid nightblue fruit" (*U* 17.1039) when they move from the house to the garden, it is Bloom who meditates on "the parallax or parallactic drift of so called fixed stars, in reality ever moving wanderers from immeasurably remote eons to infinitely remote futures" (*U* 17.1052–54) and who, alone after Stephen leaves, feels "the cold of interstellar space, thousands of degrees below freezing point on the absolute zero of Fahrenheit, Centigrade or Reaumur. The incipient intimations of proximate dawn" (*U* 17.1246–48). And in the de Quincey passage from "Oxen of the Sun" which J. S. Atherton rightly sees as "a most remarkable example of Joyce's 'power of combination,' "[12] "Bloom gazes at the triangle on the label of the bottle of bass until it becomes a 'triangled sign upon the forehead of Taurus' (*U* 14.1108–9)— combining lingam and yoni in one symbol, which itself replicates the underlying symbol of the chapter, and placing it in the depths of space." It is the relentlessly tedious "Ithaca," with its nearly unreadable "scientific" expositions of such things as the many uses and virtues of water, and the recent restrictions on water consumption in Dublin (when Bloom turns on a faucet), which, precisely because of the impersonality of its technique, becomes a kind of Pascalian meditation on the lack of connectedness not only between human beings but also between the human and the cosmos. We might of course also be tempted to see in the lostness of Bloom an image for the historical situation of Ireland itself: a country with no consensus about its past, little hope for its future, and cut off, both physically and culturally, from the rest of Europe. The anxiety which *Ulysses* massively, encyclopedically struggles to transcend—however we choose to understand its origins—is that of disconnectedness. It is perhaps here that Joyce's dependence on his readers is most pronounced, for it is *their* intra- and extratextual work which reconstitutes his mind as the serene repository of the resources of our language and our culture. From this perspective, it hardly matters if the Homeric correspondences are, to say the least, not always exact, or that the pastiches of "Oxen of the Sun" are not always very close to their originals. *Ulysses* is composed as a model of the cultural fragmentation which it represents in various ways. Furthermore, Joyce's authority depends on the idiosyncratic nature of the culture which he reconstructs; *Ulysses* gives us back our culture as *his* culture.

For authors, the anguish of paternity is experienced as an uncertainty about the property of their work, about who owns it and if it is indeed their own. "Fatherhood, in the sense of conscious begetting," Stephen announces in "Scylla and Charybdis," "is unknown to man." It is "on that mystery and not on the madonna which the cunning Italian intellect flung to the mob of Europe the church is founded and founded irremovably because founded, like the world, macro and microcosm, upon the void, upon incertitude, upon unlikelihood" (*U* 9.837–42). In our tireless elucidation of *Ulysses*, we certify Joyce's paternity, we bring his work back to him, we eliminate what Stephen describes as the natural enmity between father and son by showing how the book gives birth to its author. Exegesis reveals that *Ulysses* signifies Joyce's multitudinous stylistic and structural intentions; it demonstrates that the work glorifies its creator just as Christ—concentrating and purifying in His Person a universal human truth—

glorifies the Father. And for the worthy disciples of *Ulysses*, which we should now be able to recognize as modernism's most impressive tribute to the West's long and varied tribute to the authority of the Father, there are of course enormous rewards. *Ulysses* does not restore cultural continuities presumably broken by the modern age. Indeed, in a manner consistent with its nihilistic indifference to any relation between our experience of reading it and those concealed structures which it signifies, Joyce's novel asks only that we reconstruct the structurally coherent fragments of Joyce's own cultural consciousness. It is not Western culture that matters, but the coherence of a particular broken version of it. Joyce is faithful to our humanist tradition at a deeper level, in his reenactment of its assumptions and promise that the possession of culture will transcend anxiety and perhaps even redeem history.

Intertextual criticism is the practical activity which testifies to our espousal of a cultural ethos of the redemptive authority and mastery of art; it is, in the case of *Ulysses*, the *imitatio* which allows us to join Joyce in a community built on identifications and recognitions. Verbal consciousness in *Ulysses* is not—as it is in Lawrence or Bataille—a process of clarification repeatedly menaced by the personal and social pressures antagonistic to any clarifications whatsoever; rather, it is a conquest the multitudinous forms of which are disguised but never threatened by the novel's textures. The community of *Ulysses* and its exegetes is redemptive in its failure to acknowledge any operative relation between experience—of this text or of reality—and the forms of intelligibility which it proposes. It is the Vita Nuova in which Joyce thrillingly proposes that we spend our life with him. The call is very hard not to heed. Even in writing "against *Ulysses*," we can only feel a great sadness in leaving it; to stop working on *Ulysses* is like a fall from grace.

Notes

1. John Paul Riquelme, *Teller and Tale in Joyce's "Ulysses": Oscillating Perspectives* (Baltimore, Md.: Johns Hopkins University Press, 1983), 202.

2. Hugh Kenner, *Joyce's Voices* (Berkeley: University of California Press, 1978), 17.

3. Kenner, *Joyce's Voices*, 69–70.

4. Ibid.

5. Stephen Heath, "Ambiviolences: Notes for Reading Joyce," in *Post-structuralist Joyce: Essays from the French*, ed. Derek Attridge and Daniel Ferrer (Cambridge: Cambridge University Press, 1984), 33, 57.

6. See Richard Poirier, "The Difficulties of Modernism and the Modernism of Difficulty," *Humanities in Society* 1 (spring, 1978).

7. D. H. Lawrence, *Women in Love*, ed. David Farmer, Lindeth Vasey, and John Worthen (Cambridge: Cambridge University Press, 1987), 485–86.

8. Georges Bataille, *Blue of Noon*, trans. Harry Matthews (New York: Urizen, 1978; reprint, Marion Boyars, 1985), 153–55; *Le Bleu du ciel*, in *Oeuvres Complètes*, vol. 3 (Paris: Gallimard, 1971), 381–82.

9. Richard Ellmann, *Ulysses on the Liffey* (London: Faber, 1972), 136–39.

10. Kenner, *Joyce's Voices*, 40.

11. In Leo Bersani, *The Death of Stéphane Mallarmé* (Cambridge: Cambridge University Press, 1982).

12. J. S. Atherton, "The Oxen of the Sun," in *James Joyce's "Ulysses": Critical Essays*, ed. Clive Hart and David Hayman (Berkeley: University of California Press, 1974), 331.

Intentional Error

The Paradox of Editing Joyce's Ulysses

VICKI MAHAFFEY

❖ ❖ ❖

I N T H E S P R I N G O F 1990, I had an informal conference with
a graduate student in architecture who was auditing my course
in Yeats and Joyce. I asked him about his work, and he explained
the project he was currently working on:

> I want to design a contemporary library, one that takes into
> account the change in the way readers are increasingly en-
> countering the texts they read: on computer screens, with
> characters that are not inked, but which emit light. When you
> research the architecture of famous libraries, it becomes clear
> that throughout the era of the printed book, architects have
> had to factor in an awareness that light damages books. I am
> anticipating a situation in which we *read* light, and I'd like to
> design a library in which the architecture would express and
> reflect this startling reversal.

The student's comments crystallized for me some of the thoughts
I had been having about textual editing. Although I am not my-

self an editor, I started reading editorial theory in 1984, when I was reviewing Hans Walter Gabler's new edition of *Ulysses* for the *Philadelphia Inquirer.*[1] One thing that has emerged as incontrovertible is that editorial theory is inextricably bound to our conception of what a work of literature is and how it is authorized.[2] Our popular conception of the work of literature as fixed and monumental will increasingly be affected, perhaps eroded, not only by the substitution of lighted characters for inked ones, but by the fluidity, productiveness, and (as anyone who works on a computer knows) the potential for loss that computers bring to us. Computers are subtly drawing power *from* the individual writing in isolation and bringing it *to* the overall system or network of interconnection, and this change in the material process of writing (which has become less laborious, more ephemeral) must, in time, silently but dramatically transform our assumptions about the authority and permanence of individual labor. Increasingly, computers are contributing to and may even eventually replace the printing of books in a way that will inevitably affect our theories of editing.

Given the dramatic transformation in the idea of the book that we are in the process of witnessing, in which the old contrast between black and white is being redrawn via different intensities of light, it is significant that one of the innovative features of Hans Walter Gabler's celebrated and maligned edition of *Ulysses* was his pioneering use of computers to help him assemble and edit his critical text.[3] Computers were not only pragmatically instrumental to the production of the edition (even the typesetting was done by computer), they also analogically reinforce the conception of writing (composition) as *process* rather than product, which is perhaps the single most important (and controversial) rationale behind Gabler's editorial methodology. My emphasis here is not on the future of editing in a world of revolutionary technological change, although such a future is relevant to what I want to suggest about editing Joyce. Instead, what I propose to do is to chart Gabler's editorial procedures against a broad background of continuity and change in the idea of the book, and especially Joyce's idea of the book as suggested by his methods of composing (and anticipating the decomposition of) both *Ulysses* and *Finnegans Wake*.[4] I will argue that Gabler is conservative (traditional) in the premium he sets on authorial intention at the expense of accident and circumstance, but radical in his decision to define authorial intention as multiple and changing; moreover, I hope to show that what is most crucial for the stability and reliability of the text is a balance of tendencies, and that Gabler achieves one such balance among many possibilities. What Gabler's methods allow us to perceive more sharply is the theory of text production encoded in *Ulysses* and expanded in *Finnegans Wake*, a theory licensed by the oxymoronic concept of "intentional error" as the basis of continued productivity and a stimulus for deeper and more complicated textual understandings.

Gabler's edition of *Ulysses* has stirred controversy that is unusual partly because it has been so public (much of it has been carried out in the popular press or in widely circulated literary newspapers, the *Washington Post* and especially the *New York Review of Books*). A brief summary of the edition's publication and reception is this: in June 1984, Garland published Gabler's three-volume critical and synoptic edition of *Ulysses*. This edition, which ran to 1,919 pages, provided two "versions" or interpretations of the text on facing pages: a "synopsis" of different stages of the text's autograph composition (from final draft through the last set of proofs) on the versos, and a clear reading text on the corresponding rectos (which was the basis for the trade editions published by Random House, Bodley Head, and Penguin in 1986). The synoptic text, through the use of a complex set of diacritical marks, enables a reader in theory to reconstruct what Gabler calls the "continuous manuscript" of *Ulysses*, which he controversially assembled to use as the copy-text of his edition. This is the most unusual feature of the entire edition: Gabler's decisions not to "correct" the most authoritative printed edition (in this case the 1922 first edition) nor to choose one manuscript as his copy-text, but to assemble a compound "manuscript" out of the diverse fair copies, corrections, and additions in Joyce's hand (or dictated by him; a small portion of the Rosenbach manuscript was dictated by Joyce to Frank Budgen).

The publication of Gabler's edition was widely publicized and almost universally celebrated in the popular press when it appeared, and for good reason. Anyone who has worked closely with the 1961 Random House edition (*RH*) knows how appalling the state of that text was, and how many of its misprints gratuitously obscure the finer points of an already difficult text. When I taught the "Circe" episode out of the old Random House edition, I had to hand out lists of misprints that I had been able to ascertain as such, a strategy I devised when I realized how much unproductive trouble the misprints were causing in a text designed around verbal precision. In the stage directions that open "Circe," for example, it is difficult enough for students to recognize a nighttown reprise of a moment in "Wandering Rocks":

> *Round Rabaiotti's halted ice gondola stunted men and women squabble. They grab wafers between which are wedged lumps of coral and copper snow. Sucking, they scatter slowly, children. The swancomb of the gondola, high-reared, forges on through the murk, white and blue under a lighthouse.* (*U 15.4–9*)

In the 1961 edition, what was wedged between the wafers was "lumps of *coal* and copper snow" (emphasis added; *RH* 429). In an early discussion of the implications of the Gabler edition at the first Philadelphia conference, Bonnie Kime Scott objected that this change from "coal" to "coral" made it seem as if the menu had changed from coal (which Scott saw as appropriately grotesque) to ice cream sandwiches; she used this change to support her claim that the new edition was responsible for a "loss of some interpretative possibilities."[5] Ironically, however, a closer look at the work shows that what we get in this instance (as in many others) is not a loss but a gain in interpretative clarity. The "stunted men and women" who open "Circe" *are* eating ice cream, a perception essential to the realization that this is a nightmarish reenactment of the scene in "Wandering Rocks" in which children are eating ice cream around Rabaiotti's ice cream car when a one-legged sailor passes by, growling, "*For England. . . . home and beauty*" for alms (10.228–56). The deaf-mute idiot that jerks past the children in "Circe," only to be imprisoned in a chain of their hands until he salutes and answers their question about the great light, *is* this one-legged sailor (it is because he is a sailor that the children order him to "salute"). The reader's ability to identify the ice cream provides a crucial link in the momentary connection between the two episodes, a connection that allows us to see at the outset how "Circe" works on the book as a whole, how the text of this episode, like Homer's sorceress, retrieves and grotesquely transforms bits of text that we as readers have half-forgotten into disgruntled stylistic equivalents. Joyce's Circean revisions, like dreams, offer us the opportunity to re-view what we passed by earlier as trivial, and to apprehend more vividly the sinister or troubling implications of what we may have glossed over as normative. Looking back, we can see that even in "Wandering Rocks" the one-legged sailor is presented as grotesque, a freak whom "barefoot urchins" halt to stare at, "gaping at his stump with their yellowslobbered mouths" (10.244–45). If we notice him at all in "Wandering Rocks," it is from the perspective of the children, or as the target of a coin thrown out the window by Molly's plump arm. When we see him again in "Circe," his role as semicoherent master of ceremonies in a red-light district makes his prostituted position—and our earlier blindness to it—troublingly unmistakable: despite his service to England (which presumably cost him his leg), he is forced to sing for his supper on the streets of Dublin. The red lights of nighttown signal *both* prostitution and British domination, and the one-legged sailor aptly appears to induct us into the district that represents Dublin under British rule, a self-betraying urban underworld.

The celebration of Gabler's edition as a superior replacement for the 1961 Random House edition still seems to me to be both understandable and warranted. But on April 26, 1985, nine months after the edition was published, it was challenged by John Kidd in a paper he delivered to the Society for Textual Scholarship in New York City.[6] Since that time, controversy has raged between those who call the validity (or, less damagingly, the sufficiency) of the edition into question (usually on Kidd's authority) and those who defend its integrity. The publicity escalated in June 1988, when Kidd published another attack, this time in the *New York Review of Books*, called "The Scandal of *Ulysses*."[7] There followed an exchange that appeared in six subsequent issues over the next year[8] in which eleven readers besides Kidd participated; the controversy was heightened by a similar exchange in the *Times Literary Supplement*.[9] In June 1988, Random House announced that it was setting up a committee (chaired by G. Thomas Tanselle) to conduct an inquiry into the Gabler edition, and to advise them whether they should put the old Vintage (1961) copy back into print (which they have since done), and whether they should withdraw the Gabler edition from the market (which they have chosen not to do). The committee was dissolved before issuing a report in February 1990, when Jacob Epstein of Random House dissociated himself from his own advisory committee.[10]

The controversy over the Gabler edition has unearthed some errors in the edition, many of which have been corrected (but not attributed—emendations seldom are). Although it has been valuable in its investigation of the accuracy of individual readings, the controversy has been damaging in another way: many of the most widely publicized attacks are based on premises about textual editing that the general reading public takes for granted, so when a critic proves that Gabler has violated these guidelines, his editorial competence is implicitly or explicitly called into question. It takes a reasonably specialized reader to realize that the weakness of such arguments, which seem logically convincing on their own terms, is at the level of the premise, since Gabler does not share many of the premises on which the critique is based. For example, when Robin Bates (taking his cue from Kidd) alleges that Gabler failed to collate an important edition of *Ulysses* (the 1935 edition illustrated by Matisse, which is demonstrably important in the history of the book's *transmission in print*), thereby violating conventional editorial guidelines, he makes Gabler seem irresponsible in a way that undermines the scholarship behind the edition.[11] However, what most general readers may not realize is that Gabler's decision not to collate a particular edition does not affect his edition at all; what it affects is his list of "historical collations" in the three-volume edition, which is for Gabler mainly an apparatus devised for the reader's convenience, to facilitate a comparison between Gabler's text and notable variants that have appeared in print.

Gabler's edition is not founded on printed editions (as many Anglo-American editions have been, either wholly or in part); instead, Gabler chose to edit the autograph documents up to but not including the first published edition in 1922. As he says in his first response to Kidd, "it makes little sense to hold against the edition that it does not do what it expressly sets out to avoid."[12] What Gabler tried to produce was an "ideal" record of the process of composition, an "authoritative text free of corruption [transmissional error]"[13]: "This edition's whole rationale is based on the assumption that the legal act of first publication did not validate the actual text thereby made public to the extent of lending authority to its high incidence of corruption. Instead, . . . the edition [presents] an ideal text freed of the errors with which *Ulysses* was first published" (1892). As Jerome McGann has explained most clearly, Gabler differentiates between "documents of composition and documents of transmission," giving preemptive authority to the former. Gabler's text, therefore, "represents the ultimate state of the work's composition (not its transmission)." This ultimately leads McGann to assert:

> Gabler's is an imagination of Joyce's work and not its reconstitution. Gabler invents, by a process of brilliant editorial reconstruction, *Joyce's Ulysses* (as it were), a work that existed, if it ever existed at all in fact, for Joyce the writer rather than Joyce the author. Gabler's edition does not give us the work which Joyce wanted to present to the public; rather, he gives us a text in which we may observe Joyce at work, alone, before he turns to meet his public.[14]

McGann started a process of investigating the theoretical implications of the edition that the Kidd controversy aborted, or at least deflected, by measuring Gabler's scholarly competence against norms that Gabler had (rightly or wrongly) modified to suit the extraordinary circumstances of *Ulysses* composition and production. After five years of debate, it seems time to return to the theoretical axioms Gabler articulated as the basis of the edition in order to determine what exactly is at stake in his theoretical choices, what the implications of these choices are, how those implications are related to other poststructuralist theories of intentionality and text production (most notably deconstruction and New Historicism), and what other choices might be possible.

The first question about the choices subtending Gabler's edition is not theoretical but practical: for what audience was the synoptic text intended? On one level, the answer to this is obvious: insofar as the layers of the continuous manuscript are designed to bring us by stages to the clear reading text, it is designed for all readers, and insofar as it represents a modification of the accepted practices of textual editing, it is addressed to editors. However, Gabler's article "The Synchrony and Diachrony of Texts" suggests a third audience, which may be the most important one of all for understanding the rationale behind the edition: critics. Here Gabler emphasizes the importance of access to authorial variants for a critical understanding of a work of literature, a point he illustrates through critically analyzing two authorial versions of a Faulkner story, "That Evening Sun." He argues that "the articulation of *critical understanding* . . . will reach its highest degree of definitiveness from a critical interpretation of the work's revisional variation," and he identifies the variations within an evolving manuscript as "stimuli to *interpretation*" (emphases added). He then proceeds from the critical desirability of a genetic manuscript text to the fact that Anglo-American editing has no model for such texts: "we have currently no methodology or model for the constitution of critical texts, or of variance recording and presentation, that will answer sufficiently to the concepts of 'work' and 'text' as I have outlined them."[15] He goes on to rehearse the reason for this, a commonplace within textual studies that Gabler's editorial assistant Wolfhard Steppe explains most simply: the methodology of Anglo-American textual scholarship grows out of an engagement with "texts for which autograph sources are rare or lacking completely (e.g., for Elizabethan drama), so that printed sources—the second-best choice—have to be depended on."[16]

Given Gabler's editorial aim to make the process of authorial composition accessible to critical interpretation, one legitimate question is whether the synoptic text actually succeeds in stimulating such interpretations. The answer at this point in time seems to be "no," partly because the three-volume edition, being expensive, is not widely available, and partly because the system of diacritical marks used to designate the different levels of composition have proven difficult to interpret.[17] This prompts me to ask whether the synoptic text should not be marketed separately, without the reading text, perhaps in a more readable format. (Could colors or different typefaces be used instead of half-brackets to indicate the most important levels?[18] Would it be practicable to print the fair copy on the verso and additions—at all subsequent levels—on the recto?) The question remains whether the synoptic text could be simplified and redistributed in such a way as to make it a more useful tool for the critical analyses it was (partly) designed to facilitate.

To move from practical questions to more theoretical ones, I propose to explore Gabler's response to major theoretical concerns in both editing and criticism—the status of the text as product (whether authorial, cultural, or both), the text as authorized by authorial intention, and the relevance of transmissional corruption—and to show where the Gabler edition positions itself in relation to each concept, with what implications.

Let us begin by positing a conceptual field for editing that ranges from the isolated author at one end to a heterogeneous group of well-intentioned but sometimes inaccurate "scribes" and an undifferentiated (and possibly uncomprehending or resistant) public at the other. One formulation of the editor's task is to restore the now-dead author's literary *product*, stripping it of the grime of history, the "impurities" occasioned by multiple transmissions. Conceived this way, editing seeks to produce a kind of literary monument.[19] An understanding of texts as monumental implicitly upholds a canonical view of literature, and it favors certain kinds of authority: the authority of the author over that of his or her readers, the authority of the individual over that of the public, the authority of genius over collaborative production and reproduction, the authority of preservation over decomposition, and the authority of the conscious will (intention) over the authority of unconscious need and desire (chance). It is important to defer judgment on these implicit preferences, since how we judge them should have an integral relationship to what we want an edition to accomplish under a specified set of circumstances.

The preferences outlined above might be said to describe a set of typical expectations about what an edition should do. The Gabler edition may be seen as subscribing to such a view of the editor's task only up to a point: Gabler does not challenge the authority of the individual author; if anything, he intensifies it by choosing to focus almost exclusively on what Joyce actually wrote (what McGann calls "documents of composition"), relegating the "documents of transmission" (the typescripts, proofs, and the editions of *Ulysses* actually published) to a "historical collation" (they are also mentioned in the footnotes at the bottom of the page in the synoptic text). With respect to authorial intention, then, Gabler is quite conservative; in this respect his edition is *not* the "postmodern text" that McGann labeled it. Gabler's synoptic text (and his editorial theory) *is* postmodern in another way, however—in his questioning of the privilege of an author's final intentions over the process of writing itself.

Gabler's edition might be envisioned as a kind of Scylla and Charybdis of editing: like Odysseus, in his first pass through the channel he hugs the rock of Scylla, which is roughly equivalent here to *what the author actually wrote*.[20] But when he is buffeted back into the channel to choose between extremes a second time, Gabler goes into the whirlpool, conceiving texts as "diachronous" as well as "synchronous." This puts him in a situation aptly described as "postmodern," since what he is attacking is nothing less than our assumptive falsification of writing as product rather than process. In "The Synchrony and Diachrony of Texts," Gabler presents his position almost in the form of a manifesto:

Ulysses presents an amply documented case from which to work out the implications of the basic assumption that the object of scholarly and critical analysis and study—as opposed to an author's object of publication, and a general public's reading matter—is not the final product of the writer's art alone, but beyond this, the totality of the Work in Progress. It is an assumption that follows from the theoretical premise that the work of literature possesses in its material medium itself, in its text or texts, a diachronic as well as a synchronic dimension. The act of publication which confers upon it a synchronous structure does not at the same time have the power to obliterate the coexisting diachronous structure of the work, to which the discrete temporal states of its text coalesce by complex hierarchical interrelationship. The synchronous and diachronous structures combine to form the literary work in the totality of its real presence in the documents of its conception, transmission, and publication.[21]

Gabler suggests earlier in the essay that "the synoptic apparatus for *Ulysses* should encourage a reader to move . . . forwards and backwards along the axis of diachrony of the work's total text" ("Synchrony and Diachrony," 320); his Scylla and Charybdis, like Joyce's, turns out to be a way of making time a two-way street— Gabler's synoptic edition, in theory, clears the way for us to read backward as well as forward in narrative time.

Gabler's emphasis on the process over and above the product of writing is an approach particularly suitable to the works of Joyce, who continued to write *Ulysses* in the margins of anywhere from two to nine sets of proof per episode, right up until two days before its date of publication on his fortieth birthday. *Finnegans Wake* was known only as "Work in Progress" for years; its compositional process lasted seventeen years, and the progress it depicts is in a sense eternal (since the book itself is syntactically circular). An aspect of the edition that could be questioned is the apparent arbitrariness of where Gabler decided to begin and end his chart of Joyce's progress: why begin with the fair copy? Why not begin with notes and drafts? And why exclude other kinds of progress, including the progress of the book through different printings? There are good practical answers to such questions, but questions geared toward Gabler's theory are harder to answer. Gabler excludes all errors of transmission in the synopsis: why do this on *theoretical* grounds? Gabler's references to the public odyssey of *Ulysses* in print seem at times to suggest objections that are aesthetic and even moral: transmissional errors (in a usage commonly found in textual criticism) are referred to as "corruptions" and "impurities"; the implication is that the public text has been adulterated by the other hands through which it has passed. In contrast, what Gabler offers us is an "ideal" genetic approach that he describes as "essentially *virgin* land for criticism" ("Synchrony and Diachrony," 325; emphasis added). Gabler does not make a neutral distinction between documents of composition and those of transmission; he ranks them in a way that clearly privileges individual composition as potentially "pure," as opposed to transmitted texts that are presented as less desirable in their adulteration. Such an attitude seems sensible enough in a traditional editorial context, but it stands out conspicuously against the background of *Ulysses*, which takes adultery and adulteration (sexual and verbal "wanderings") as a primary subject and method. The privileging of "purity" and the dismissal of scribal departures is what Fritz Senn objects to in the edition; evoking Joyce's characteristic emphases on sin and chance, he writes that the synoptic text "refines corruptions out of visible existence. . . . It pretends that no accident ever intervened. The documents (typescripts, placards, page proofs, etc.) that Joyce actually had in front of him, naturally, were not immaculate but showed all those corruptions."[22]

Since Gabler clearly advocates the presumptive authority of authorial intention as it progresses, it makes sense to test his preference for the "pure" (conscious and intentional) over the adulterated (unconscious and accidental) in terms of what Joyce has to say about these categories in both *Ulysses* and *Finnegans Wake*. First of all, we can point to Stephen's famous celebration of error in his disquisition on Shakespeare, which clearly runs counter to an ethic of ideal purity: "A man of genius makes no mistakes.

His errors are volitional and are the portals of discovery" (*U* 9.228–29). Stephen here suggests that error can be volitional, even (in a sense) intentional. He implies that Shakespeare refuses to label his errors "mis-takes"; instead of closing the door on alternative, unexpected possibilities, he perceives them as openings, as "portals of discovery" through which he can proceed. In *Finnegans Wake*, Joyce fleshes out the view of mistakes as tantalizing and potentially productive possibilities by personifying them as women, "misses in prints," punningly identified with misprints: "For that (the rapt one warns) is what papyr is meed of, made of, hides and hints and misses in prints. Till ye finally (though not yet endlike) meet with the acquaintance of Mister Typus, Mistress Tope and all the little typtopies" (*FW* 20.13). Joyce suggests that misprints become the occasion for future productivity, producing a "tiptop" family of type.

Finnegans Wake also challenges the privileged view of the author as an individual writing in isolation: in the letter chapter, the "objective" narrator insists that the idea of an individual author is a fiction, that what we call the "writer" is an illusion born of reading with our eyes closed to an entire palimpsest of historical conflicts: "Closer inspection of the *bordereau* would reveal a multiplicity of personalities inflicted on the document or documents. . . . In fact, under the closed eyes of the inspectors the traits featuring the *chiaroscuro* coalesce, their contrarieties eliminated, in one stable somebody" (*FW* 107.23–30). A few pages later the narrator attributes literature not to an author but to "the writer complexus (for if the hand was one, the minds of active and agitated were more than so)" (*FW* 114.32–35). If we look to Joyce's texts for evidence of his intentions, we discover him minimizing the importance of authorial intentions by stressing the ways in which they are modified and reframed by the variable processes of writing, transmission, and reception. Joyce, then, uses his authority to recontextualize that authority against the broader backgrounds of history and production, insisting upon the irreducible oscillation between intention and circumstance.

Ulysses and, to an even greater extent, *Finnegans Wake* welcome adulteration, chance, the transmigration of written characters through time. Joyce's most emphatic presentation of writing as a process involving many hands and instruments is found in an editor's description of writing in the *Wake*:

> every person, place and thing in the chaosmos of Alle anyway connected with the gobblydumped turkery was moving and changing every part of the time: the travelling inkhorn (possibly pot), the hare and turtle pen and paper, the continually more and less intermisunderstanding minds of the anticollaborators, the as time went on as it will variously inflected, differently pronounced, otherwise spelled, changeably meaning vocable scriptsigns. (*FW* 118.21–119.1)[23]

Ironically, although the Gabler text does not register the obliterations that time and usage have worked on *Ulysses* historically (it seeks to obliterate them), although it resists the way that coincidence has operated *on Ulysses*, its "ideality" has sharpened the representation of the way that coincidental misprints work *within* the text, thereby stimulating the very critique I just articulated. One of the most famous examples of the several typos that the Gabler edition has restored is in the telegram Stephen recalls having received from his father recalling him from Paris. We find from Gabler's historical collation that all the editions he collated from 1922 through 1961 read:

> a blue French telegram, curiosity to show:
> —Mother dying come home father.

As several people have pointed out, this telegram is not much of a "curiosity," but Gabler identifies "Mother" as a scribal error on the last (fifth) set of proofs for "Nother," so that the telegram in his edition reads "Nother dying come home father" (*U* 3.199). This is indeed a "curiosity to show," one that reveals the chance significance of scribal error within the fiction that the scribal "correction" to the fiction had inadvertently obscured. The unreliability of print—"the line of botched type" and the misspelling of Bloom's name as "L. Boom" in the *Telegraph*—nettles Bloom

"not a little" in "Eumaeus," along with "the usual crop of nonsensical howlers of misprints" (*U* 16.1262–67). One of the difficulties of editing *Ulysses* involves preserving the misprints that
Bloom and Stephen register without allowing the misprints in
Ulysses itself to upstage the inculcated awareness that, as the narrative shows, print itself can "tell a graphic lie" (*U* 16.1232). The
difference between the tolerant, even opportunistic attitude the
book encourages its readers to take toward the vagaries of print
and the precise, scholarly attitude an editor must take to allow
the narrative to convey this message is something that should be
explicitly stated: the book's theory is necessarily and meaningfully
at odds with editorial *and* critical practice.

In *Finnegans Wake*, one of the substitutions for "Ireland" is "Er-
rorland" (as Yeats punned on "Eire" and "air" in *The Wind among
the Reeds*, Joyce puns on "Eire" and "err" in *Finnegans Wake*). Errancy
(modeled on odyssey) provides the very structure of *Ulysses*
("Longest way round is the shortest way home"; *U* 13.1110–11),
and the texture of language in "Penelope" and the *Wake* is satu-
rated with apparent "errors." The main task of the editor is to
eliminate error,[24] which if literally carried out in the editing of
Joyce would obscure his modus operandi in *Ulysses* and eliminate
Finnegans Wake almost entirely. (Many of the erroneous "corrections" made by typists and compositors of *Ulysses* resulted from
just such an attempt to eliminate error, but in eliminating Joyce's
intentional errors they homogenized the interplay between intention and chance that is such an important part of Joyce's subject.)
What editors need in the case of Joyce is an oxymoronic category
of "volitional error," but how can an editor determine which
errors are "volitional" without relying solely on individual critical
judgment? Gabler's controversial and not altogether unproble-
matic strategy was to follow the authorial inscriptions whenever
possible, thereby construing *Ulysses* less as a commodity given to
the public in 1922 than as a representation of one man's thought
as it grew under his hand. Gabler has made a judgment: that
Joyce's critical choices as he constructed his text are more precise
and meaningful than corrections and accidents introduced later
by other hands, that Joyce's work is more "his" than "ours." What

makes Gabler's verdict interesting is that when he chooses the act of authorial composition as the basis for his copy-text, he not only privileges active over passive authorization, individual and private determinations over more public and social ones, and the author's labor over that of others involved in the process, but his choice also has the unexpected and paradoxical effect of amplifying the author's critique of authorial intention. In effect, Gabler focuses his attention as editor on what Roland Barthes has called the "work" as opposed to the "text," which has the effect of emphasizing Joyce's investment in text. Barthes argues that "the work is held in the hand, the text is held in language . . . *the Text is experienced only in an activity, in a production.*"[25] One of the main differences between Barthes's "work" and "text" is in what authorizes each: he argues that the work is something that we attribute to an author, who "is reputed to be the father and owner of his work," whereas "the Text . . . is read without the Father's inscription"; the metaphor of the work is the image of a growing *organism*, whereas "the metaphor of the Text is that of the *network* . . . no vital 'respect' is therefore due to the Text." In Barthes's terms, Joyce uses his works to draw the reader's attention to what Barthes calls "text," the dynamic process of reading/writing, theory/practice. By enhancing Joyce's authority, Gabler therefore promotes Joyce's miniaturization of such authority. As Barthes explains, the author does not necessarily disappear from the Text, but when he returns, "he does so, one might say, as a guest; if he is a novelist, he inscribes himself there as one of his characters, drawn as a figure in the carpet; his inscription is no longer privileged, paternal, alethic, but ludic: he becomes, one can say, a paper author."

Joyce's use of "volitional errors" may be the most far-reaching of his many innovations: it is one of the guiding principles behind the evolution of Joyce's style, and it also provided him with a way of intertwining conscious and unconscious awareness, intentional and unintentional expression, individual purpose and an almost providential appreciation of chance and coincidence. Joyce's exploration of error began with the epiphanies, which he defined as records of inadvertent "slips" by which people unintentionally gave away what they cared most to conceal. Error in *Dubliners* is offered as a point of entry for the reader, a threshold through which we can see that what the characters do not know *does* hurt them. A dramatized moment of willed ignorance or arrogance, a punctiliously recorded "mistake" that no one points out—these are given to us as the vortices of the narrative, where we can begin to see a character's intention unraveling into its opposite, paralysis. Most critics would now agree that the "meaning" of *Dubliners* is found in its gaps, "between the acts"—not in the narratives that the characters construct about themselves, but in the errors that show us, as readers, how to deconstruct those narratives.[26] In *Ulysses* error takes many forms—of errancy, excess, gleeful self-parody. Characters suffer themselves to be transposed and transformed, but willful obscurity increasingly infiltrates the narrative, and in the obscurity of the later episodes the real novelty of the book's transgressive language begins to work its dark magic. *Finnegans Wake* leaves us largely in the dark; it could be described as a book composed entirely of misprints—volitional errors—carefully selected to show that when meaning is obscured, we find ourselves inventing new principles of interconnection, or rediscovering a host of old ones. What we find when we turn away from enlightenment is what the "light" of conscious reason and intention has whited out, as the sun outshines the stars: what Stephen in *Ulysses* calls the "darkness shining in brightness which brightness could not comprehend" (2.160). Stephen always knows that "Darkly they [the stars] are there behind this light, darkness shining in the brightness, delta of Cassiopeia, worlds" (3.409–10). One of the narratives of *Ulysses* is a search for the stars behind the sun, for the Greek constellations behind the Christian concentration on the one son/sun, for the "heaventree of stars hung with humid nightblue fruit" (17.1039) that is the book's Ithaca. That hidden tree of light with its dark fruits, always with us somewhere beyond the light of reason and the fire of individual purpose, is what all Joyce's works try to lead us toward.

Editing is an enlightenment activity; the word comes from "edere," to bring forth, and it means "to publish" (*Oxford English Dictionary*), to bring to light. Webster's is even more specific: to edit is "to alter, adapt, or refine esp. to bring about conformity to a standard or to suit a particular purpose." Joyce poses a particular problem for the editor because he situates many of his characters' thoughts and utterances on the line between wanting to "bring forth" a word or idea and wanting to suppress it. This conflict produces meaningful error (a "Freudian slip"), which should not be regularized or brought into conformity with a standard. What this error has the power to represent in miniature is the conflict between an individual's "ideal purpose" and its incompatibility with historical contingency—our inability to ensure the realization of that purpose in exactly the form in which it was conceived. To edit *Ulysses* with reference to texts that have already been intentionally "corrected" *and* accidentally corrupted is to see history at work on print in exactly the ways Joyce described, but it is to obscure that description itself. Anyone who has had occasion to use the title *Finnegans Wake* in her own writing has experienced in miniature the challenges and frustrations of editing Joyce, of preserving Joyce's solecisms against the almost universal impulse to standardize a familiar usage. If you write *"Finnegans Wake"* nine people out of ten will transcribe it as *"Finnegan's Wake"*; one of the functions of Joyce's title is to inculcate an awareness that we are all editors, that reading is itself a transitory editorial practice. It is unconscious editing that produces transmissional errors, and it takes a different, more self-aware, and responsible kind of editing to delete them.

Other editions of *Ulysses* are certainly possible. We can imagine editions with a textual apparatus that is easier to use, or a historical collation of *all* the extant printings of *Ulysses* (which would be invaluable for a detailed assessment of how accident has operated on Gabler's "ideal" text). But given what we know about the 1922 edition, and how it was prepared, it is hard to imagine a better strategy for preserving Joyce's volitional errors than the one Gabler devised. Gabler has recovered *Joyce's* garbles, and most important, he has done so in a way that makes public his own procedures and assumptions. He has given up the anonymity, the veil of editorial authority (invisibility) that is the editor's traditional privilege, presenting it instead as grounded in specific (if controversial) historical and textual contingencies. In the process, he has done more to make public the difficulties of textual editing than any other editor of the last twenty-five years. In a sense, his explicit representation of his editorial procedures has invited readers to collaborate in the recreation of the edition, as an almost unprecedented number of readers, led by John Kidd, have tried their hand at doing.[27]

By editing *Ulysses* in the way that he has, Gabler has done two things, then: first, he has challenged the fetishizing of texts as the product rather than the process of composition. Second, by questioning the definitiveness of the fact of publication, he has transformed the role of the editor: in some ways, he has amplified that role, assuming for his own construction of Joyce's "continuous manuscript" the authority that he had disallowed in the first edition of 1922 (just as he amplified the voice of the author by multiplying its articulations as they evolve through time). Although his methodology has enhanced the editor's authority to select individual readings (from among authorized variants), it has diminished the apparent absoluteness of that authority, its invisibility to the general public.

Gabler unveils his editorial authority to be as provisional, dynamic, and contingent on judgment and accuracy as Joyce's, although his eyesight and "memory," aided by documents not available to Joyce and by computerized collations of those documents, are better; moreover, like Joyce, Gabler invites his reader to participate in the process of reconstructing (or constructing) the text.

Gabler's edition—in conjunction with Joyce's text—has the effect (if not the intention) of advertising the insufficiency of any one edition of a book with so many previous lives. We could perhaps fault Gabler for his intention of producing an "ideal," private text rather than an actual public one, for his apparent preference for individual intentions (conceived severally) instead of multiple realizations (integrated through "correction"). What makes the debate exciting is the new possibilities it engenders, but what validates the theory behind Gabler's edition, making it successful on its own terms (if necessarily insufficient), is the way that its effects counterbalance its published intentions. If it once hoped to present itself as definitive (the impossibility of such a hope was not acknowledged until the second impression of the Garland edition), its effect is to call definitiveness into question; if it intends to give us ideal perfection, it allows us a surer glimpse into Joyce's depictions of the operations of the real. Gabler chose to reconstruct Joyce's process of composition, replicating in his edition even the number of years it took Joyce to complete the book (seven); interestingly, his effort reproduced the controversy that followed publication as well. John Kidd has emerged as a contemporary avatar of Wyndham Lewis, attacking the assumptions that subtend the edition as Lewis attacked the world view reflected in *Ulysses*. What Joyce's script would seem to demand is that we put the antagonists together, as warring twins, to produce a new and much-needed edition of *Finnegans Wake*.

Interestingly, despite its productive (and modernist) contradiction between intention and effect, the ideology behind Gabler's edition is nevertheless harmonious with many of the most recent (postmodern) tendencies in literary theory. Its implicit critique of the overwhelming product orientation of a writer's labor, the traces of which are erased in the publication of a cleaned-up printed book to be sold to the public, has a distinctively materialist overtone. Gabler presents *Ulysses* not as a sacred book, but as a labor-intensive process the intricacies of which are (theoretically if not always practically) recoverable. Similarly, Gabler's privileging of authorial intentions, which paradoxically highlights both the power and the limitations of conscious and intentional uses of language, amounts to a restaging of a "deconstructive" insight attributable to Joyce. Intentionality (as an ideal) versus the production of the real; the corrosive power of a communally authored, metaphorically suggestive, sensual language to undermine and complicate individual intent; laborious production as it invisibly underwrites idealized and sanctified (i.e., privileged) "creation"—these are the issues of our time. Gabler's edition of *Ulysses* has revitalized these debates, not as they affect the abstract realm of ideas, but as they destabilize our notion of what constitutes and authorizes literary "work"—from the author to print, from

an apparently transcendent "origin" of a work to its most im-
manent "ends"—and what connects them: those "variously inflected, differently pronounced, otherwise spelled, changeably
meaning vocable scriptsigns" (*FW* 118.26–28), the "radiooscillating
epiepistle" in black and white (or electricity and light) to which
"we must ceaselessly return" (*FW* 108.24, 26).

Notes

1. James Joyce, *Ulysses: A Critical and Synoptic Edition,* prepared by Hans
Walter Gabler, with Wolfhard Steppe and Claus Melchior (New York:
Garland, 1984), 3 vols. My review appeared on Sunday, September 9,
1984, 7.

2. See, for just one example, David F. Hult's excellent article, "Reading It Right: The Ideology of Text Editing," *Romanic Review* 79 (January
1988):88: "What is crucial about the editor's craft is its direct placement
at that spot where modern concerns meet medieval ones in the very
conception of the literary object."

3. Cf. Gabler's afterword (1905–7) for a description of how his editorial team used TUSTEP, "an autonomous system of computer programs for text data processing developed at the computing center of
the University of Tubingen," and also Gabler, "Computer-Aided Critical
Edition of *Ulysses,*" *AALC* (Association of Literary and Linguistic Computing) *Bulletin* 8 (1981): 232–48. The clearest account of the way the
edition was put together (and the role played by computers in that
process) is Michael Groden's "Editing Joyce's *Ulysses:* An International
Effort," *Scholarly Publishing* 12 (October 1980): 37–54. Some of the criticism
leveled at the edition has suggested that the use of computers made the
process of editing too mechanical, a protest I see as being directed not
so much at Gabler as at technological change in general.

4. There is some disagreement over whether the theories of writing
and reading found in *Finnegans Wake* are applicable to a discussion of
Ulysses, whether it is legitimate to "read backwards." I am taking the
position that *Finnegans Wake* is directly relevant to *Ulysses,* that it is (among
other things) an elaborate response to the ways in which *Ulysses* was
printed and received (or misconceived). Joyce frequently used critical
responses to a previous work (including his own criticisms) to help him
design its successors, and the emphasis on problems of textual trans-

mission in *Finnegans Wake* lends itself to an analysis of comparable problems with (and in) *Ulysses*.

5. See Jane Ford, Bonnie Kime Scott, Jean Kimball, and Fritz Senn, "The New Edition of *Ulysses*. An Assessment of Its Usefulness One Year Later," in *New Alliances in Joyce Studies*, ed. Bonnie Kime Scott (Newark: University of Delaware Press, 1988), 221.

6. John Kidd, "Errors in Execution in the 1984 *Ulysses*," printed together with Gabler's reply in the special issue on editing *Ulysses* edited by Charles Rossman, *Studies in the Novel* 22 (Summer 1990): 243–49 and 250–56. This issue also concludes with an annotated bibliography of what has been written on the Gabler edition (257–69). Kidd's attack on Gabler was effectively advertised before the fact by an article in the *Washington Post* by David Remnick called "The War over *Ulysses*," April 2, 1985, B1–4, in which a picture of Kidd bears the caption, "I think what I have to say is going to blow the whole Joyce establishment wide open."

7. Kidd, "The Scandal of *Ulysses*," *New York Review of Books* 35 (June 30, 1988): 32–39. See Peter du Sautoy (one of the trustees of the James Joyce estate), "Editing *Ulysses*. A Personal Account," *James Joyce Quarterly* 27 (Fall 1989): 76, for a reasonable objection to the hyperbole of the headline: "I must conclude by saying that I am surprised the *New York Review of Books*, a reputable journal though little known in Britain, should indulge in a scare headline, 'The Scandal of *Ulysses*,' thus turning what is essentially a dispute between scholars into a sort of prize fight."

8. The issues concerned are those of August 18, 1988; September 29, 1988; December 8, 1988; January 19, 1989; March 30, 1990; and June 1, 1989. My thanks to John Crowther for assembling copies of these articles for me.

9. The *Times Literary Supplement* (*TLS*) exchange was sparked by a review of new editions of Proust by Roger Shattuck and Douglas Alden, "Searching for the True Text," *TLS*, June 10–16, 1988, 640–41; Gabler responded with a letter, July 1–7, 1988, 733; followed by Peter du Sautoy, July 8–14, 1988, 755. John Kidd replied to Gabler, July 22–28, 1988, 907, who countered in the issue of August 12–18, 1988, 733. Charles Rossman then entered the fray with "Editing *Ulysses*," *TLS*, September 2–8, 1988, 963; and Peter du Sautoy answered on September 9–15, 1988, 989. In the same issue (and on the same page) Stephen Joyce responded to Alden, Shattuck, and Rossman. Michael Groden replied to Kidd in *TLS*, October 7–13, 1988, 1109; and Kidd answered in TLS, October 21–27, 1988, 1175. Ian Gunn's response to Kidd appeared in the issue of November 4–10,

1988, 1227; and Gabler finished off the exchange in *TLS*, December 16–22, 1988, 1395.

10. For an account of why Epstein might have taken such a step, see Robin Bates's "Postscript: February 1990" to his "Reflections on the Kidd Era," *Studies in the Novel* 22 (Summer 1990): 136–38.

11. See Bates, "Reflections on the Kidd Era," 123–24. See also Kidd's much more extreme charge in his "An Inquiry into *Ulysses: The Corrected Text*," *Papers of the Bibliographical Society of America* 82 (December 1988): 514: "Somehow Gabler overlooked seven typesettings of *Ulysses* which came before his own, making his [edition] not the eleventh [as Gabler says in the *Critical and Synoptic Edition*] but the eighteenth."

12. Hans Walter Gabler, "A Response to John Kidd, 'Errors of Execution in the 1984 *Ulysses*', " *Studies in the Novel* 22 (Summer 1990): 252.

13. Hans Walter Gabler, "The Synchrony and Diachrony of Texts: Practice and Theory of the Critical Edition of James Joyce's *Ulysses*," *Text* 1 (1981 [published in 1984]): 310. Hereafter cited as "Synchrony and Diachrony."

14. Jerome J. McGann, "*Ulysses* as a Postmodern Text: The Gabler Edition," *Criticism* 27 (Summer 1985): 286, 287, 290–91.

15. Gabler, "Synchrony and Diachrony," 309–10.

16. Wolfhard Steppe, "Reply to Paola Pugliatti's 'Who's Afraid of the 1984 *Ulysses*?' " *James Joyce Quarterly* 27 (Fall 1989): 60.

17. See, once again, Steppe's "Reply," 55–57, where he argues that Pugliatti has misread the diacritical symbols. An added complication is that the symbols sometimes designate different documents in different episodes. See also Fritz Senn, "*Ulysses* between Corruption and Correction," in *Assessing the 1984 "Ulysses,"* ed. C. George Sandulescu and Clive Hart (Gerrards Cross, Buckinghamshire, England: Colin Smythe, 1986), 188–206.

18. See, for example, *The Cornell Yeats* project for instances of editions that use different typefaces to represent different stages of composition (general editors Phillip L. Marcus, Stephen Parrish, Ann Saddlemyer, Jon Stallworthy).

19. See, for example, G. Thomas Tanselle, who concludes *A Rationale of Textual Criticism* (Philadelphia: University of Pennsylvania Press, 1989) with the claim that "our cultural heritage consists, in Yeats' phrase, of 'Monuments of unageing intellect' " (93). See also Michael Groden's inquiry into the monumental view of editing and its relation to New Criticism in "Contemporary Textual and Literary Theory," in *Representing*

Modernist Texts: Editing as Interpretation, ed. George Bornstein (Ann Arbor: University of Michigan Press, 1991), 259–86.

20. But see Clive Hart's corrective to Gabler's view, which clarifies the extent to which Gabler does not strictly adhere to what Joyce actually wrote. Hart would have an edition of *Ulysses* in which Joyce's errors and evidence of his forgetfulness are preserved, and he disagrees with Gabler's preference for the best formulations of a given phrase, and with Gabler's decision to correct obvious authorial errors. "Art Thou Real, My Ideal?" in Sandulescu and Hart, *Assessing the 1984 "Ulysses,"* 58–65.

21. See Gabler, "Synchrony and Diachrony," 325. It is interesting to compare Gabler's insistence on writing as process with Derrida's "The end of the book and the beginning of writing" (*Of Grammatology,* trans. Gayatri Chakravorty Spivak [Baltimore, Md.: Johns Hopkins University Press, 1976], 6–26) as well as to contrast the premium he puts on individual agency with that of Benjamin in "The Work of Art in the Age of Mechanical Reproduction" (*Illuminations,* ed. Hannah Arendt, trans. Harry Zohn [New York: Harcourt, Brace & World, 1968], 219–54).

22. Fritz Senn, "Inherent Delicacy: Eumaean Questions," *Studies in the Novel* 22 (Summer 1990): 184.

23. For a fuller account of the *Wake*'s emphasis on the conditions of its own production and printing, see John Paul Riquelme, *Teller and Tale in Joyce's Fiction: Oscillating Perspectives* (Baltimore, Md.: Johns Hopkins University Press, 1983), 14–19.

24. As A.E. Housman put it, "Textual criticism is . . . the science of discovering error in texts and the art of removing it." See his "The Application of Thought to Textual Criticism," *Proceedings of the Classical Association* 18 (1921): 67–84, reprinted in *Art and Error: Modern Textual Editing,* ed. Ronald Gottesman and Scott Bennett (Bloomington: Indiana University Press, 1970), 2. The best article on error and the Gabler edition to date is that of Patrick McGee, "The Error of Theory," *Studies in the Novel* 22 (Summer 1990): 148–62. See in particular McGee's assertion, "For all of its errors, Gabler's edition represents a theoretical breakthrough even if it is editorially flawed. It may even be necessary to consider the errors as a byproduct of the theory. . . . Theory as a discourse is always in error, always moving away from certainties of the law. But the law itself is never stable and produces theory as the sediment of its own process. Any editorial practice taking place within our academic institutions can be read as theory. The language of the text is transformed by the editor into the discourse of theory" (157, 160).

25. Roland Barthes, "From Work to Text," in *The Rustle of Language*, trans. Richard Howard (Berkeley: University of California Press, 1986), 56–64.

26. See, for example, Margot Norris, "Narration under a Blindfold: Reading Joyce's 'Clay,' " PMLA 102 (1987): 206–15; and Jean-Michel Rabaté, "Silence in *Dubliners*," in *James Joyce: New Perspectives*, ed. Colin MacCabe (Sussex, England: Harvester, 1982), 45–72.

27. See the replies to Kidd's "The Scandal of *Ulysses*" by Jon N. Elzey and Beverly Fields in " 'The Scandal of *Ulysses*': An Exchange," *New York Review of Books* 35 (August 18, 1988): 64. On a more serious level, see Sandulescu and Hart, *Assessing the 1984 "Ulysses"*; Philip Gaskell and Clive Hart, *Ulysses: A Review of Three Texts* (Gerrards Cross, England: Colin Smythe, 1989); and Rossman's special issue on editing *Ulysses*, *Studies in the Novel* 22 (Summer 1990).

Conversations with Joyce (1934)

FRANK BUDGEN

◆ ◆ ◆

IT WAS SHORTLY AFTER OUR meeting at Taylor's pension that I again met Joyce, by chance this time, and we strolled through the double avenue of trees on the Utoquai from Bellevue towards Zürich Horn. To the left of us were the solid houses of Zürich burgesses, on our right the lake and on the far shore of the lake the green slopes and elegant contours of the Uetliberg ridge.

"I am now writing a book," said Joyce, "based on the wanderings of Ulysses. The *Odyssey*, that is to say, serves me as a ground plan. Only my time is recent time and all my hero's wanderings take no more than eighteen hours."

A train of vague thoughts arose in my mind, but failed to take shape definite enough for any comment. I drew with them in silence the shape of the Uetliberg-Albis line of hills. The *Odyssey* for me was just a long poem that might at any moment be illustrated by some Royal Academician. I could see his water-colour Greek heroes, book-opened, in an Oxford Street bookshop window.

Joyce spoke again more briskly:

"You seem to have read a lot, Mr. Budgen. Do you know of any complete all-round character presented by any writer?"

With quick interest I summoned up a whole population of invented persons. Of the fiction writers Balzac, perhaps, might supply him? No. Flaubert? No. Dostoevsky or Tolstoy then? Their people are exciting, wonderful, but not complete. Shakespeare surely. But no, again. The footlights, the proscenium arch, the fatal curtain are all there to present to us not complete, all-round beings, but only three hours of passionate conflict. I came to rest on Goethe.

"What about Faust?" I said. And then, as a second shot "Or Hamlet?"

"Faust!" said Joyce. "Far from being a complete man, he isn't a man at all. Is he an old man or a young man? Where are his home and family? We don't know. And he can't be complete because he's never alone. Mephistopheles is always hanging round him at his side or heels.* We see a lot of him, that's all."

It was easy to see the answer in Joyce's mind to his own question.

"Your complete man in literature is, I suppose, Ulysses?"

"Yes," said Joyce. "No-age Faust isn't a man. But you mentioned Hamlet. Hamlet is a human being, but he is a son only. Ulysses is son to Laertes, but he is father to Telemachus, husband to Penelope, lover of Calypso, companion in arms of the Greek warriors around Troy and King of Ithaca. He was subjected to many trials, but with wisdom and courage came through them all. Don't forget that he was a war dodger who tried to evade military service by simulating madness. He might never have taken up arms and gone to Troy, but the Greek recruiting ser-

---

* This sentiment is apparently shared on the other side of the footlights. Many years afterward I asked Joyce why his friend Sullivan, the Paris-Kerry tenor, was so loth to sing in an opera that has become the standby of the Académie Nationale, and he replied: "That Samson of the land of Dan has told me that what bothers him is not so much the damnation of Faust as the domination of Mephistopheles."

geant was too clever for him and, while he was ploughing the
sands, placed young Telemachus in front of his plough. But once
at the war the conscientious objector became a jusqu'auboutist.
When the others wanted to abandon the siege he insisted on
staying till Troy should fall."

I laughed at Ulysses as a leadswinger and Joyce continued:

"Another thing, the history of Ulysses did not come to an end
when the Trojan war was over. It began just when the other
Greek heroes went back to live the rest of their lives in peace.
And then"—Joyce laughed—"he was the first gentleman in Europe. When he advanced, naked, to meet the young princess he
hid from her maidenly eyes the parts that mattered of his brine-
soaked, barnacle-encrusted body. He was an inventor too. The
tank is his creation. Wooden horse or iron box—it doesn't matter.
They are both shells containing armed warriors."

History repeats itself. The inventor of the tank also found his
Ajax at the War Office in the shape of Lord Kitchener.

It seems to me to be significant that Joyce should talk to me
first of the principal character in his book and only later of the
manifold devices through which he presented him. If the two
elements of character and material can be separated this is the
order in which he would put them. On the home stretch back
to Bellevue a question grew in my mind.

"What do you mean," I said, "by a complete man? For example,
if a sculptor makes a figure of a man then that man is all-round,
three-dimensional, but not necessarily complete in the sense of
being ideal. All human bodies are imperfect, limited in some way,
human beings too. Now your Ulysses . . ."

"He is both," said Joyce. "I see him from all sides, and therefore
he is all-round in the sense of your sculptor's figure. But he is a
complete man as well—a good man. At any rate, that is what I
intend that he shall be."

. . .

A COLD WIND WAS BLOWING when I met Joyce one evening on
the Bahnhofstrasse. The brown overcoat buttoned up to his chin
lent him a somewhat military appearance.

"I'm glad you liked the 'Portrait'," said Joyce. I had returned the book with a letter recording some of my impressions of it.

"That simile of yours, 'a young cat sharpening his claws on the tree of life,' seems to me to be very just applied to young Stephen."

I enquired about *Ulysses*. Was it progressing?

"I have been working hard on it all day," said Joyce.

"Does that mean that you have written a great deal?" I said.

"Two sentences," said Joyce.

I looked sideways but Joyce was not smiling. I thought of Flaubert.

"You have been seeking the *mot juste*?" I said.

"No," said Joyce. "I have the words already. What I am seeking is the perfect order of words in the sentence. There is an order in every way appropriate. I think I have it."

"What are the words?" I asked.

"I believe I told you," said Joyce, "that my book is a modern *Odyssey*. Every episode in it corresponds to an adventure of Ulysses. I am now writing the "Lestrygonians" episode, which corresponds to the adventure of Ulysses with the cannibals. My hero is going to lunch. But there is a seduction motive in the *Odyssey*, the cannibal king's daughter. Seduction appears in my book as women's silk petticoats hanging in a shop window. The words through which I express the effect of it on my hungry hero are: 'Perfume of embraces all him assailed. With hungered flesh obscurely, he mutely craved to adore.' You can see for yourself in how many different ways they might be arranged."

A painter is, perhaps, more originality proof than any other artist, seeing that all recent experimental innovations in the arts have first been tried out on his own. And many a painter can labour for a day or for many days on one or two square inches of canvas so that labor expended on achieving precious material is not likely to surprise him. What impressed me, I remember, when Joyce repeated the words of Bloom's hungrily abject amorousness to me, was neither the originality of the words themselves nor the labour expended on composing them. It was the sense they gave me that a new province of material had been found. Where that province lay I could not guess, but as our talk proceeded Joyce spoke of it himself without question of mine. We were by this time sitting in the Astoria Café.

"Among other things," he said, "my book is the epic of the human body. The only man I know who has attempted the same thing is Phineas Fletcher. But then his *Purple Island* is purely descriptive, a kind of coloured anatomical chart of the human body. In my book the body lives in and moves through space and is the home of a full human personality. The words I write are adapted to express first one of its functions then another. In "Lestrygonians" the stomach dominates and the rhythm of the episode is that of the peristaltic movement."

"But the minds, the thoughts of the characters," I began.

"If they had no body they would have no mind," said Joyce. "It's all one. Walking towards his lunch my hero, Leopold Bloom, thinks of his wife, and says to himself, 'Molly's legs are out of plumb.' At another time of day he might have expressed the same thought without any underthought of food. But I want the reader to understand always through suggestion rather than direct statement."

"That's the painter's form of leverage," I said.

We talked of words again, and I mentioned one that had always pleased me in its shape and colour. It was Chatterton's "acale" for freeze.

"It is a good word," said Joyce. "I shall probably use it."

He does use it. The word occurs in the "Oxen of the Sun" episode of *Ulysses* in a passage written in early English, describing the death and burial of Bloom's son Rudolph: "and as he was minded of his good lady Marion that had borne him an only manchild which on his eleventh day on live had died and no man of art could save so dark is destiny. And she was wondrous stricken of heart for that evil hap and for his burial did him on a fair corselet of lamb's wool, the flower of the flock, lest he might perish utterly and lie akeled."

In leaving the café I asked Joyce how long he had been working on *Ulysses*.

"About five years," he said. "But in a sense all my life."

"Some of your contemporaries," I said, "think two books a year an average output."

"Yes," said Joyce. "But how do they do it? They talk them into a typewriter. I feel quite capable of doing that if I wanted to do it. But what's the use? It isn't worth doing."

. . .

I stopped at the door as I was about to leave.

"You know, Joyce," I said, "when Stephen sees that three-masted schooner's sails brailed up to her crosstrees."

"Yes," he said. "What about it?"

"Only this. I sailed on schooners of that sort once and the only word we ever used for the spars to which the sails are bent was 'yards.' 'Crosstrees' were the lighter spars fixed near the lower masthead. Their function was to give purchase to the topmast standing rigging."

Joyce thought for a moment.

"Thank you for pointing it out," he said. "There's no sort of criticism I more value than that. But the word 'crosstrees' is essential. It comes in later on and I can't change it. After all, a yard is also a crosstree for the onlooking landlubber."

And crosstree does recur in the pattern in that episode where Stephen discusses Shakespeare with some Dublin scholars. "Who, put upon by his fiends, stripped and whipped, was nailed like bat to barndoor, starved on crosstree."

Joyce told me that some admirers of *A Portrait of the Artist as a Young Man,* Americans, I understood, had expressed disappointment at the way *Ulysses* was shaping.

"They seem to think," he said, "that after writing the *Portrait* I should have sat down to write something like a sermon. I ought to have a message, it seems."

. . .

ONE IMPORTANT PERSONALITY THAT emerges out of the contacts of many people is that of the city of Dublin.

"I want," said Joyce, as we were walking down the Universitätstrasse, "to give a picture of Dublin so complete that if the city one day suddenly disappeared from the earth it could be reconstructed out of my book."

We had come to the university terrace where we could look down on the town.

"And what a city Dublin is!" he continued. "I wonder if there is another like it. Everybody has time to hail a friend and start a conversation about a third party, Pat, Barney or Tim. 'Have you seen Barney lately? Is he still off the drink?' 'Ay, sure he is. I was with him last night and he drank nothing but claret.' I suppose you don't get that gossipy, leisurely life in London?"

. . .

JOYCE'S FIRST QUESTION WHEN I had read a completed episode or when he had read out a passage of an uncompleted one was always: "How does Bloom strike you?"

Technical considerations, problems of homeric correspondence, the chemistry of the human body, were secondary matters. If Bloom was first it was not that the others were unimportant but that, seen from the outside, they were not a problem. At about the time of the publication of the "Lestrygonians" episode he said to me:

"I have just got a letter asking me why I don't give Bloom a rest. The writer of it wants more Stephen. But Stephen no longer interests me to the same extent. He has a shape that can't be changed."

. . .

EARLY IN 1919, when the deeds of militant Sinn Fein were becoming world news, I was sitting with Joyce one evening in my workroom in the Usteristrasse. It was a quiet room overlooking the Sihl, and it had for furniture two quite comfortable chairs, a table, and a copious litter of newspaper files, English, Swiss and German. Thither we often went at that time to continue a conversation interrupted by *Polizeistunde* in the *Wirtschaft*, and to be stayed with a further flagon. We spoke of the happenings in Ireland. Joyce stated no positive, personal opinion on the solution to the conflict, but I put my own in this way:

"All this fighting with Ireland is absorbing too much English energy. History is leading us up the garden. We are being ruined by politics. Let us give economics a chance. The Irish want political autonomy. Why not give them what they want, give them at any rate what will satisfy them? Then, perhaps, when history is satisfied, the two islands will be able to realise their unity on an economic basis."

"Ireland is what she is," said Joyce, "and therefore I am what I am because of the relations that have existed between England and Ireland. Tell me why you think I ought to wish to change the conditions that gave Ireland and me a shape and a destiny?"

"But what about us?" I said with indignation. "Do you think that we English exist to further the spiritual development of the Irish people?"

Joyce's eyes flickered laughter behind their powerful lenses. He made no answer, and I took his silence to mean that he did think that that was one of our useful functions. Meeting Joyce a day or two later, he referred to our conversation in my room and laughed again, this time loudly.

"That talk of ours the other evening amuses me," he said. "You, an Englishman, trying to convince me, an Irishman, of the necessity of home rule for Ireland on the premises of the British Consulate, representing more or less the British Empire in Zürich."

We were strolling along the Bahnhofstrasse one evening after he had read to me a passage where the Fenian giant, representative of the most one-eyed nationalism, denounces the bloody and brutal Sassenach.

"I wonder," said Joyce suddenly, "what my own countrymen will think of my work?"

"I think they won't like it," I said. "The ardent party man is apt to believe that he who is not with him is against him. He understands opposition, but doesn't like criticism. Your countrymen are men of violent beliefs, and your book is the book of a sceptic."

"I know it is," said Joyce. "It is the work of a sceptic, but I don't want it to appear the work of a cynic. I don't want to hurt or offend those of my countrymen who are devoting their lives to a cause they feel to be necessary and just."

. . .

A VISITOR TO JOYCE'S apartment alluded to a picture on the wall as a photograph. In mentioning the fact to me, Joyce said:

"Now I couldn't see anything ridiculous in that. It isn't the usual word, but surely light-writing is a beautiful word to apply to a painted picture."

Seeing words as mysterious means of expression as well as an instrument of communication made Joyce sometimes a severe critic of his contemporaries. Not that he often praised or condemned or even mentioned their productions. I once alluded to one of his contemporaries as a great writer.

"Is he?" said Joyce. "What has he written?"

I began to describe a dramatic scene in a provincial hotel, when Joyce interrupted:

"Tell me something of it in his own words."

"Ah, the words. I can't remember the actual words of the book."

"But why can't you?" said Joyce. "When you remember a scene or a sonnet of Shakespeare you can tell me about it in the words that conveyed it to you. Why can't you do so in this case? Some one passage ought to stick."

"Do you think that is necessary?"

"I do. When you talk painting to Taylor, Sargent or Suter you don't talk about the object represented but about the painting. It is the material that conveys the image of jug, loaf of bread, or whatever it is, that interests you. And quite rightly, I should say, because that is where the beauty of the artist's thought and handiwork become one. If this writer is as good as you say he is, I can't understand why some of his prose hasn't stuck in your otherwise excellent memory."

Joyce's memory for the words of his own compositions and for those of all writers he admired was prodigious. He knew by heart whole pages of Flaubert, Newman, de Quincey, E. Quinet, A. J. Balfour and of many others. Most human memories begin to fail at midnight, and lapse into the vague and *à peu près*, but not that of Joyce. It was while we were at Locarno that we returned once to our pension at about midnight, and sat for a while in Joyce's room. We had been talking about Milton's *Lycidas*, and I wanted to quote some lines of it that pleased me. My memory gave out, but Joyce said the whole poem from beginning to end, and followed it up with *L'Allegro*. I wonder if Macaulay could have done as much at midnight after a litre of Nostrano? Dante he knew as lover and scholar, and he was an ardent admirer of Verlaine. One evening in my studio in the Seefeldstrasse Paul Suter recited that poem of Verlaine which begins:

> Les roses étaient toutes rouges
> Et les lierres étaient tout noirs.
> Chère, pour peu que tu te bouges,
> Renaissent tous mes désespoirs.

Joyce asked him to repeat it.

"That," he said, "is perfection. No more beautiful poem has ever been made. And yet I wonder at what hour, A.M. or P.M., are roses quite red and ivy perfectly black?"

Appendix

The Schema of Ulysses

Joyce allowed his friends to see two versions of the schema; the following table is based on the one used by Stuart Gilbert for his book *James Joyce's "Ulysses": A Study* (1930) and on Clive Hart's adaptation of it in his *James Joyce's "Ulysses"* (1968). I have incorporated additional elements from the earlier schema Joyce lent to Carlo Linati in 1921 (which differs in many places from the later one).

TITLE	SCENE	HOUR	ORGAN	ART	COLOR	SYMBOL	TECHNIC
I. Telemachia							
1. Telemachus	The Tower	8 A.M.	——	theology	white, gold	heir	narrative (young)
2. Nestor	The School	10 A.M.	——	history	brown, chestnut	horse	catechism (personal)
3. Proteus	The Strand	11 A.M.	——	philology	green, blue	tide	monologue (male)
II. Odyssey							
4. Calypso	The House	8 A.M.	kidney	economics, mythology	orange	nymph	narrative (mature)
5. Lotus Eaters	The Bath	10 A.M.	genitals, skin	botany, chemistry	——	eucharist	narcissism
6. Hades	The Graveyard	11 A.M.	heart	religion	white, black	caretaker	incubism
7. Aeolus	The Newspaper	12 noon	lungs	rhetoric	red	editor	enthymemic
8. Lestrygonians	The Lunch	1 P.M.	esophagus	architecture	blood color	constable	peristalsis
9. Scylla and Charybdis	The Library	2 P.M.	brain	literature	——	Stratford, London	dialectic
10. Wandering Rocks	The Streets	3 P.M.	blood	mechanics	rainbow	citizen	labyrinth
11. Sirens	The Concert Room	4 P.M.	ear	music	coral	barmaid	fuga per canonem
12. Cyclops	The Tavern	5 P.M.	muscle, bones	politics, surgery	green	Fenian	gigantism
13. Nausikaa	The Rocks	8 P.M.	eyes, nose	painting	grey, blue	virgin	tumescence, detumescence
14. Oxen of the Sun	The Hospital	10 P.M.	womb	medicine, physics	white	mother	embryonic development
15. Circe	The Brothel	12 midnight	locomotor apparatus, skeleton	magic, dance	violet	whore	hallucination

TITLE	SCENE	HOUR	ORGAN	ART	COLOR	SYMBOL	TECHNIC
				III. *Nostos*			
16. Eumaeus	The Shelter	1 A.M.	nerves	navigation	—	sailor	narrative (old)
17. Ithaca	The House	2 A.M.	skeleton, juices	science	starry, milky	comet	catechism (impersonal)
18. Penelope	The Bed	—	fat	—	starry, milky, then new dawn	earth	monologue (female)

Suggested Reading

Adams, R. M. *Surface and Symbol: The Consistency of James Joyce's "Ulysses."* New York: Oxford University Press, 1962.

Attridge, Derek. *Peculiar Language: Literature as Difference from the Renaissance to James Joyce.* London: Methuen; Ithaca, N.Y.: Cornell University Press, 1988.

——. *Joyce Effects: On Language, Theory, and History.* Cambridge: Cambridge University Press, 2000.

——, ed. *The Cambridge Companion to James Joyce.* Second ed. Cambridge: Cambridge University Press, 2004.

Attridge, Derek, and Daniel Ferrer, eds. *Post-structuralist Joyce: Essays from the French.* Cambridge: Cambridge University Press, 1984.

Attridge, Derek, and Marjorie Howes, eds. *Semicolonial Joyce.* Cambridge: Cambridge University Press, 2000.

Beja, Morris. *James Joyce: A Literary Life.* Columbus: Ohio State University Press, 1992.

Benstock, Bernard. *Narrative Con/Texts in "Ulysses."* Urbana: University of Illinois Press, 1991.

Benstock, Bernard, and Shari Benstock. *Who's He When He's at Home: A James Joyce Directory.* Urbana: University of Illinois Press.

Bowen, Zack, and James Carens. *A Companion to Joyce Studies.* Westport, Conn.: Greenwood, 1984.

Brown, Richard. *James Joyce: A Post-Culturalist Perspective.* Basingstoke, England: Macmillan, 1992.

Budgen, Frank. *James Joyce and the Making of "Ulysses."* 1934. Bloomington: Indiana University Press, 1960; London: Oxford University Press, 1972 (with additional articles).

Connor, Steven. *James Joyce.* Plymouth, England: Northcote House, 1996.

Deming, Robert H., ed. *James Joyce: The Critical Heritage.* 2 vols. London: Routledge & Kegan Paul, 1970.

Derrida, Jacques. "Ulysses Gramophone: Hear Say Yes in Joyce." In *Acts of Literature,* ed. Derek Attridge. New York: Routledge, 1992. 253–309.

Devlin, Kimberly J., and Marilyn Reizbaum, eds. *"Ulysses": En-Gendered Perspectives.* Columbia: University of South Carolina Press, 1999.

Duffy, Enda. *The Subaltern "Ulysses."* Minneapolis: University of Minnesota Press, 1994.

Ellmann, Richard. *Ulysses on the Liffey.* London: Faber, 1972.

———. *James Joyce.* Rev. ed. New York: Oxford University Press, 1982.

Froula, Christine. *Modernism's Body: Sex, Culture, and Joyce.* New York: Columbia University Press, 1996.

Gibson, Andrew. *Joyce's Revenge: History, Politics, and Aesthetics in Joyce's "Ulysses."* Oxford: Oxford University Press, 2002.

Gifford, Don. *"Ulysses" Annotated.* Berkeley: University of California Press, 1989.

Gilbert, Stuart. *James Joyce's "Ulysses": A Study.* 1930. Rev. ed., London: Faber, 1952; New York: Random House, 1955.

Groden, Michael. *"Ulysses" in Progress.* Princeton, N.J.: Princeton University Press, 1977.

Hart, Clive. *James Joyce's "Ulysses."* Sydney, Australia: Sydney University Press, 1968.

Hart, Clive, and David Hayman, eds. *James Joyce's "Ulysses": Critical Essays.* Berkeley: University of California Press, 1974.

Hart, Clive, and Leo Knuth. *A Topographical Guide to James Joyce's "Ulysses."* Colchester, England: A Wake Newslitter Press, 1975; rev. ed., 1986.

Hayman, David. *"Ulysses": The Mechanics of Meaning.* Rev. ed. Madison: University of Wisconsin Press, 1982.

Herring, Philip. *Joyce's Notes and Early Drafts for "Ulysses."* Charlottesville: University Press of Virginia, 1977.

Jameson, Fredric. "Ulysses in History." In *James Joyce and Modern Literature,* ed. W. J. McCormack and Alistair Stead. London: Routledge & Kegan Paul, 1982. 126–41.

Jones, Ellen Carol, ed. *Feminist Readings of Joyce.* Special issue of *Modern Fiction Studies* 35 (Autumn 1989).

Kain, Richard M. *Fabulous Voyager: A Study of James Joyce's "Ulysses."* New York: Viking, 1947.

Kenner, Hugh. *Dublin's Joyce.* Bloomington: Indiana University Press, 1956.

———. *Joyce's Voices.* London: Faber, 1987.

———. *Ulysses.* Rev. ed. Baltimore, Md.: Johns Hopkins University Press, 1987.

Lawrence, Karen. *The Odyssey of Style in "Ulysses."* Princeton, N.J.: Princeton University Press, 1981.

Levin, Harry. *James Joyce: A Critical Introduction.* Rev. ed. New York: New Directions, 1960.

Litz, A. Walton. *The Art of James Joyce: Method and Design in "Ulysses" and "Finnegans Wake."* London: Oxford University Press, 1961.

Lloyd, David. "Adulteration and the Nation." In *Anomalous States: Irish Writing and the Post-Colonial Moment.* Dublin: Lilliput Press, 1993. 88–124.

MacCabe, Colin. *James Joyce and the Revolution of the Word.* Basingstoke, England: Macmillan, 1979.

McGann, Jerome J. "*Ulysses* as a Postmodern Text: The Gabler Edition." *Criticism* 27 (1985): 283–306.

Mahaffey, Vicki. *Reauthorizing Joyce.* Cambridge: Cambridge University Press, 1988.

Manganiello, Dominic. *James Joyce's Politics.* London: Routledge & Kegan Paul, 1980.

Moretti, Franco. "The Long Goodbye: *Ulysses* and the End of Liberal Capitalism." In *Signs Taken for Wonders: Essays in the Sociology of Literary Form.* Rev. ed. London: Verso, 1988. 182–208.

Newman, Robert D., and Weldon Thornton, eds. *Joyce's "Ulysses": The Larger Perspective.* Newark: University of Delaware Press, 1987.

Nolan, Emer. *James Joyce and Nationalism.* London: Routledge, 1995.

Norris, Margot. *Joyce's Web: The Social Unraveling of Modernism.* Austin: University of Texas Press, 1992.

———, ed. *A Companion to James Joyce's "Ulysses."* Boston: Bedford Books, 1998.

Osteen, Mark. *The Economy of "Ulysses": Making Both Ends Meet.* Syracuse, N.Y.: Syracuse University Press, 1995.

Parrinder, Patrick. *James Joyce.* Cambridge: Cambridge University Press, 1984.

Pearce, Richard, ed. *Molly Blooms: A Polylogue on "Penelope" and Cultural Studies.* Madison: University of Wisconsin Press, 1994.

Rabaté, Jean-Michel. *James Joyce: Authorized Reader.* Baltimore, Md.: Johns Hopkins University Press, 1991.

———. *Joyce upon the Void: The Genesis of Doubt.* New York: St. Martin's, 1991.

———. *James Joyce and the Politics of Egoism.* Cambridge: Cambridge University Press, 2001.

Raleigh, John Henry. *The Chronicle of Leopold and Molly Bloom: "Ulysses" as Narrative.* Berkeley: University of California Press, 1977.

Restuccia, Frances. *Joyce and the Law of the Father.* New Haven, Conn.: Yale University Press, 1989.

Schutte, William M. *Index of Recurrent Elements in James Joyce's "Ulysses."* Carbondale: Southern Illinois University Press, 1982.

Seidel, Michael. *James Joyce: A Short Introduction.* Oxford: Blackwell, 2002.

Senn, Fritz. *Joyce's Dislocutions.* Ed. John Paul Riquelme. Baltimore, Md.: Johns Hopkins University Press, 1984.

———. *Inductive Scrutinies: Focus on Joyce.* Ed. Christine O'Neill. Baltimore, Md.: Johns Hopkins University Press, 1995.

Sherry, Vincent. *James Joyce, "Ulysses."* Cambridge: Cambridge University Press, 1994.

Spoo, Robert. *James Joyce and the Language of History: Dedalus's Nightmare.* New York: Oxford University Press, 1994.

Staley, Thomas F., ed. *"Ulysses": Fifty Years.* Bloomington: Indiana University Press, 1974.

Steppe, Wolfhard, with Hans Walter Gabler. *A Handlist to James Joyce's "Ulysses."* New York: Garland, 1986.

Thornton, Weldon. *Allusions in "Ulysses": An Annotated List.* Chapel Hill: University of North Carolina Press, 1968.

Tymoczko, Maria. *The Irish "Ulysses."* Berkeley: University of California Press, 1994.

Valente, Joseph. *James Joyce and the Problem of Justice.* Cambridge: Cambridge University Press, 1995.

———, ed. *Quare Joyce.* Ann Arbor: University of Michigan Press, 1998.

Wollaeger, Mark A., Victor Luftig, and Robert Spoo, eds. *Joyce and the Subject of History.* Ann Arbor: University of Michigan Press, 1996.